FAILING TO WIN

FAILING TO WIN

Perceptions

of Victory

and Defeat in

International

Politics

DOMINIC D. P. JOHNSON

DOMINIC TIERNEY

HARVARD UNIVERSITY PRESS
Cambridge, Massachusetts
London, England
2006

Library of Congress Cataloging-in-Publication Data

Johnson, Dominic D. P., 1974–
  Failing to win : perceptions of victory and defeat in
international politics / Dominic D. P. Johnson and
Dominic Tierney.
      p.   cm.
  Includes bibliographical references and index.
  ISBN-13: 978-0-674-02324-6 (alk. paper)
  ISBN-10: 0-674-02324-2 (alk. paper)
    1. War—Public opinion. 2. War—Psychological
aspects. 3. International relations—Public opinion.
4. International relations—Psychological aspects.
5. World politics. I. Tierney, Dominic, 1977– II. Title.
  U21.2.J626 2006
    303.6′6—dc22   2006043575

To our parents

CONTENTS

FAILING TO WIN

1 | INTRODUCTION

Victory has a thousand fathers, but defeat is an orphan.

—JOHN F. KENNEDY

AT 10:50 P.M. ON 30 APRIL 1945, triumphant Soviet soldiers raised a fluttering hammer and sickle over the Reichstag in Berlin. In a ferocious war, the Red Army had ground the Germans back all the way from the gates of Moscow. Around the world, people celebrated the fall of Berlin as a defining moment in the destruction of the Nazi regime. It was a classic case in which perceptions of victory matched the result on the battlefield.

But people do not always judge victory this way. Observers' perceptions of who won and who lost in a war or a crisis often diverge widely from the realities on the ground. Armies can win brilliant triumphs in battle and observers may nevertheless see the outcome as a defeat. Diplomats can make major concessions in crisis negotiations and observers may nevertheless see the outcome as a victory. In this book we dissect the psychological, political, and cultural factors that predispose observers to perceive outcomes of international disputes as victories or defeats. By observers we mean anyone paying attention to the event—the public, the media, political elites, leaders themselves, or foreign governments. By perceptions we mean observers' personal interpretations of the world. Sometimes perceptions and reality match, sometimes they do not.

Observers can end up judging similar events very differently.

1

Compare, for example, perceptions of success in the 1975 *Mayaguez* incident, in which 41 Americans died, with perceptions of success in the 1992–1994 U.S. intervention in Somalia, in which 43 Americans died.

In May 1975 the Cambodian Khmer Rouge seized the U.S. merchant ship *Mayaguez* and 39 crewmembers. The U.S. president, Gerald Ford, ordered a force of marines to land on the Cambodian island of Koh Tang to rescue the crew. Unfortunately for the Americans, the crew had already been transferred to the mainland, and instead of a small force of captors the marines encountered an elite unit of well-armed Khmer Rouge troops, sparking an unexpectedly bitter fight. The United States began bombing the Cambodian mainland, and the *Mayaguez* crewmembers were released. But it is unclear what role, if any, U.S. military action played in the Cambodians' decision to free the crew: the men were released before the bombing began. When the dust settled on Koh Tang, 41 U.S. soldiers had been killed, dozens more had been wounded, several helicopters had been shot down, and the marines' position had been very nearly overrun. Three U.S. soldiers were left behind by accident, captured, and executed. Overall, this was a bungled operation based on poor intelligence, in which more U.S. servicemen died than there were hostages to be rescued. Furthermore, the U.S. military's use of a base in Thailand for the rescue mission led to a diplomatic crisis between Bangkok and Washington. Remarkably, though, most Americans perceived the episode to have been a striking success: in one poll 79 percent of the public rated Ford's handling of the incident positively. Far from regretting the Mayaguez incident, Ford highlighted it when running for reelection in 1976.[1]

Compare these perceptions of success in the *Mayaguez* incident with perceptions of success in the U.S. intervention in Somalia in 1992–1994. In November 1992 President George H. W. Bush decided to send U.S. military forces to secure the delivery of humanitarian aid to Somalia, an impoverished state racked by civil war and starvation. This intervention is now widely acknowledged to have saved the lives of tens or hundreds of thousands of Somalis. Operation Restore Hope, as it was called, proved to be far more effective than existing UN efforts in Somalia. Overall it was one of the great, if unheralded, American moral actions of the twentieth century.

As U.S. and UN forces expanded their mission in 1993 to try to stabilize Somalia's political chaos, a labor of Herculean proportions, they unsurprisingly encountered increasing obstacles and dangers. This phase of the U.S. intervention culminated in the infamous "Black Hawk Down" battle in the Somali capital, Mogadishu, in early October 1993, in which 18 U.S. soldiers were killed. In response to the downing of two Black Hawk helicopters, U.S. soldiers fought their way to the crash site to retrieve survivors. In a prolonged and complex battle in Mogadishu's maze of hostile streets, U.S. forces demonstrated a remarkable effectiveness despite the circumstances, performing an extremely difficult withdrawal while killing perhaps fifty opponents for every loss of their own. Indeed, the mission succeeded in capturing its targets: two associates of General Aidid, the Somali warlord blamed for earlier attacks on UN forces. The U.S. intervention in Somalia was a noble humanitarian effort, which included an Alamo-style battle against the odds in Mogadishu.

But Somalia was not remembered as another Alamo—far from it. Instead, as we will see in more detail in Chapter 8, the mission is usually judged as an unmitigated failure. Soon after the "Black Hawk Down" battle, a poll found that only 25 percent of Americans thought the intervention "to provide humanitarian relief" in Somalia had been successful, while 66 percent thought it had been unsuccessful.[2]

The perception that the United States had suffered a defeat in Somalia would have terrible consequences for hundreds of thousands of people in another African country: Rwanda. In April 1994, just months after the battle in Mogadishu, Hutus in Rwanda began a systematic genocide of Tutsis and moderate Hutus, killing eight hundred thousand people in a matter of weeks. Although military intervention could have saved thousands of lives, the United States, under President Bill Clinton, decided to do almost nothing. According to the political scientist Robert DiPrizio, the "ghost of Somalia" was the primary factor sealing Rwanda's fate.[3] The tragedy is that, had American leaders and the American public perceived Somalia as at least a partial success, the Clinton administration might have pursued a more robust policy against genocide in Rwanda. American perceptions of the events in Somalia may ultimately have determined whether many Rwandans would live or die.

In the 1975 *Mayaguez* incident, 41 Americans died in an operation that may have played little or no role in saving the 39 hostages, but the episode was widely viewed as a triumph for the United States. In the 1992–1994 Somalia intervention, 43 Americans died in a mission that saved tens or hundreds of thousands of Somalis, but the operation was viewed as the greatest U.S. failure since Vietnam. American judgments about these two missions suggest a puzzle in international relations: How can we account for substantive failure on the ground accompanied by widespread perceptions of success, or alternatively, for success on the ground perceived as failure? This prompts a larger set of questions: How do people decide which side has won or lost in international disputes, or how well their leaders have performed? What factors shape the process of judgment? What are the implications for policymakers and for democracy? We take up these important questions in this book.

On the face of it, evaluating winners and losers in wars and crises might seem to be a straightforward task: Which country made the greater gains or achieved more of its aims in the final outcome? In international relations, however, achieving military victory, or indeed any tangible prize at all, is neither necessary nor sufficient for people to think a leader has won. Not necessary, because a widespread perception of victory can be obtained despite net losses; not sufficient, because even substantial gains do not guarantee that people will view the events as a success. Sometimes, as in 1945, battlefield victory and perceived victory are synonymous. Quite often, though, a battlefield victor will emerge as the perceived loser, with all the tribulations that this status involves.

Human nature being what it is, the interpretation of success or failure can become a matter of great uncertainty and controversy. Unless the outcome on the ground is heavily one-sided, it can be unclear how to cast judgment. In the Vietnam war, for example, some insisted that relative "body counts" were the best way to tell who was winning. Others believed they were a useless measure of success. The same dilemma is playing out today in Iraq. Newt Gingrich, a prominent Republican and a former speaker of the U.S. House of Representatives, criticized the G. W. Bush administration for its choice of metrics: "The real key here is not how many enemy do I kill. The real key is how many allies do I grow . . . And that is a very important metric that they just don't get."[4]

People's beliefs about winners and losers, both during an event and after it is over, can be influenced as much by psychological biases as they are by the actual material changes on the ground. Quite often, people end up evaluating outcomes on the basis of factors that are largely independent of the battlefield: their preexisting beliefs, the symbolism of events, and manipulation by elites and the media. Understanding these sources of bias is vital because perceptions of victory can make or break the careers of leaders, shape relations between countries, and skew the historical lessons that guide future policymaking.

As international relations become more complex and interdependent, people's evaluations of international outcomes become increasingly prey to bias. Victory and defeat used to be far more obvious than they are today. The winner was often determined by who had control or possession of the battlefield. Marauding kings or warlords would conquer their enemies outright, steal their treasures, sack their towns, kill their warriors, and imprison whoever was left. In such cases, the reality of defeat was self-evident for both the victor and the vanquished. After the seven-month siege of Tyre in 332 BC, Alexander's forces slaughtered eight thousand Tyrians, and the remaining thirty thousand inhabitants were enslaved. Since 1945, however, the wholesale conquest of rival states and populations has become a rarity. Increasingly, in a world of limited conflicts, multi-ethnic civil wars, UN peace deals, international interventions, and secret wars on terror, the relative winners and losers in the global chess game (or, indeed, in any single move) are much more ambiguous, and evaluations are more open to interpretation and influence by psychological biases.[5]

| Imagined Victories and Defeats

There are many historical examples in which interpretations of victory and defeat bear surprisingly little relation to the outcomes on the ground. As time goes on, dominant perceptions about who won tend to become established wisdom.

The War of 1812 between the United States and Britain ended with a commitment to return to the prewar status quo. The outcome on the ground was basically a draw, but in the United States it quickly came to be seen as a great triumph. This evaluation emerged even though the United States had failed in its objective to annex Canada, the British had razed much of Washington, D.C., and Americans had been deeply divided by the war. The dominant perception was of a young United States standing up to the forces of the mighty British Empire. This viewpoint ignored the fact that the British had their hands full dealing with the even mightier Napoleon. The British won many of the clashes in the war, but Americans focused on the U.S. victory in the final battle at New Orleans, won by Andrew Jackson and an unlikely collection of U.S. soldiers, Haitian slaves, Kentucky mountain men, and pirates under the legendary Jean Lafitte. However, this battle was largely irrelevant because, unknown to the combatants in New Orleans, the two sides had already signed a peace treaty.

The historian Donald Hickey wrote that as the years passed, Americans forgot the costs and defeats of the war: "According to the emerging myth, the United States had won the war as well as the peace. Thus the War of 1812 passed into history not as a futile and costly struggle in which the United States had barely escaped dismemberment and disunion, but as a glorious triumph in which the nation had single-handedly defeated the conqueror of Napoleon and the Mistress of the Seas." After the war, many opponents of the conflict suffered politically, while its supporters and participants prospered—in the case of James Monroe, John Quincy Adams, Andrew Jackson, and William Henry Harrison, by becoming president of the United States. American history textbooks today continue to convey a favorable impression of the war as one that left "a feeling of pride as a nation," helped "Americans to win European respect," and (the main outcome for some textbook authors) led to the composition of "The Star-Spangled Banner."[6]

Similarly curious evaluations were evident in Italy after World War I, but in this case a country that had been victorious on the battlefield believed itself to have lost. Italy had been on the winning side in the Great War, and yet many Italians came to see the conflict as a defeat. In the words of two historians of the period: "It seems strange, at least in terms of the final outcome, that Italy fought a successful war yet emerged psychologically a loser."[7] Unlike the other victors—Britain, France, and the United States— many Italians had bitter perceptions of the war because Italy had not made all the territorial gains it had hoped for. With the emergence of Mussolini, extreme nationalism, and revisionism, Italy's postwar society quickly came to resemble those of the states that *had* lost the war: Germany and the former Austria-Hungary.

Meanwhile, in the German population, the myth developed that their country had not actually been beaten in the Great War, that the German army had remained undefeated in battle, and that domestic forces had stabbed the military in the back. According to the historian Hew Strachan: "Despite its defeat, Germany manufactured its own feeling of victory out of the war." Germany's chancellor Friedrich Ebert told veterans after the armistice: "I salute you, who return unvanquished from the field of battle." This is a phenomenon that has been common throughout history. As Wolfgang Schivelbusch wrote in *The Culture of Defeat*: "Nations do not usually embrace defeat in their mythology. Indeed, they do everything in their power to deny it or to turn the tables by imagining the victor as the loser of the next round of warfare."[8]

In the 1938 Munich crisis, Hitler succeeded in acquiring the Sudetenland from Czechoslovakia, in return for agreeing not to use force. In spite of this apparently clear-cut outcome, the Munich settlement generated a variety of contrasting assessments and reassessments about which side had really won and which had lost. Opinions shifted over time, sometimes conforming to the result on the ground (a German victory), sometimes deviating widely from it. The notion that a negotiated agreement had averted war led British Prime Minister Neville Chamberlain to declare the settlement a diplomatic coup that had established "peace with honour . . . peace for our time." The *Times* of London rejoiced: "No conqueror returning from victory on the battlefield has come home adorned with nobler laurels than Mr. Chamberlain from Munich."[9] However, within a few weeks criticism mounted that Germany had been significantly strengthened by the settlement, with predictions that Berlin would soon make additional demands. Yet in 1945 Hitler himself looked back on the Munich settlement as a defeat for Germany because it had prevented him from starting a war in 1938, when German military advantage had been, he thought, at its greatest. In the years since World War II, Munich has been widely seen as a major reverse for the Western democracies, and it is commonly cited as categorical evidence that dictators should never be appeased. Despite this generally negative view of Munich, the historian A. J. P. Taylor maintained in the 1960s that, by delaying war to allow for rearmament, British policy was "a triumph."[10]

Even military defeats can be perceived as victories. After World War II broke out, British forces were rushed to France to help stall the German advance. Although they were quickly overwhelmed by the massive onslaught of the German Blitzkrieg, their emergency withdrawal from France in 1940 was transformed into a kind of victory at Dunkirk, in which 340,000 troops were shipped to safety as German tanks pressed on their heels all the way to the coast. Civilian sailors became heroes by making the cross-channel voyage to rescue the desperate men on the beaches. A perception of success arose despite the fact that the British had crumbled under the German advance and had left almost all their equipment on the beaches of northern France. Dunkirk in itself *was* a success—thousands of soldiers escaped. But the drama focused attention away from the wider picture: a disastrous military defeat for Britain and France. The historian Roy Jenkins remarked that in Britain "there was a seductive tendency to treat Dunkirk as a victory and not just as a deliverance." But as Winston Churchill wryly noted: "Wars are not won by evacuations."[11]

In 1949 U.S. Republicans accused President Truman and the Democrats of "losing" China to the communists during the Chinese civil war. While the outcome ran counter to U.S. interests, the notion that America had been defeated implied that it had made serious efforts to prevail—which it had not. It also implied that China could have been saved at an acceptable cost, but the United States would have had to send hundreds of thousands of ground troops to avert a communist triumph. Nevertheless, as a result of these perceptions of failure in China, future Democratic administrations were fearful of being seen to "lose" Vietnam to communism, and this fear was a major reason for their decisions to escalate U.S. military intervention. President Johnson declared that the setback for the Democrats over China would be "chickenshit compared with what might happen if we lost Vietnam."[12]

In 1950, shortly after the supposed defeat for the United States in China, North Korea invaded South Korea. U.S. and allied forces succeeded in preventing a communist takeover of South Korea, and drove the North Koreans back across their border to the Yalu River. Following Chinese intervention, U.S. forces lost virtually all their gains in the North, and the front lines returned almost exactly to the prewar boundaries. The war became increasingly unpopular in the United States, and by 1952 it was widely considered an attritional failure. By the mid-1950s, however, opinion polls showed that Americans had changed their minds and now viewed the Korean War as a qualified success.[13] Thus a conflict whose outcome had been a draw was seen initially as a failure and later as a success.

In the 1962 Cuban missile crisis, the United States and the USSR hammered out a deal that pulled the world back from the brink of

nuclear war. The settlement involved compromises and concessions on both sides: the Soviet Union pulled its missiles out of
Cuba, and the United States pledged not to invade Cuba and
agreed to withdraw its own missiles from Turkey. Yet all over the
world, in capitalist and communist states alike, the crisis was seen as
a major defeat for Moscow and an unalloyed triumph for the Americans. The Soviet leader, Nikita Khrushchev, was soon thrown out
of office.[14]

Six years later, in 1968, at the high point of the Vietnam war, the
U.S. military achieved a remarkable battlefield victory in reversing
the communists' Tet offensive—a massive surprise attack across the
country. Yet Tet was perceived in the United States as a major defeat—with significant consequences. Just as the American military
was finally able to exploit its technological advantages by fighting
communist forces in the open, President Johnson halted the bombing campaign, offered negotiations to North Vietnam, withdrew
from the presidential election, and set in motion the disengagement of U.S. ground forces from Vietnam.

Similarly, in 1973, Egypt and Syria launched a surprise attack on
Israel, which, after early Arab successes, led to a complete reversal
and a significant Israeli victory on the battlefield. When a ceasefire
was agreed upon, Israeli forces were on the counterattack within a
few miles of both Cairo and Damascus. Despite this outcome, in
both Israel and the Arab states the war was seen as a failure or a defeat for Israel. Even though the Israeli forces captured far more territory in the war than they lost, even though many more Arabs died
than Israelis, and even though a large part of the Egyptian army was
surrounded in the Sinai and on the brink of surrender when the
conflict ended, the Yom Kippur War is remembered in Egypt as a
historic triumph, and in Israel as one of the most shocking and disastrous events in the country's history.

As noted earlier, Americans viewed the bungled rescue mission in the 1975 *Mayaguez* incident as a triumph, but saw the quite successful 1992–1994 U.S. mission in Somalia as a prominent failure. Similarly puzzling perceptions of victory are apparent in relation to the Israeli withdrawal from Lebanon in 2000. Israel had arguably accomplished many of the original aims of its invasion of Lebanon, and it made sense to pull out. Yet, in the view of Gershon Baskin of the Israel-Palestine Center for Research and Information: "Israel's rapid withdrawal from south Lebanon, after a 20-year occupation was widely perceived in the Arab world as a victory by the Islamic Hezbollah group over the Jewish state. That perception became one of the triggers for the Palestinian decision to resort to armed struggle against Israel after the collapse of Camp David peace negotiations in the summer of 2000."[15]

Today, with Iraq and the war on terror dominating the U.S. foreign policy agenda, the American public and media are deeply divided over whether the United States is winning or losing these complex new struggles. America's ongoing wars are, evidently, the latest in a long line of wars of perception.

Why Imagined Victories and Defeats Are Important

In these wars, battles, interventions, and crises, simple comparison of the gains and losses of the opposing sides cannot explain the dominant perceptions of victory and defeat. Neither can the material result explain a diversity of perceptions of victory and defeat. We are, therefore, left with a puzzle: What *does* drive the process of evaluating victory and defeat? This question, which we will address in Chapters 2–4, has considerable implications for leaders, for society and democracy, for current foreign policy, and for future foreign policy.

Impact on Leaders

Leaders ought to be particularly concerned with perceptions of their success and failure because their domestic political survival may well depend on being viewed as the victors, whether or not they did, in fact, achieve significant tangible gains. President Kennedy derived great political benefit from the Cuban missile crisis; Khrushchev quite the opposite. After the Tet offensive, President Johnson decided not to seek reelection, while the American military commander in Vietnam, General Westmoreland, was "kicked upstairs." Israel's investigations into the Yom Kippur War led to the resignation of Prime Minister Golda Meir and her entire cabinet, while in Egypt President Anwar Sadat's prestige rose considerably. Put simply: if leaders want to stay in office, it is imperative that they be seen to win.[16] One might cynically recommend that leaders should exert greater effort in winning over the minds of observers than in winning the war itself. Indeed, at the extreme, a political victory can be levered from the jaws of a military defeat. This offers both opportunities and dangers. A skilled politician can lay a smokescreen over failure, but a less able (or less lucky) politician may face an undeserved collapse in political support.

Impact on Society and Democracy

Perceptions of victory and defeat also have crucial implications for the public, interest groups, and the media. Defeat, or perceived defeat, often proves to be a traumatic experience for society at large. It can lead to a number of complex psychological and cultural responses, which may consume subsequent domestic politics for many years (think of the intense and continuing unease over the Vietnam war in U.S. politics). Defeat often comes to define a country's self-image. Losing states tend to rewrite histories, generate myths to explain failure, emulate victors, and find domestic scapegoats (for example, the Jews in Germany after World War I).[17]

A prerequisite for democracy is that citizens be able to fairly and accurately evaluate their current and prospective leaders, and vote accordingly. If a leader is reelected primarily because of perceptions of success rather than actual success, or loses office because of perceived rather than actual failure, this raises troubling questions for democracy. Understanding how perceptions of victory are formed will enable the use of more accurate criteria with which to hold policymakers accountable.

Impact on Current Policy

Perceptions of success also matter because they shape current foreign policy options and decisions. The American public tends to withdraw its approval, and to become much less tolerant of U.S. casualties, when it perceives a foreign policy mission as failing. When a mission is deemed to be going well, as in Panama in 1989 or the Gulf War in 1991, approval for the president can rise even as casualties increase. When the U.S. public thinks a war is going badly, as in Vietnam after 1968, further casualties have a much greater negative effect on presidential approval ratings. As the political scientists Peter Feaver and Christopher Gelpi put it: "The public is defeat phobic, not casualty phobic."[18] General George Patton told U.S. troops just before D-Day in 1944: "Americans love a winner and will not tolerate a loser. Americans play to win all the time. I wouldn't give a hoot in hell for a man who lost and laughed. That's why Americans have never lost and will never lose a war. Because the very thought of losing is hateful to Americans." Patton was right that Americans are very sensitive to winning and losing, but he was wrong in his prediction that the United States would never lose a war—it was defeated in Vietnam. In fact, the United States is sometimes less successful than it might be precisely because Americans are so sensitive to perceptions of winning and losing. Hints of failure can produce a self-fulfilling prophecy, whereby public or congressional discontent leads to reduced U.S. military expenditure or a withdrawal of American troops, thus increasing the probability of a bona fide defeat on the ground.[19]

Perceptions of victory and defeat also influence international alliances and bargaining. The perceived defeat of the Soviet Union in the Cuban missile crisis, for example, widened the Sino-Soviet split, one of the major dynamics of the Cold War. States whose leaders and publics *believe* they lost act much like states that really *did* lose. The fact that Israel saw the 1973 war as a defeat opened the way for it to trade land for peace with Egypt. Whether positive or negative, perceptions of victory and defeat have significant and lasting effects on international relations.

Impact on Future Policy

Beliefs about success also affect subsequent foreign policy decisionmaking because they influence popular and institutional learning. This phenomenon seems to be a feature of mammalian behavior. Researchers who sent mice that were inexperienced at fighting into combat with other mice, and then fixed the matches so that the inexperienced mice always won, found that within a few days the inexperienced mice became far more aggressive and would even attack females and young. As the psychologist Ralph White concluded about the experiment: "Unless counterbalanced by the pain and frustration of defeat, victory alone is enough to keep the fighting behavior going or even increase it."[20]

People, too, learn from their experiences and change their behavior accordingly. Yuen Foong Khong and Ernest May have demonstrated that decisionmakers commonly perceive their policy options to widen or narrow in accordance with the lessons they draw from salient historical events. Where observers place an outcome along the spectrum between victory and defeat strongly determines what those lessons will be. Human actors will readily repeat strategies that produced outcomes perceived as successes. In contrast, strategies that led to perceived failures become warnings about what not to do. Having "failed" in Somalia in 1992–1994, the Clinton administration thought it should avoid intervening in Rwanda. As another example, the political scientist Dan Reiter found that the decisions made by small and medium-sized states about whether to join alliances or stay neutral are based to a large extent on the perceived success of previous alliance strategies. If a state was neutral in the last regional conflict, and this strategy is viewed as a success, then the state will tend to adopt a similar policy of neutrality in the future.[21]

The danger is that states will readily repeat policies that were perceived as successful in the past, even if those policies, in tangible terms, had neutral or negative effects or produced positive results simply because of good fortune. As the political scientist Robert Jervis pointed out decades ago, achievements may lead to erroneous conclusions: "With a successful outcome relatively little attention is paid to the costs of the policy, the possibility that others might have worked even better, or the possibility that success was largely attributable to luck and that the policy might just as easily have failed."[22]

The perceived U.S. victory in the 1962 Cuban missile crisis produced the "lessons" that nuclear crises were manageable or inherently winnable, and that a tough stand would always make the Soviets retreat. Members of the Kennedy and Johnson administrations thought that this same logic would apply if they were steadfast in Vietnam. The political scientist Richard Lebow, writing about the Cuban missile crisis, has argued that "Kennedy's successful use of coercive diplomacy led ineluctably to American intervention in Vietnam." President Johnson's press secretary, Bill Moyers, said that in Johnson's inner circle "there was a confidence, it was never bragged about, it was just there—a residue, perhaps of the confrontation over the missiles in Cuba—that when the chips were really down, the other people would fold." However, a closer examination of the missile crisis reveals that it was the willingness of both sides to compromise that defused the situation. Such caution about reading too much into supposed triumphs echoes Plato's warning: "Many a victory has been and will be suicidal to the victors." If genuine triumphs can breed an unhealthy hubris, the danger is even greater when the victory is more imagined than real.[23]

On the other side of the coin, states will avoid repeating policies that were perceived as unsuccessful, despite any virtues those policies might have. In 1998, for example, President Clinton ordered the firing of cruise missiles at al-Qaeda training camps in Afghanistan in response to terrorist attacks on U.S. embassies in East Africa, but Osama bin Laden apparently had left a few hours before the missiles arrived. Missile strikes might be seen as a useful tactic that happened not to work on this occasion because of bad luck. However, the administration of Clinton's successor, George W. Bush, consigned the cruise missile strikes to the defeat category, largely for symbolic reasons. Bush remarked: "The antiseptic notion of launching a cruise missile into some guy's, you know, tent, really is a joke. I mean people viewed that as the impotent America . . . It was clear that bin Laden felt emboldened." With the cruise missile strikes perceived as a failure, any similar tactics were taboo after the terrorist attacks of 11 September 2001. When the Pentagon presented the Bush administration with three options for the war in Afghanistan, the first was cruise missile strikes. According to the journalist Bob Woodward: "It might as well have been labeled the Clinton Option . . . There was palpable disgust at the mere mention of cruise missiles."[24]

In summary, perceptions of victory not only affect the account book of history but also shape the fate of leaders, democratic processes, support for foreign policies, and the lessons used to guide decisions in the future. In this book we examine the formation of those perceptions: how observers perceive the outcomes of international disputes, whether they are wars, crises, interventions, or individual battles, and whether they are ongoing, recently ended, or long past.[25] Our scope is broad because the factors that shape evaluations tend to operate in similar ways across these different types of disputes. We are especially interested in the origins of differences of opinion and — the converse — how a dominant view of which side won can emerge and become established wisdom.

To understand evaluations of outcomes, we bring to bear recent findings from psychology, mass communication, and studies of elite manipulation and the cultural construction of historical narratives. We focus on how three classes of bias influence people's perceptions of victory: mind-sets, salient events, and social pressures. In addition, we examine the many and varied interactions between these processes: entrenched mind-sets, for example, may provide opportunities for leaders to exploit. We aim to map out and develop an exciting new area for research. In tackling the puzzle of imagined victories and imagined defeats, we draw from a wide range of theoretical and historical literatures and utilize a number of methodologies, including experiments and analysis of polling data.

In Chapters 2 and 3 we offer a taxonomy of the primary factors that shape evaluations of victory and defeat, which we draw together into two theoretical frameworks. Framework 1 we label "score-keeping" (adding up gains and losses). Framework 2 we label "match-fixing" (by which the result becomes fixed or preordained in the minds of observers because of mind-sets, salient events, and social pressures). In Chapter 4 we explain the conditions under which people tend to score-keep and the conditions under which they tend to match-fix; and which side in a dispute usually benefits or suffers from match-fixing (that is, which country is judged more leniently and which is judged more harshly than performance on the ground would indicate). The following five chapters trace the formation of perceptions of victory in a number of critical disputes: the 1962 Cuban missile crisis, the 1968 Tet offensive in the Vietnam war, the 1973 Yom Kippur War, the 1992–1994 U.S. intervention in Somalia, and America's ongoing wars—the war on terror and the war in Iraq.

Perceptions of victory and defeat result from competition between the reality on the ground and biases produced by mind-sets, salient events, and social pressures. Any attempt to judiciously weigh up gains and losses for each side is in conflict with deep-seated cognitive and motivational biases, ingrained over millennia in a life and an environment very different from the one in which we now live. In certain clear-cut outcomes, skewed evaluations are swept aside by the undeniable triumph of one side. In ancient wars of conquest, such clarity of result was more common. But undeniable triumph is the exception in most of the crises and wars of today. In these more ambiguous circumstances, observers searching for an evaluation—pushed by elite manipulation, pulled by the media—fall back on cognitive shortcuts and gut feelings to make their way through the complex information available to them. On their highly subjective and often deeply skewed judgments rests the destiny of leaders, their states, and their peoples.

2 | SCORE-KEEPING

With Alexander as an able partner [Philip] beat the Athenians in
a pitched battle and took total control of mainland Greece. It was
a crushing victory, with the famous "Sacred Band," which had
never retreated, being killed to the last man.

—THOMAS WILLIAM-POWLETT

The results of the battles near Moscow and in Stalingrad, the
courage of Leningrad under siege, the success in the Kursk and
Dnieper battles, determined the outcome of World War II. The
Red Army marked the victorious end to the war by liberating
Europe, waging the battle for Berlin.

—VLADIMIR PUTIN

IN THIS CHAPTER we examine the hypothesis that people's judgments of victory and defeat simply reflect the material outcome: a
phenomenon we call score-keeping. But first there is a very basic
question to answer: Do we know that observers actually make judgments about success at all? It could be that people typically decline
even to reach an evaluation about international events. Americans,
for example, differ markedly in terms of their interest, attention, and
involvement in politics. The political scientist W. Russell Neuman
divided the American population into three categories: 5 percent
who are political activists, with high levels of interest and involvement; 75 percent in the "middle mass," who pay scant attention to
politics but do vote quite regularly; and 20 percent who pay little or

no attention to politics and rarely vote. Except during major crises, Americans tend not to follow the international news. According to one survey conducted in 2002, 11 percent of Americans aged 18–24 could not locate the United States on an unlabeled world map. Consequently, many people would not have an opinion about who won, say, the 1998 war between Ethiopia and Eritrea, since they would be unaware that this war even took place.[1]

However, people will offer evaluations on issues that are either personally important, or are widely covered in the media, even when they lack the information to make a truly informed judgment. When asked by polling agencies if the United States is winning the war on terror (an issue even experts acknowledge is exceptionally difficult to judge), fully 90–97 percent of Americans offer an opinion, and only 3–10 percent say they are not sure or don't know. Similarly, when asked how likely a terrorist attack is against the United States "within the next few months," only 5 percent claim to be unsure, with the other 95 percent offering an apparently firm view, one way or the other. Many of these evaluations are probably quasi-attitudes made up on the spot, half-hearted, even random reactions. They nevertheless exist in people's minds, or can be readily formed when prompted. The complex nature of international relations should make observers cautious about their judgments, but people often believe that their evaluations about winners and losers are *obviously* true. At times people disagree strongly about the performance of their leaders or armies; at other times almost everyone agrees about who won and who lost. The questions we examine are: How are these judgments made? And why and when do they vary?[2]

| Evaluating Victory

We begin with the most basic model of how people evaluate victory. Judgments of success (whether by a computer or a person's con-

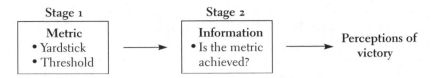

CHART 2.1. The process of evaluating victory.

scious or unconscious mind) must involve a two-stage process (see Chart 2.1):

1. Observers need a *metric* for what constitutes success and failure. A metric is the criterion against which to measure an outcome, and comprises two parts: a *yardstick* of what to measure (e.g. territory or body counts); and a *threshold* on the yardstick to mark the point when success is considered to be achieved (e.g. a strategic target captured or an enemy army destroyed).

2. Once observers have a metric, they need *information* about the outcome of the dispute to determine if country X has been successful (whether or not the relevant threshold on the yardstick has been reached).

People sometimes have in their minds a very specific metric for victory. For example, military personnel may have an explicit set of goals that would constitute mission success. Other observers may not even realize that they are utilizing a metric for victory. But any judgment of success requires at least an implicit metric. To say that an outcome is a defeat is to say that it falls short of some (perhaps unstated or even unacknowledged) standard for what victory would be. Such a metric may be vague, arbitrary, or changing, but it exists. Metrics are therefore a necessary and logical part of the judgment process. Now we can move on to ask: How do people select metrics? And how do they match them to information?

| Framework 1: Score-keeping

Our first explanation for perceptions of victory and defeat is called score-keeping. According to this approach, observers decide the winners and losers on the basis of a scorecard listing material gains and losses. When people score-keep, their views about who won and who lost directly reflect the material outcome of the war or crisis.

Score-keeping is one potential explanation of how people make judgments. It is not merely a "straw-man" argument; on the contrary, score-keeping is quite often effective at explaining evaluations of victory and defeat. Indeed, we argue later that score-keeping is the way people *should* judge victory and defeat. It's the Occam's Razor approach: if you are trying to understand why someone evaluated a battle in a certain way, then before invoking anything more complex, it makes sense to ask what happened on the battlefield. Why does someone believe that the Chicago White Sox won the 2005 World Series? Before choosing a complicated explanation based on psychological phenomena, we should check to see if the White Sox really did win more World Series games than the opposing team in 2005. A Chicago victory would offer a simple and convincing explanation of the perception of success: it reflected events on the ground.

Unfortunately, in most circumstances we cannot directly observe whether people are score-keeping or not—we cannot peer over their shoulders to see if they are tallying material results on a scorecard. We can, however, test the congruence between the material scorecard outcome and the beliefs people hold about the performance of each side. If such beliefs are congruent with the material outcome, then this suggests (although it does not prove) that the beliefs are products of score-keeping. This causal link would be reinforced, of course, if observers overtly cited material gains and losses as the basis for their perceptions. Either way, if beliefs are *not* congruent with the material scorecard outcome, we must look elsewhere for an explanation. But before getting into that, what exactly is a material scorecard outcome in a war or a crisis?

Definitions of Victory

There are at least five definitions of material victory:

Type 1. *Absolute gains.* Logic: The actor gains in some way from the conflict compared with its antebellum position (any gains made by the adversary are ignored). Example: "France won World War I because it regained Alsace-Lorraine."

Type 2. *Relative gains.* Logic: The actor does better than the adversary on some dimension. Example: "Israel won the 1967 Six-Day War because it conquered more territory than the Arab states did."

Type 3. *Achieving core aims.* Logic: The actor accomplishes important aims. Example: "NATO succeeded in the 1999 Kosovo air campaign because it achieved its core aim of forcing a withdrawal of Serb forces from Kosovo."

Type 4. *The price of peace.* Logic: As a result of the conflict, the actor is better off than if the conflict had never been fought. Example: "The United States was a victor in the 2003 Iraq War because without the conflict Iraq would have developed WMD and supplied them to terrorists."

Type 5. *Optimal policy.* Logic: The policy chosen by the actor achieved the best possible result of all the available policies. Example: "The United States was victorious against Japan in World War II because the island-hopping campaign and the use of atomic weapons led to the surrender of Japan at a lower cost than any other strategy."

These definitions do not necessarily correlate closely with one another, because they use different metrics for victory. I can win by achieving all my objectives (according to a type 3 victory) but still lose if the other side gains more (according to a type 2 victory). But each definition has some merit in determining who *really* won on the battlefield. Therefore, if we are to assess the argument that people's evaluations reflect the battlefield result, we need a model that integrates all these definitions of victory.

Score-keeping incorporates the first three definitions of victory by noting two key elements of the outcome: (1) material *gains* and *losses*, such as territory, casualties, and resources; and (2) whether or not each side achieved its material *aims*. It is essential to separate gains and aims. If you win X, but wanted Y, have you achieved a victory? This clearly depends on additional aspects of the outcome. A situation in which a state achieved all its material aims, yet emerged with substantial overall material losses, could only be described as an ambiguous victory. Similarly, achieving substantial gains but failing to realize one's basic aims would at best be an unclear result. In reality, since leaders usually aim for material gains, the dual assessments of gains and aims often converge to provide the same conclusions about which side won and which side lost. But whether they match or not, a score-keeping analysis must account for aims as well as gains, and weigh up both in determining overall victory.

An examination of gains and aims must also take account of both the *importance* and the *difficulty* of the gain or aim for the state in-

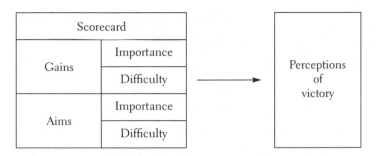

CHART 2.2. With Framework 1 (score-keeping), perceptions of victory are derived from a scorecard comprising evaluations of both gains and aims, each weighted by its importance and difficulty.

volved (see Chart 2.2). Greater *importance* of a gain or aim produces extra credit for achieving it (compared with other gains and aims): capturing 50,000 soldiers warrants more credit than capturing 50 soldiers. Greater *difficulty* of a gain or aim (measured in terms of likely costs incurred in its attainment) also produces extra credit for successfully achieving it (compared with other gains and aims). For example, the U.S. defeat of Grenada in 1983 warranted less credit for Washington than a hypothetical defeat of China would have, because the difficulty of the Grenada operation was much lower.

Accounting for the difficulty of gains and aims is essential for a fair score-keeping analysis because it adjusts for the existing material strength of each side in the dispute. David deserves more credit for defeating Goliath than Goliath would deserve if the outcome had been the other way around. What score-keeping really measures, therefore, is the success of each side's *strategy*, or how effectively the sides use their resources given the particular environment, to make gains (especially those that constitute their core aims).[3]

Should aims and gains be measured in absolute terms (type 1

victory) or in relative terms (type 2 victory)? This depends upon the nature of the dispute. For certain types of wars it is appropriate to judge success in relative terms. If the sides are rivals with a probable future of conflict, then a country that makes gains while its rival makes even greater gains cannot be considered victorious. In contrast, in some situations it is appropriate to focus on the gains and aims achieved by just one side. For example, we should assess U.S. gains and aims achieved in the 1992–1994 intervention in Somalia in absolute rather than relative terms, because the United States did not face a coherent adversary and Washington's objectives were mainly humanitarian.[4]

One of the thorniest issues is whether to incorporate type 4 and type 5 victories into score-keeping: the "price of peace" and "optimal policy" victories. David Baldwin has argued that to judge success one needs to compare the outcome that did occur with outcomes that would have occurred if an alternative strategy had been employed. Otherwise a supposedly "failed" policy might actually have produced the best possible outcome under the circumstances because all the other strategies would have fared even worse.[5] For example, to judge U.S. success in Somalia we would have to compare the gains and losses that did arise in 1992–1994 with the gains and losses that would have arisen from strategies that were *not* employed (such as economic sanctions or purely diplomatic methods).

However, we are more cautious than Baldwin about the utility of this method of defining material success. A counterfactual analysis of gains and losses in hypothesized scenarios can end up as little more than guesswork. To determine how successful economic sanctions would have been in Somalia, we have to construct a fictional alternative universe. One could argue that we have enough difficulty score-keeping in the world that exists, without trying to score-keep in worlds that do not exist. Nevertheless, in those rare circumstances where reliable information allows confident judgments about the probable gains and losses that would have accrued from alternative strategies, such an analysis can be incorporated into a score-keeping approach: the gains and aims actually achieved can be weighed against the counterfactual gains and aims achieved.

When Does Score-keeping Begin and End?

Any score-keeping analysis requires a "before" time point and an "after" time point, so that the gains and aims achieved between these two points can be measured. How do we decide where these points fall?

Wars start with the first shot fired. Crises start with the first precipitating act. At this stage an observer can begin to keep track of the score. The end point can in principle be as late as the moment at which the observer makes a judgment, because wars or crises can produce gains and losses after the fighting or diplomacy stops. A victorious side might force further concessions a month after the peace treaty was signed. However, in order to be counted in the scorecard, a gain or an aim achieved must be a direct product of the war. Including later gains in the scorecard is often ill-advised because, as time goes on, confidence that these gains were really caused by the war rapidly declines. Gains and losses during the war are often direct products of the fighting; changes a few weeks afterward may also be fairly clearly caused by the war; but after several months thousands of other events will have occurred, rendering claims of causality highly suspect. Once years have passed, it is very difficult to demonstrate that some new gain or loss was directly caused by the original war or crisis. In summary, score-keeping includes only gains and losses that we know with a high degree of certainty are the product of the war or the crisis itself.

Is Score-keeping Objective or Subjective?

Score-keeping includes both objective and subjective elements. The objective element is the importance of aims; the subjective elements are the importance of gains, the difficulty of aims, and the difficulty of gains. Why is this?

Let's start with the objective element: the importance of aims. Given leaders at a given time will have some set of aims that they want to achieve. Thus observers can, in principle, discern what these aims are and how the leaders rank them in importance, and then give extra credit for the achievement of aims that are ranked highly. Few doubt that Hitler sought to dominate Europe, or that Stalin wanted to remain in power at almost any price. Both aims were of high importance — to those leaders — and different observers can agree on this.

However, the importance of gains is inherently subjective. Whereas the importance of an aim is measured in terms of a leader's desires, the importance of a gain is measured in terms of an observer's subjective view of its worth. It is logical that a leader's aims should be weighted by how much they mattered to the leader personally. It is also logical that the importance of gains should be weighted by their worth as perceived by an observer. Most people consider the capture of 50,000 soldiers to be a more important gain than the capture of 50 soldiers, not because the leader happens to think so, but because most people perceive the former achievement to have greater worth. If Hitler won a scrap of territory that he valued highly (say, a patch of desert that he was emotionally attached to), but an observer perceived the territory to be worth very little,

then in score-keeping the observer would note both its high importance as an aim for Hitler and its low importance as a gain,
measured in terms of its subjectively perceived worth. Considering
only one of these dimensions of importance would produce an inadequate understanding of the significance of the winning of the
territory.

Why is measuring the worth of a gain a subjective process? Because we cannot say for sure that any one material gain is more important than any other material gain. Even individuals with full information about the outcome, who lack any unconscious biases,
and who process information perfectly, will probably vary somewhat in their views about the importance of particular gains because of different personal preferences—and no single observer can
be said to be "right" or "wrong." For example, the Dalai Lama and
Genghis Khan might assess the importance of the same set of material gains and losses in the light of very different beliefs. The Dalai
Lama might attribute more importance to the human costs, and
Genghis Khan might attach more importance to territorial gains.
Neither would necessarily be assessing the importance, or worth, of
material gains and losses any more "accurately" than the other. In
contrast, preferences do not matter for the importance of aims, because the Dalai Lama and Genghis Khan could, in principle, agree
on what *another actor* wanted, regardless of whether they themselves would want these things or not.

For similar reasons, the difficulty of both aims and gains is subjective. High difficulty indicates that certain gains and aims are
likely to incur greater costs in their attainment. Weighing up likely
costs, however, is an inherently subjective process because it involves ranking certain types of costs (such as casualties) over other
types (such as monetary costs). The Dalai Lama and Genghis Khan
might disagree over the ranking of particular costs even if they had

full information and lacked any unconscious biases, because of varying preferences, and neither would be "right" or "wrong."

Since score-keeping involves a subjective component, the overall scorecard will not be entirely objective. However, this is not particularly important for our analysis. Although in a group of score-keepers the importance and difficulty attached to particular material gains and losses will nearly always vary, score-keeping evaluations will nevertheless tend to cluster together, in a fairly predictable manner, as reasonable approximations of each side's performance on the ground. Most people are not as different from one another as the Dali Lama and Genghis Khan (and thus may be expected to diverge less in their preferences). There is considerable consensus, and common sense, in people's views about the importance of various gains and losses: territory captured and casualties incurred by an army are seen as more important than, say, the amount of recreation time an army has. All in all, in the real world, major discrepancies among people who are properly score-keeping will be rare.

In summary, score-keeping may appear to be a complicated explanation for people's evaluations of victory and defeat, but it is founded on some simple principles. People score-keep if their judgments (1) are measured in terms of material gains and aims achieved, (2) are adjusted for difficulty and importance, and (3) cover the relevant period. All of these factors are quite intuitive. If people's evaluations do *not* reflect these principles, then we must find another explanation.

Is Score-keeping the Best Way to Evaluate Victory?

Score-keeping is primarily used in this book as a candidate explanation for the way people actually evaluate victory and defeat in real life (a null hypothesis, if you like). We compare people's perceptions of success with the outcome on the ground to determine whether or not they were score-keeping.

However, score-keeping is also the way we think people *ought* to evaluate success and failure. Score-keeping is a mode of judgment that focuses on tangible gains and losses and aims achieved and not achieved. It also explicitly incorporates the dimensions of difficulty and importance, and it seeks to clarify the relevant time points. Score-keeping integrates all of the major definitions of victory and is therefore sufficient to provide a sound basis of judgment.

Score-keeping focuses on *material* changes and ignores psychological gains such as increasing perceived resolve or credibility. Why do psychological gains not also deserve credit? There are two good reasons for ignoring them. First, including them would require measuring an endless series of psychological effects: not just resolve and credibility, but also prestige, reputation, and so on. It is unclear which ones should be included (let alone how to measure them). Second, and more fundamentally, these factors should not be taken into account in judgments of victory even if they could be measured. Resolve and credibility are important only inasmuch as they are a means to a material end, and it is this *end* that we evaluate. When judging the success of a sports team we do not measure the players' resolve on the field; we measure the *fruits* of their resolve in terms of points scored. Similarly, in international politics, we do not measure resolve itself; we measure the fruits of a state's resolve in terms of material gains and losses. The strengthening of resolve may translate into material gains in the future, but then again it may not, and credit is awarded only when the material gains actually occur. Therefore, observers ought to judge victory on the basis of material gains and losses and material aims achieved and not achieved.

But there is one very important caveat. Score-keeping is the recommended mode of judgment *only if everyone else is score-keeping too*. If other people are *not* score-keeping, their false view of the outcome may rebound to alter the reality of gains and losses. For example, once observers in the United States decide, perhaps inaccurately, that one country is the victor in a war or crisis, this judgment can alter subsequent U.S. policy (via congressional action, voting behavior, and so on), producing new gains for one side or the other.

An ideal judgment must therefore consider not only the scorecard but also the material changes that result from the prevailing opinion about who has won. For this reason, judgments formed through score-keeping alone are often incomplete. For example, if we score-keep the Tet offensive of 1968, we find that the United States won. But this is a misleading view because it fails to account for the fact that some Americans were not score-keeping, and their perception of American defeat led to U.S. de-escalation that benefited the North Vietnamese (who were, as a consequence, the real victors, achieving the greatest net gains). The Tet offensive illustrates that an inaccurate perception of victory, if sufficiently widespread, can become a self-fulfilling prophecy: the perceived winners become the real winners. Therefore, although score-keeping is the method people *should* use to evaluate outcomes, if some people are not score-keeping, one must take into account the dominant perceptions of who won and who lost and their consequences.

| Do People Score-keep?

Is score-keeping the way people *do* evaluate victory and defeat? The short answer is yes—sometimes. There are hundreds of examples in history of situations in which one protagonist was widely recognized as being victorious because it attained greater material gains than its opponent. No one doubts that Germany, Japan, and Italy were defeated in World War II, or that Napoleon lost the wars that bear his name. Not only do observers in very different cultures and with very different beliefs agree on who won and who lost these wars, they would probably offer similar *reasons* for assigning victory and defeat in each case, based on the material scorecard. Germany, Japan, and Italy lost on the battlefield, Germany and Japan were physically occupied, and Germany was dismembered.

Even though people tend to score-keep World War II, not all evaluations of that war are identical. As already suggested, observers who score-keep assess the importance of material gains and losses according to their own preferences. As we would predict, some people highlight the civilian costs on all sides of World War II (an emphasis that might slightly temper views of an Allied victory) while others focus on narrowly defined military gains (and thus see a clear-cut victory for the Allies). There is therefore some variation, but, nevertheless, evaluations are clustered around the consensus position that the Allies won and the fascist states lost.

In other cases, score-keeping may account only partially for judgments about victory and defeat. American evaluations of U.S. success in the Kosovo campaign in 1999 became more favorable once the major U.S. material aims had been achieved and Serb forces had retreated from Kosovo. At the same time, beliefs about success were strongly influenced by partisanship: Democrats were more positive about Democratic President Bill Clinton's performance than Republicans were. Similarly, the American public's evaluations of the Iraq War and its aftermath were influenced by tangible material gains and losses such as U.S. casualty figures. But they were influenced to an equal or greater extent by a wide range of other factors such as partisanship, race, gender, symbolic events, and media manipulation, factors that are substantially independent of the success and failure of American troops fighting in Iraq (see Chapter 9).

World War II, Kosovo, and Iraq are illustrative examples in which score-keeping at least partly accounts for perceptions of victory and defeat. But there are a number of puzzling disputes in which score-keeping has little explanatory power at all. Indeed, the role of score-keeping in explaining evaluations can vary from zero to 100 percent. Examples of international disputes in which score-keeping fails to explain perceptions of victory and defeat, ranging from the War of 1812 to Israel's withdrawal from Lebanon in 2000, were outlined in Chapter 1. These cases suggest that evaluations of victory and defeat often strongly depend on who the observers were, when and where they evaluated the outcome, and how it was reported to them. In other words, victory was a matter of perception.

3 | MATCH-FIXING

Victory always starts in the head. It's a state of mind. It then spreads with such radiance and such affirmations that destiny can do nothing but obey.

— DOUCHAN GERSI

Appearances to the mind are of four kinds. Things either are what they appear to be; or they neither are, nor appear to be; or they are, and do not appear to be; or they are not, and yet appear to be.

— EPICTETUS

IN JOHN HUGHES'S 1986 movie *Ferris Bueller's Day Off*, the dean of students, Ed Rooney, is in search of his wayward pupil, Ferris Bueller. On his travels, Rooney visits a fast-food restaurant, where a grease-covered television set broadcasts a Chicago Bears game. Rooney glances at the screen and asks, "What's the score?" The server replies, "Nothin' to nothin'." Rooney, not really listening, asks, "Who's winning?" The server pauses before replying, as if the answer is obvious: "The Bears!" After a moment's surprise, Rooney nods and exits, just missing Ferris Bueller cheering in a close-up of the crowd.[1]

Rooney's experience at the fast-food stand alludes to our central puzzle. The gains and losses made by each side often fail to explain people's perceptions of victory, whether in wars, crises, or other events (even when there is a fifty-foot scoreboard declaring the distribution of points). In fact, material gains and losses often fail to explain three distinct phenomena: the *dominant* perception of victory and defeat; the *diversity* in perceptions of victory and defeat; and the *changes* in these perceptions over time. Why do states that win narrowly, achieve a draw, or even suffer greatly, sometimes come to be perceived as the triumphant victors? And why do other states that lose narrowly, achieve a draw, or even seize the lion's share of gains, sometimes come to be perceived as the defeated parties? If perceptions of victory and defeat are only loosely related to what actually happens on the ground, what factors *do* explain these evaluations?

| Fixing the Match

In this chapter we suggest a new approach for explaining people's perceptions of victory and defeat (our dependent variable) when score-keeping fails to do so. We propose that perceptions of victory and defeat do not just depend on score-keeping, but are also influenced by three types of phenomena rooted in human nature: mindsets; salient events; and social pressures. We may believe ourselves to be judging outcomes fairly and objectively, but as thinking, feeling, social beings, we often cannot help seeing portentous international events through a series of subconscious lenses, subject to prior biases, the drama of events, and manipulation by the media and elites. Collectively, these phenomena constitute our alternative explanatory framework: *match-fixing*.

The term match-fixing comes, of course, from deliberate meddling in the outcome of sporting events (often in return for bribes from gambling syndicates), a problem dating to the ancient Greek Olympics. The victory of the Chicago White Sox in the 2005 World Series, for example, marked their first win since 1917. That long wait might have been two years shorter if members of the 1919 team had not deliberately thrown the match in an infamous gambling conspiracy known as the Black Sox Scandal. In international politics, match-fixing occurs not in material reality but in the minds of observers. Perceptions favoring victory or defeat can become fixed by mind-sets, salient events, and social pressures so that people are bound to see one side as the winner, regardless of what happens on the ground.

Why does match-fixing arise? The process of reaching a verdict of victory or defeat is deeply problematic for human beings for two main reasons: informational biases, and psychological biases. First, the content of the available information changes people's perceptions, whether or not they have any psychological bias. Fair evaluations are hard to make, therefore, even for a purely rational agent. If we fed *New York Times* reports of the 1968 Tet offensive into a computer, on the basis of this information the computer would probably determine that the United States had lost. The computer might process the information in an unbiased manner, but the editorial selection of stories, and the newspaper reports themselves, might be misleading in the information they contain.

Second, whether or not the information we receive is biased, in the process of sorting and interpreting this information, we are subject to numerous psychological biases.[2] People tend to reach and hold biased opinions of people and events, to form them quickly, and to be influenced by others. Other systematic tendencies are for emotional responses to shape opinions, for people to find it hard to shake off established images, and for memory to become distorted over time. Our brains generate many beliefs and images without our even being aware of the process. Indeed, such beliefs often dominate our thinking precisely *because* we are unaware of their formation. Psychological biases in perception, judgment, and decisionmaking can arise from a number of sources: cognitive processes, affective processes, learning, and cultural influences. We draw on all of these sources throughout the book.

Cognitive biases arise from constraints on information processing. Daniel Kahneman and Amos Tversky have shown that when faced with complex problems, the brain employs a number of systematic "heuristics and biases" which lead to judgments that deviate substantially from expectations based on mathematical cost-benefit analysis.[3] The brain does not easily or impartially integrate probabilities and utilities. Real-world judgments are at the mercy of a number of systematic biases in the way the brain processes information, such as recalling information according to its availability to the brain rather than its relevance to the situation; matching stereotypes to new scenarios; being more averse to losses than positive about equivalent gains; and favoring gambles when losses are at stake more than when gains are at stake. Many of these cognitive biases are clearly important for judgments of victory and defeat. One widely documented bias known as "beneffectance," for example, means that people recall success more easily than failure and, moreover, give themselves credit for causing successes but see outside forces as the cause of failures.[4]

Affective biases arise from emotional states such as desire and fear, especially when there is a threat to people's core values.[5] It should be noted that cognitive and affective processes often interact, and that some of their circuitry actually overlaps. Indeed, cognitive processing is derailed when emotional components are absent or damaged. Affective biases have powerful influences on behavior. For example, the limbic system (which is commonly but not exclusively involved in emotions) sometimes conducts information-processing tasks before or without passing the data on to higher-level-cognition areas of the brain. Emotions such as fear and anger can alter arousal, steer the organization and interpretation of information, increase the speed of decisionmaking, and produce a reliance on hunches. Emotional events are often seared into memory, with vivid associations of feelings, threats, time, place, and context—so-called flashbulb memories. People tend to have a great deal of confidence in such memories even when they are inaccurate, and subsequent encounters with analogous events can trigger the same emotional states, significantly influencing judgment even in quite different circumstances.[6]

Learning biases arise from applying the experience of the past to shape perceptions of current or future events. Our understanding of history can be flawed; for example, we may think that certain events happened that did not actually occur. The ways in which we use history can also be biased. In international relations, historical analogies commonly influence perceptions of events, with both the public and policymakers seeing, say, Vietnam as another Korea, or Iraq as another Vietnam.[7] Such analogies are easily assumed to provide useful guides to how to react "this time," but they often mislead because of important differences between the cases.

Cultural biases arise from features of society itself; they can be rooted in common values, cultural traditions, and/or shared history. Different cultural groups can view similar events in widely differing ways.[8] According to the memory researcher Daniel Schacter: "Societies often hold beliefs about their pasts that are based on stories and myths that develop and change over time, often bearing little resemblance to the events that initially gave rise to them." War magnifies such differences. The psychologist Lawrence LeShan notes that during major wars there is a shift to a "mythic perception" of reality in which simplistic notions like good and evil or "us" and "them" take precedence: issues are black or white; God is on "our" side; winning is all important; "they" act out of self-interest; "we" act out of self-defense or morality; the enemies are evil so they

41

lie, whereas "we" tell the truth; identical acts are good when we do them, criminal when they do them.[9]

We know that decisionmakers often hold biased perceptions of international relations, even when they have strong incentives not to because of the high stakes involved for their nation and their careers, and even when they have vast intelligence organizations to help them perceive as accurately as possible.[10] By contrast, when observers in the general population judge a foreign policy outcome, they usually have few pressing incentives to be accurate: their careers will probably not suffer because they see a battle as a victory or as a defeat. Nor will such observers have anything like the breadth or depth of information and analysis that decisionmakers enjoy. We should, therefore, expect bias to be even more prevalent among the general population than, say, within the White House.

The four sources of psychological bias we have described, in addition to informational bias, make the choice of metrics and information on which to base a verdict of victory or defeat highly subjective. The problems include the ambiguity of what constitutes an appropriate metric; the difficulty of receiving, selecting, and interpreting information; the difficulty of accurately matching metrics with relevant information; and the difficulty of determining when a particular war or crisis started and ended.

Subjective Metrics

To judge success we need a metric, but psychologists have firmly established that people inadvertently use self-serving metrics that corroborate their beliefs, expectations, and desires rather than expending the mental effort to achieve objectivity.[11] When the thing being assessed is ambiguous, a wider range of metrics can potentially be employed, making it easier to use self-serving criteria. Foreign policy therefore generates particular problems for metric selection. Ambiguity is inherent on the international stage, where there is a lack of agreed-upon evaluative standards and an enormous variety of worldviews, ideologies, and cultures. Partly because of this, as Yaacov Vertzberger noted, "the criteria for success in foreign policy are often vague in the minds of the general public."[12] What constitutes success for the United States in the war in Iraq is more ambiguous, for example, than what constitutes success in the domestic fight against crime. People experience the impact of domestic policy every time they visit banks, shops, hospitals, or workplaces, and they hear such issues discussed at home, among friends, or on television and radio. The greater familiarity with domestic issues produces consensus about how to measure success. In the case of crime the measure would be crime rates; in the case of the economy it would be rates of growth or unemployment. In contrast, many people simply do not have preexisting metrics for evaluating foreign policy. Observers often cannot locate the latest crisis on a map, let alone integrate the complexity of two or more polities and cultures in collision. The public may have little familiarity with the general issues at stake or the aims of each side in a dispute. Indeed, for people in general, most foreign countries exist only as mental constructions, which they have never experienced at first hand. Therefore, foreign policy metrics are often invented on the spot, and they tend to be both more arbitrary and more open to suggestion than domestic policy metrics.

Subjective Information

In addition to subjectivity in selecting metrics, the information required to evaluate whether or not the selected metric has been achieved is susceptible to bias. There are at least four major problems in obtaining and utilizing accurate information: access, selection, distortion, and recall.[13]

Access. Observers are often bombarded with data about foreign policy issues by leaders, opposition politicians, the media, family, friends, colleagues, and so on. The more information one has, the more difficult it is to arrange and filter that information into a coherent pattern. Despite this volume of data, however, there is often a paucity of *reliable* information with which to evaluate even a perfect metric. The media offer only part of the picture, so the information that reaches the average person depends upon the whims and policies of reporters and editors. For example, score-keeping requires knowledge about a leader's aims, and while in principle such aims objectively exist (see Chapter 2), it is very easy to interpret them inaccurately. Even with costly intelligence organizations, national leaders repeatedly fail to understand other leaders' aims, with surprise attacks, for example, being quite common.[14] Professional historians who analyze government documents regularly hold completely divergent views about a leader's aims. Since most people lack the access, time, and incentive to study archives or the secret workings of government, their understanding of the objectives of leaders (especially foreign leaders) often amounts to guesswork. Of course, many observers do not even attempt a reasoned analysis of aims and whether or not they were achieved. While observers may consider their judgments to be fair, in reality they often evaluate idiosyncratic metrics on the basis of very superficial information.

Selection. Human brains are not equally open to all information. A number of psychological predispositions tend to focus our attention on some types and sources of information and to discount others. We are particularly good at ignoring, discounting, or rejecting information that does not fit with our cherished or well-established beliefs (the discomfort we feel when confronted with such information is called cognitive dissonance). Although the information we do take in may be accurate, it may represent only half the story— and that half is unlikely to be a random sample but instead is likely to be biased to fit with our preconceptions and desires.

Distortion. Whatever information does survive the vagaries of access and selection to reach our brains then faces a large number of cognitive and affective biases, which reinterpret incoming information to maintain psychological comfort, coherence, and computational ease. Even contradictory information can be turned on its head to fit with favored or established ideas.

Recall. When we evaluate victory and defeat after the event, particular chunks of information will vanish while other chunks remain vivid in our memories. Think of the way most Americans remember the U.S. intervention in Somalia. Is it pictures of starving people and a successful humanitarian mission, or of crashed helicopters and dead soldiers in Mogadishu? People tend to recall certain events or aspects of events and not others, depending on media coverage, emotional arousal, the degree of shock generated, and the personal salience of each event.[15]

Subjective Linking of Information to Metrics

The problems do not stop there: even if one had appropriate metrics and balanced information about the outcome of a war or a crisis, linking the metrics and information together requires difficult information processing tasks. One of the core ideas in political psychology is the mismatch between a complex and incoherent world and the limited information-processing capabilities with which human beings comprehend this world. As an example, although our long-term memory can retain a vast amount of information, our working memory is limited: we are commonly able to handle and integrate only a few pieces of information at a time.[16]

To accurately link together metric and information requires an ability to separate out the dimensions in which a given policy was a success from those in which it was a failure. Human belief systems, however, often display what Robert Jervis calls "overkill": we view a favored policy as likely to succeed on *all* dimensions, while we see a policy we do not favor as likely to fail on *all* dimensions. Before the invasion of Iraq in 2003, for example, people who supported an invasion also tended to hold a number of other beliefs that were psychologically consistent with their pro-war position—that Iraq had weapons of mass destruction (WMD), that a military victory would be swift, and that the war was popular in other countries around the world. People who were against the war tended to hold *all* of the opposite beliefs. An unbiased observer might conclude, say, that a given policy succeeded on most dimensions, failed on a few dimensions, but still deserved an overall verdict of success. However, once people have decided that a policy will be a success in the future, is currently a success, or was a success, they are disinclined to admit any significant negative aspects. We have a tendency to categorize even complex issues into black-or-white binary choices, and to single out a winner and a loser in a war or crisis, as if all interactions were zero-sum. In reality, of course, both parties in a dispute may make gains, and both parties may suffer losses. People are intolerant of ambiguous or complex judgments, preferring a single familiar category like victory or defeat.[17]

Subjective Choice of Time Period

The selection of metrics and information can also be biased by the time period employed to judge success. Verdicts of victory or defeat rely on a mental comparison of a "before" time point and an "after" time point to decide who has won and lost what in the selected period. This is necessary for the most basic score-keeping analysis (as discussed in Chapter 2). However, the choice of time points is often not self-evident, is therefore open to interpretation, and can have a major effect on how the outcome is perceived. Psychological experiments have shown, for example, that people see gains or losses in relation to a self-established reference point: change the reference point and the same outcome is judged differently.[18]

The choice of a "before" time point substantially determines the extent of apparent gains as measured at the "after" time point. If you were to judge the success of a person's weight-loss diet by comparing a "before" photo with an "after" photo, the evaluation would depend to a large extent on when the "before" picture was taken: the results would look most impressive if the "before" picture was taken at the person's heaviest. In a similar vein, the outcome of a war might appear far more impressive when compared with the situation, say, five years earlier, than it would if the "before" point was either three or seven years earlier. Shifting the "after" time point can also alter evaluations, especially if the dispute continues over a long period, with the fortunes of both sides waxing and waning, and if the length of the particular battle or campaign being judged is open to question. Varying either time point means that even a computer that processed information perfectly would come up with a different tally of gains and losses.

The effect of bias in choosing time points is illustrated by the Israeli and Palestinian perceptions of the relative concessions each side offered in the 2000 peace proposal. Both sides had the same "after" time point, which was the deal on the table: Israel would give up control of the Gaza Strip, most of the West Bank, and part of Jerusalem. The Israelis tended to compare this proposal with a "before" point in the 1990s, and thereby argued that Israel had made unprecedented concessions which would represent significant gains for the Palestinians. However, the Palestinians tended to compare the proposal with a "before" point in the 1940s: from this perspective the deal only offered them 22 percent of pre-1947 Palestine, and they were the ones who were being asked to make extraordinary concessions in giving up the rest of the land.[19]

Another example comes from the Russian experience in World War II. In this case, moving the "before" time point forward allowed for a more comfortable view of history: "When Russians commemorate the 'Great Patriotic War,' their beginning point is June 1941 when Germany invaded the Soviet Union. This enables Russians to pay homage to the 20 million war dead but at the same time conveniently helps them to overlook the 1939 Hitler-Stalin Non-Aggression Treaty that so significantly aided the build-up of the German military machine."[20]

To sum up the way people form subjective verdicts of victory, the metrics for judgment are susceptible to bias. But even if they are not biased, the information used by observers to check those metrics is prone to bias. And even if observers could be armed with appropriate metrics and unbiased information, the ability of the brain to link these elements is subject to cognitive limitations. Finally, the time period over which to analyze gains and losses can easily be biased.

None of this makes Framework 1, score-keeping, a realistic model for explaining human evaluations much of the time. Indeed, understanding judgments of victory in international relations will require paying at least as much attention to the factors that predispose observers toward particular metrics and information as to the battlefield outcome itself. In the minds of observers, these predisposing factors often fix the match so that one side is bound to win, almost irrespective of its gains or losses on the ground.

| Framework 2: Match-Fixing

If observers often fail to evaluate victory or defeat on the basis of a Framework 1 score-keeping analysis, how exactly do they evaluate? What determines their choices of metric and information? And what explains how they link them together?

In this section we construct an alternative approach to understanding perceptions of victory and defeat, which we call Framework 2, or match-fixing. In contrast to score-keeping's focus on striving for a fair evaluation of material gains and aims achieved, match-fixing offers a model of perceptions of victory and defeat based on a more realistic view of human beings: as actors whose beliefs about the world are shaped by constraints on information and well-established psychological biases. Match-fixing factors always represent deviations from a purely Framework 1 score-keeping model of evaluation, either because the evaluation process, although fair and balanced, is compromised by incomplete or inaccurate information, or because the evaluation process is itself biased, regardless of good or bad information.

Chart 3.1 shows that perceptions of victory and defeat have inputs from both score-keeping and match-fixing. Each framework may play a greater or lesser relative role in any given case, either at the aggregate level (as when some members of the population match-fix while others score-keep) or at the individual level (as when a person's perception of victory involves the score-keeping of certain dimensions and the match-fixing of other dimensions). Score-keeping accounts for gains and aims, modified by their importance and their difficulty. Match-fixing accounts for three categories of factors

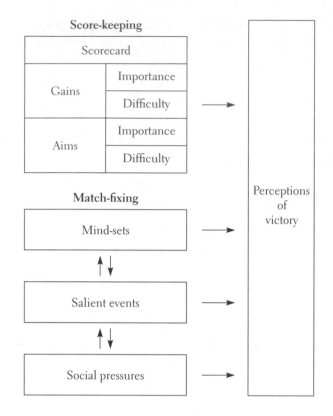

CHART 3.1. Score-keeping and match-fixing as sources of perceptions of victory.

that influence perceptions of victory and defeat: mind-sets; salient events; and social pressures.

The rationale for focusing on mind-sets, salient events, and social pressures is as follows. First, each of these categories is linked to an established literature on perceptual biases. Second, these three categories cover the chronology of the formation of perceptions, from prior mind-sets (before the war/crisis), to the salient events themselves (during the war/crisis), to social pressures from peers, media, and elites (during and after the war/crisis). Third, the three categories cover bottom-up processes (preexisting mind-sets), contextual processes (salient events), and top-down processes (media and elite pressures).

Match-fixing category	Biases influencing perceptions of victory	
	Acting on metric	Acting on information
Mind-sets	Cognitive dissonance	Cognitive dissonance
	Expectations	
Salient events	Settlement process	Symbolic events
		Rally phenomenon
Social pressures	Manipulation of metrics	Manipulation of information

CHART 3.2. Key biases influencing perceptions of victory and defeat.

Each category of match-fixing factors produces bias in perceptions of victory and defeat by influencing both the choice of metrics and the use of information. The key biases are summarized in Chart 3.2.

Mind-sets

An observer's mind-set exists before the crisis or war begins and "represents all the hypotheses and theories that he is convinced are valid at a given moment in time." Mind-set is produced by national culture, bureaucratic position, individual experience, personality traits, and other psychological phenomena. Sometimes people's attitudes and values are idiosyncratic; at other times many or all members of a society share the same beliefs.[21]

An observer's mind-set shapes evaluations of victory by influencing both stages of the judgment process: the choice of metrics for evaluating success, and the selection and interpretation of information to determine whether such metrics have been achieved.

Mind-sets and Metrics of Success

Mind-set narrows the choice of metrics for judging victory and defeat from a range of conceivable alternatives. When observers' beliefs determine their selection of metrics in a biased or self-serving manner, the observers are match-fixing. We focus here on two mind-set biases crucial for metric selection: expectations and cognitive dissonance.

Expectations. People often judge victory and defeat in terms of deviations from an explicit or implicit baseline: their own *expectations*. The problem is that observers' expectations may have little relationship to the capabilities of the countries involved or the difficulties each side faces. Even well-informed decisionmakers often find it problematic to estimate the likely outcomes of wars and crises. Overconfidence, for example, is very common in war.[22] If one is overconfident about one's own side, or underestimates the opponent, then one may interpret anything less than complete triumph as a defeat. The Korean War, despite being essentially a draw on the ground, was initially seen as a failure by the U.S. public because Americans were used to, and therefore tended to expect, outright victory in war.

Furthermore, surprises have a more powerful impact than expected events. Surprises can feel more pleasant (if positive) or more painful (if negative) than actions that are predicted in advance. In fact, in the words of the political scientist Rose McDermott: "surprising smaller wins make people happier than larger expected ones; a loss can feel like a gain if a larger loss was expected (as when a utility bill is less than anticipated); and a gain can feel like a loss if a better but unobtained result was possible, as when a person gets a small grant instead of a large one."[23]

In politics, even moderate gains can look impressive if expectations are low enough. After the tumultuous downfall of Richard Nixon in 1974, the new U.S. president, Gerald Ford, received credit for quite ordinary characteristics. As the political scientist

Fred Greenstein put it: "In the weeks following his abrupt elevation to the presidency, Ford was showered with praise, much of it for attributes that in another context would have marked him as pedestrian." Ford's attempt in 1975 to rescue the thirty-nine crewmembers of the *Mayaguez* from their Cambodian captors led to the deaths of more than forty U.S. personnel, in what was on paper a costly, poorly planned, and largely unsuccessful operation. But in the aftermath of the fall of Saigon and Phnom Penh to communist forces, American observers, accustomed to recent news of U.S. retreat and incapacity, applauded the resolute style of the rescue operation. In one poll 76 percent of Americans agreed that "after losing Vietnam and Cambodia, the United States had no choice but to take decisive action, even risking a bigger war, to get back the ship and crew."[24]

When are observers likely to have optimistic expectations (and employ hard-to-achieve metrics for success), and when are they likely to have pessimistic expectations (and employ easy-to achieve metrics for success)? Psychologists have demonstrated that people in general have a baseline optimistic bias about themselves, their control over events, and the future. This optimistic bias, however, is known to vary depending upon specific circumstances. First, optimism varies among individuals (it is greater among Westerners than Asians, greater among men than women, greater among people with egoistic and narcissistic personality types, and almost absent among people suffering from depression). Second, optimism varies among different policy contexts (overconfidence is greater if, for example, contradictory information is not available, or in closed policymaking structures where critical debate is absent). To caricature these findings, an egoistic American man in a closed peer group is far more likely to have overly optimistic expectations than a depressed Korean woman in a diverse decisionmaking environment.[25]

Recent history is another major source of variation in expectations about victory and defeat. Reasoning by historical analogy is a classic cognitive shortcut in an uncertain world, enabling people to interpret a current situation by inferring information from past events deemed to be similar.[26] Just as militaries are often said to fight the last war, observers tend to build their expectations in reference to the last conflict or crisis. In 1973 observers often explicitly judged the performance of countries in the Yom Kippur War according to a standard based on the staggering Israeli triumph in the 1967 Six-Day War. Seen through the lens of 1967, anything less than a rout of the Arab armies looked like an Israeli failure.

Overly negative expectations in one war sometimes encourage overly positive expectations in the next war. When people are pessimistic they employ easy-to-achieve metrics for success, and thus they are inclined to judge the outcome as a victory. These feelings of success can breed unjustified confidence and expectations about the outcome of the next war. Even if this next dispute produces a favorable scorecard, the expectations may not be met. For example, very cautious Israeli expectations in 1967 exaggerated the sense of triumph after the Six-Day War. That feeling of triumph engendered overconfident expectations about the results of the war in 1973.

The reverse can also happen. If overconfident expectations lead observers to judge a country as having lost, they will tend to underplay that country's chances in the next war, find its performance surprisingly positive, and form new overconfident expectations that start the whole process again. Arab observers were overconfident in 1967 and therefore perceived the Six-Day War as a complete debacle. As a result of this trauma, their expectations were very low in 1973, a situation that encouraged perceptions of Egyptian and Syrian victory.

Those who remember how their low or high expectations previously biased their judgment may be particularly prone to this "boomerang" effect, because they may recognize their initial bias and then overcorrect by engaging in perceptual distortion in the reverse direction. As Robert Jervis wrote: "Those who remember the past are condemned to make the opposite mistakes."[27]

Cognitive dissonance. Mind-sets also shape metric selection because of cognitive dissonance: the discomfort of maintaining a belief system with inconsistent elements leads people to subconsciously suppress or eliminate inconsistencies as they present themselves. The phenomenon is partly cognitive, but it also has an affective component, in that dissonance may be especially potent when core values are at stake. As a way of rationalizing favored policies, observers will tend to expect such policies to succeed, and will resist evidence suggesting that they have failed. Therefore metric selection can be strategic: an intellectual device designed to avoid cognitive dissonance by allowing one to perceive the "correct" side as having won. Work by the psychologist David Dunning has shown that people routinely invoke self-serving criteria in all sorts of assessments. Idiosyncratic criteria are used to justify success on grounds favorable to the observer, a tendency that can result in, for example, a majority of people seeing their own skills or traits as being above the average (which is impossible in reality).[28]

An extreme example of cognitive dissonance shaping metrics is evident in observers' beliefs about who won and who lost an American presidential debate. Many studies have shown that voters evaluate the performance of candidates in such debates to a large extent along partisan or ideological lines. Democrats seem to honestly believe that the Democratic candidate came out ahead, while Republicans have little doubt that it was the Republican candidate who emerged victorious. In the 2004 campaign, 84 percent of Republicans polled thought George W. Bush had won the second presidential debate; only 1 percent thought John Kerry had won. Among Democrats, in contrast, 85 percent thought Kerry had won this debate while 2 percent thought Bush had won.[29]

Were members of the two parties watching the same debate? Not really, since Republicans' and Democrats' preexisting beliefs ensured that those on each side accepted the words of their favored candidate almost without question, while viewing the words of the disfavored candidate in an especially harsh light. In explaining why their candidate won, people will select whatever criteria for victory best fit the performance of their favored politician. In effect, the process of judgment is reversed: the outcome is first determined by cognitive dissonance (to conform with the favored result); metrics are selected later to rationalize this perceived outcome. After the first presidential debate in 2004, in which Bush slouched a little while Kerry stood upright, Democratic commentators implied that the appropriate metric for success was "who hunched over their podium least." Undoubtedly, if Kerry had been the one who slouched, Republicans would have been the ones advocating this particular metric.[30]

Until the 1960s, divisions among Americans over questions of foreign policy tended not to fall along partisan lines. By the 1970s, however, party and foreign policy cleavages became more closely aligned, and now partisanship is a major predictor of people's positions on international issues.[31] For example, people who oppose President Bush's war on terror are predisposed to search for metrics by which this policy can be measured as a failure, such as the loss of international support, the insurgency in Iraq, and continuing terrorist attacks in other countries. They will downplay or simply ignore metrics by which the war on terror appears to be proceeding favorably: the capture of al Qaeda leaders; the removal of the Taliban regime in Afghanistan; or the lack of terrorist attacks in the United States since September 11, 2001. Because of the strategic nature of metric selection, we would predict that if the insurgency in Iraq were to die down, many Democrats would no longer regard the level of violence in Iraq as a key metric by which to judge the president (see Chapter 9 for experimental evidence on this point).

In addition to partisanship, wider beliefs about foreign policy can also shape metric selection. Americans vary in how hawkish or dovish they are, with hawks predisposed to see the use of military force as being successful, and doves predisposed to judge it as a failure.[32] The U.S. public also ascribes more importance to some goals, such as fighting terrorism and stopping the proliferation of WMD, than to others, such as spreading democracy.[33] Thus we would expect Americans to be more skeptical about the success of ventures perceived as being designed to spread democracy, and more forgiving of measures perceived as being designed to combat terrorism. An example of the way beliefs can shape metric selection occurred during the Vietnam war. For President Johnson, a key value at stake in Vietnam was the strength of U.S. will and purpose: thus he saw the rising enemy body count as a sign of success. For critics who primarily focused on the human cost of the war, the same outcome signaled a massive failure.[34]

Because mind-set influences metric selection, changing mind-sets can produce new metrics. Thus evaluations of the success of a policy sometimes change after the event. Polled in 1937, 64 percent of Americans thought U.S. entry into World War I in 1917 had been a mistake, while 28 percent thought it had been the right move. By the time of the Japanese attack on Pearl Harbor in 1941, evaluations had completely shifted: only 21 percent thought U.S. entry into World War I had been a mistake, and 62 percent supported it. The growing belief that the United States should oppose German and Japanese aggression between 1937 and 1941 produced new metrics for judging U.S. actions of more than twenty years before. Instead of focusing on whether the United States had been sucked into European power politics by financiers and munitions manufacturers, Americans began to instead judge the previous intervention in terms of standing up to German militarism. Changing beliefs produced new metrics that turned a perceived policy failure into a perceived success.[35]

Cognitive dissonance shapes metric selection to a greater extent when a judgment of success or failure would support or undermine partisan, ideological, or other deeply held or favored beliefs. In these circumstances, the discomfort of admitting that a disliked candidate was successful can be enough for the human brain to search for metrics to facilitate the preferred verdict of failure. When people judge foreign policy success today in the United States, ideological and partisan beliefs are commonly triggered, producing a perfect environment for cognitive dissonance to flourish.

Mind-sets and Information on Success

Whether or not observers' mind-sets influence metrics for victory or defeat, they can shape the information that is used to assess whether a chosen metric has been achieved. Mind-sets are the lenses through which information about a crisis or a war is received, interpreted, and often distorted.

Cognitive dissonance. To avoid concluding that their favored policy failed, observers will search for information according to which their selected metric for success has been achieved. This is an analogous and complementary process to the strategic selection of metrics outlined above.

The "confirmation bias" means that people take data they agree with at face value, often without any criticism at all, while discounting or challenging information that contradicts their established or favored views.[36] Prior to the 2003 Iraq War, Bush administration officials asked U.S. intelligence officials to recheck any information suggesting that war with Iraq was unnecessary or would go badly. In contrast, dubious and unsubstantiated evidence that Iraq had or was developing WMD was treated to a much lower level of critical scrutiny.[37] Observers initially tend to see unfolding events as representing the outcome they desire, at least until the evidence against this view is incontrovertible. In contrast, they tend to apply considerable skepticism when evaluating information about policies they do not see as worthwhile. Thus although information about the U.S. humanitarian mission in Somalia in 1992–1994 included several positive aspects, Americans who opposed the mission nevertheless saw it as having been a substantial failure for the United States. This is not to say that mind-sets typically produce ironclad opposition to a nonfavored evaluation, but they do produce more resistance than would result from an unbiased view of the evidence.

Many Americans use their party identification as a shortcut when evaluating information about the success or failure of a policy. In 1967–1968, during the Johnson administration, Republicans were more likely than Democrats to state that "we" had made a mistake in getting involved in the Vietnam war, while Democrats were more likely to state that the war would be over quickly and that the Paris peace talks were making headway. After Richard Nixon won office in 1969, these positions reversed: suddenly Democrats tended to think "we" had made a mistake, while Republicans now tended to believe that the war would be over quickly and that the peace talks were going well.[38]

Because of cultural and social norms, the Japanese at the end of World War II displayed an extreme aversion to defeat, particularly in the sense of dishonor or surrender. Information indicating the Japanese surrender in 1945 was systematically downplayed by Japan. As part of the surrender terms, the Allies demanded that the authority of the Japanese emperor and government "shall be subject to" the Allies. But the Japanese foreign ministry deliberately mistranslated this key phrase as "will be placed under the restraint of." Without the connotation of subordination, the Japanese military was able to save face, and the Japanese government agreed to the Allied terms. In the years after 1945, the most common term for the surrender in Japan was "end of war."[39]

In the American Civil War, Confederate cultural values tended to alter the perception of incoming information to create an idealized image of the heroic Southerner fighting against the massed ranks and dark satanic industries of the North. How could Southerners reconcile this self-image with the fact of defeat? The answer was that the South had displayed the greater heroism, but had been ground down by impossible odds. When Robert E. Lee announced the surrender of his Confederate army in 1865, he noted the bravery, valor, and devotion of his troops, but claimed that he was "compelled to yield to overwhelming numbers and resources." The implication was that in man-for-man terms, the South had really won the war. The notion that the Confederacy had *deserved* to succeed became part of the emerging myth of the "Lost Cause."[40]

Events can even be seen in diametrically opposite ways by two alienated groups. The Egyptologist Jan Assmann notes dramatically dissimilar interpretations of the Israelites' Exodus from Egypt: "In the biblical version, the Egyptians are shown as torturers and oppressors, idolators and magicians; in the Egyptian version, the 'Jews' are shown as lepers, impure people, atheists, misanthropes, iconoclasts, vandals, and sacrilegious criminals."[41]

Mind-set can also influence perceptions of victory and defeat through mood. People exhibit not only "mood-congruence," in which they "selectively take in information consonant with their current mood state," but also "mood-dependent retrieval," tending to recall events after the fact that match their mood at that later time.[42] A pall of negativity that appeared in the United States with the onset of the Tet offensive in 1968 may have primed people to see subsequent events as being more indicative of disaster.

Cognitive dissonance makes observers most receptive to information that confirms their expectations. In one experiment, subjects who were told beforehand that a speaker had a warm personality saw him as warm; subjects told that he was cold saw him as cold. Richard Ashmore and colleagues found that American college students evaluated a Vietnam war peace proposal much more negatively when it was attributed to North Vietnam than when it was attributed to the United States: they expected a U.S. text to have positive qualities and judged it accordingly. Examples abound from the real world. During the Yom Kippur War in 1973, the U.S. administration was confident of Israel's military superiority over the Arab states. When initial evidence suggested Israeli military defeats, this information was downplayed or simply ignored, and Washington remained confident that Israel was in fact winning.[43]

As we have seen, cognitive dissonance is more pronounced when judgments relate to strongly held beliefs. We therefore predict that the ideological and partisan nature of the current foreign policy debate in the United States means that Republicans and Democrats are likely to judge information about the international success of U.S. presidents very differently.

Salient Events

Particular events during a crisis or a war influence perceptions of victory or defeat. Some events, of course, feature in a score-keeping analysis: battlefield victories, material gains, and so on. However, we focus here on the role of events that may not represent tangible gains for either side (at least not significant ones), but that nevertheless shape judgments.

Perceptions can be influenced by the drama that is common in crises and in wars, which may elicit strong emotions, hormones, stress, depression, or hysteria. The aura of war itself has a number of effects on mass psychology. LeShan writes of "a strong tendency in us humans to shift our method of appraising an international situation from a sensory [more objective] reality to a mythic [more self-serving and other-deprecating] reality as tensions escalate."[44]

Salient Events and Metrics of Success

Settlement Process. The process by which an international outcome is reached — irrespective of the substance of the outcome — can influence metrics for judging victory. If the outcome is seen as the result of an agreed deal, perhaps accompanied by images of leaders from the opposing sides shaking hands and signing a treaty, then the immediate impression is one of a negotiated draw. However, if the exact same deal is reached after a standoff with two military forces poised for action, one side is likely to be perceived as having given up or backed down first, and thus as having lost. In the Cuban missile crisis, the fact that Soviet ships physically turned away from a U.S. naval blockade of Cuba created the image that Moscow had backed down and thereby lost the crisis, even though the USSR made tangible gains in the final settlement. Success can be judged by very simple metrics: whoever is seen to withdraw or step down loses.

The danger of basing perceptions of defeat on whoever appears to back down or lose resolve is that such psychological results may have little or no relationship with the material gains made by each side, which, as we argued in Chapter 2, ought to be the basis for the verdict of victory. Furthermore, apparent resolve may be a phenomenon largely constructed by elite manipulation, or by whatever happened to be caught (and not caught) on television cameras. The salience of images of backing down will depend upon how closely the event approximates a classic standoff and whether one side unambiguously carries out the public demands of the other side.

Salient Events and Information on Success

Salient events in a dispute also shape the information that observers employ to assess whatever metrics they may be using.

Symbolic events. Symbolic events can have an effect on perceptions of victory out of all proportion to their actual impact on the battlefield. People tend to generalize from specific phenomena to universal conclusions, and to see in symbolic events a microcosm of the bigger picture. Symbolic events therefore provide intellectual shortcuts in the assessment of information.

For example, observers judged the Reagan administration's intervention in Grenada in 1983 to be a significant success only after seeing images of rescued American medical students returning to the United States, joyfully kissing U.S. soil at the base of the air-craft steps. Larry Speakes, Reagan's press secretary, commented: "My staff and I were watching when the first students arrived in Charleston, and when we saw how happy they were to be home, we started cheering and pounding the table. 'That's it! We won!' I shouted." Edwin Meese, who was attorney general under Reagan, said it was lucky that one of the students kissed the ground: "With that simple gesture, the debate over Grenada was effectively over."[45]

As a contrary example, the attack on the U.S. embassy in Saigon by Vietcong forces during the Tet offensive in 1968 had little tangible impact (all those who invaded the compound were dead within a few hours, and they never took the main building), but in the minds of many Americans it engendered an image of significant U.S. failure. Observers whose metric for success was stability in South Vietnam could see on television that the symbolic heart of the U.S. presence—the embassy itself—in a supposedly safe city, was swarming with enemy fighters. The implication was that off camera the whole country was overrun.

The particular way in which the Dunkirk evacuation in 1940 was carried out increased the favorable impression of this operation. If the British navy had simply picked up the troops according to standard military procedures it would have looked like a fairly typical retreat. The participation of a flotilla of volunteers, sailing small vessels from England to rescue the men on the beaches, created a heroic image of the plucky British population uniting to defy the German war machine. The operation came to be known as the "miracle of the little ships" despite the fact that 80 percent of the troops were actually evacuated on large ships and destroyers.

The seizure of culturally or ethnically significant and thereby highly symbolic pieces of territory can engender dramatic reactions that a third party might consider unwarranted. People often hold certain pieces of territory in special regard at a visceral, emotional level. Monica Toft has written about the attachment of ethnic groups to their perceived homeland, even if it is impassable mountains, a war zone, or a parched desert.[46] Losing the homeland can signify abject disaster. Gaining even a small fragment of it can signify divine deliverance. The emotional power of such symbolic gains and losses can produce judgments of success and failure that diverge from a dispassionate tally of material changes.

A number of studies have found evidence that a "peak-and-end" rule operates when people look back on events: their memories are driven by the worst (or best) part, and by what the situation was like at the end. People do not remember the average, day-to-day emotions they felt at the time, or the variation in their experience. Hence a dramatic and salient negative peak experience, and then a final image of defeat, could make a person remember the episode as one of consistent failure.[47]

Symbolic events are more likely to influence perceptions of victory and defeat under two sets of circumstances: when they clearly relate to a core metric (as with the embassy attack and South Vietnamese security in 1968); and when they trigger nationalism, religious beliefs, or other strongly held values (as with seeing one's countrymen joyfully return from Grenada, or perceiving a threat to one's homeland or sacred site).

The Rally Phenomenon. Dramatic and violent events also tend to create a rally phenomenon, whereby public support for a leader rises, as do evaluations of information about his or her job performance—whether or not the events themselves are favorable to the leader. In threatening circumstances people need a figure to venerate. In the American Revolution, for example, the young nation required a hero and chose George Washington. Before independence, Washington was not recognized as charismatic or particularly heroic, yet after independence was declared, and even before he had taken charge of the army, children and ships were being named after him, and he rapidly became the most admired man in the former colonies. The lavish praise he received was quite independent of his actual performance: Washington symbolized the revolution, and lauding Washington meant lauding the cause itself.[48]

The rally phenomenon was apparent following the U.S.-backed invasion of Cuba at the Bay of Pigs in 1961, when even though the mission was a fiasco, President Kennedy's approval ratings rose 5 percent. President G. W. Bush's approval ratings shot up immediately after the terrorist attacks in September 2001; attacks that, of course, did not in themselves signal that Bush was doing a better job than before. Because of cognitive dissonance, once observers favor a leader on one dimension, such as national security, they start to view that leader as being successful across all dimensions. On 9 September 2001, 48 percent of Americans approved of Bush's handling of the economy, slightly down from 52 percent the month before. By 6 November, approval of his handling of the economy had leapt to 72 percent, even though economic conditions had actually gotten worse in the wake of the terrorist attacks. Approval of the president's handling of education also rose: from 61 percent before 11 September 2001 to 71 percent in January 2002.[49]

Most rallies are short-lived, however. Judgments about a leader's performance tend to rise sharply and then decline sharply in a "spike" pattern. Rallies produce a greater increase in public support and tend to last longer when the event is large in scale, dramatic, and shocking, such as a surprise attack, and when elites also rally and decline to criticize the leader. Partly because of these factors, the terrorist attacks of September 2001 produced one of the greatest rallies in modern American history. Even here, however, Bush's approval ratings began to fall back in 2002 on all dimensions, including national security, the economy, and education.[50]

Social Pressures

Governments, media, and other figures influence the perceptions of observers through social pressures. Such factors act as a "push" toward a particular way of thinking, which may either augment or counter the "pull" of mind-sets and salient events. Social pressures can include rhetoric by politicians, media manipulation, campaigns by lobbying groups, international opinion, peer pressure, and, on leaders themselves, influence from legislators, cabinet members, and advisors. Manipulation often targets a particular aspect of the evaluation process (as when manipulators push a preferred metric or distort a source of information).

Media Manipulation. In developed societies, mass media, including television, radio, print media, and the internet, have dramatically multiplied the amount of information available to the public. Some scholars have been skeptical about the proposition that citizens alter their views on the basis of the media presentation of issues, calling it a myth. However, it is likely that the media do exert a significant influence, at least in certain circumstances. A recent review concluded that, overall, mass communication in the United States had substantial effects in shaping opinion.[51]

Although some people distrust the media and are skeptical about what they read and hear, others take the information presented in the media at face value. In a famous example, a TV commercial for

AT&T clearly showed a group of friends cooking hamburgers on a fishing trip because a storm had ruled out any actual fishing. They nevertheless jubilantly told family members on the phone that they were cooking trout. When audiences were polled afterward, a huge majority reported that the men had been cooking trout. Even when there is no outright distortion of the facts, the media serve to frame issues and set agendas, bringing order to confusing and complex events.[52]

In reality, the effect probably works both ways: the media influence public opinion, but they also react to demand from the public. After all, people buy the newspapers they want to read and tune in to the TV shows they want to watch. Whatever the relative strength of the interacting causal arrows between the public and the media, however, the key point for our argument is that, at times, media manipulation can be powerful enough to significantly shape observers' views of victory and defeat.

Mass communication influences the metrics and information used by observers to evaluate the performance of governments and leaders. Shanto Iyengar, Mark Peters, and Donald Kinder, scholars of the media and public opinion, suggest that "fluctuations in the importance of evaluational standards may well depend on fluctuation in the attention each receives in the press." According to Kinder: "By dwelling on some problems and issues and neglecting others, media prime certain memories and not others, thereby altering the standards citizens apply when they evaluate the wisdom of a policy, the virtue of a candidacy, or the performance of their government."[53] In one experiment, after viewers were primed with stories about national defense, they tended to judge presidential performance on national defense issues rather than on domestic issues. Evidence comes from real-life scenarios as well. Following the

Iran-Contra scandal, which was widely covered in the media in the 1980s, the U.S. public showed a disposition to evaluate President Ronald Reagan more on foreign policy than on other possible issues.[54]

The ability of the media to cue metrics and information about success and failure was evident in the second U.S. presidential debate in 1976 between Gerald Ford and Jimmy Carter. Immediately after the televised debate, according to polling data, 53 percent of the American public thought Ford had won, and 35 percent thought Carter had won. However, the view conveyed in the media was that Ford had lost because he had mishandled a question about Soviet control of Eastern Europe. Polls taken between 12 and 48 hours after the debate, when this media evaluation had become widely known, found that public opinion had reversed—that now 58 percent thought Carter had won, and 29 percent thought Ford had won. Furthermore, in the earlier sample only 10 percent of respondents mentioned the statement on Eastern Europe in explaining their evaluations, but in the later sample more than 60 percent mentioned it.[55]

Following the invasion of Iraq in 2003, the media played a significant role in shaping perceptions of *when* victory was achieved—specifically on 9 April. That was the day the statue of Saddam was torn down on Firdos Square, across the street from the Palestine Hotel, where many foreign journalists were staying. Despite the continuation of serious fighting in Baghdad and around the country, the media focused heavily on this event. Fox News and CNN anchormen frequently alluded to it as a historic moment reminiscent of the fall of the Berlin Wall. Brit Hume on Fox declared: "This transcends anything I've ever seen." The toppling was shown repeatedly (once every 4.4 minutes on Fox from 11 A.M. to 8

P.M.). Perhaps most significantly, "the battlefield itself disappeared": the number of stories about the fighting fell by 79 percent on Fox and 81 percent on CNN, despite the fact that major military operations were continuing. (President Bush did not declare the end of major combat operations until 1 May.)[56]

When do the media shape judgments of victory? The media tend to independently influence perceptions of success (1) in open and democratic regimes where they are not simply the mouthpiece of the regime; (2) when they have a significant cohort of expert correspondents in the field, with the resources and contacts to challenge the government's version of events; and (3) when the media unite in offering the same biased framing of events. This third point could apply to a general approach to reporting politics. For example, the U.S. media are increasingly critical of the administration in power: each president since 1976 has received more negative coverage than his predecessor. Media unity can also apply to the presentation of a particular event, as with the consensus framing of the battle in Mogadishu in 1993 as a humiliating failure for the United States.[57]

Leader Manipulation. Niccolo Machiavelli wrote that leaders need not have all the princely qualities, such as being "a man of compassion, a man of good faith, a man of integrity, a kind and a religious man," but they "should certainly appear to have them."[58] In the same way, leaders need not actually win a war or crisis outright, but if they want to survive politically, they should certainly appear to do so. All too aware of the importance of perceptions of success, leaders seek to shape views about appropriate metrics and information to ensure the most positive interpretation of their performance.

In nondemocratic regimes, leaders can shape perceptions through strict control of information about battlefield outcomes. In George Orwell's famous novel *1984*, the protagonist, Winston Smith, lives in a totalitarian state in which the government frequently invents military victories to build domestic support:

> "Attention! Your attention, please! A newsflash has this moment arrived from the Malabar front. Our forces in South India have won a glorious victory. I am authorized to say that the action we are now reporting may well bring the war within measurable distance of its end. Here is the newsflash—" Bad news coming, thought Winston. And sure enough, following on a gory description of the annihilation of a Eurasian army, with stupendous figures of killed and prisoners, came the announcement that, as from next week, the chocolate ration would be reduced from thirty grammes to twenty.[59]

Such extreme manipulation is not limited to fiction. In 1942 the Japanese people were told that the disastrous battle of Midway had been a triumph, and wounded survivors were kept in hospitals to prevent the true outcome from becoming known.[60]

In democracies, manipulation by leaders is usually subtler, but still very much in evidence. U.S. leaders have every incentive to try and frame their own policies as a success. After all, as we saw in Chapter 1, Americans are "defeat phobic" rather than inherently "casualty phobic": if the president can promote a positive view about a war, the public will tend to tolerate casualties and still support the mission. President G. W. Bush's "Plan for Victory" speech on Iraq, delivered at the Naval Academy in November 2005, was a classic example of a leader's attempt to shape perceptions of success. Bush highlighted existing gains that had been made, outlined his favored metrics, and suggested which information was most relevant for evaluating progress toward U.S. goals: "Americans should have a clear understanding of this strategy . . . how we define victory, and what we're doing to achieve it."[61]

It is not easy for democratic leaders to shape perceptions of success. Most major presidential policy initiatives fail, and presidential rhetoric regularly falls on deaf ears. People often do not receive the president's messages, and even when they do, these messages can reinforce the beliefs of both supporters and opponents rather than actually persuade anyone.[62]

But U.S. presidents are usually better able to influence opinion on foreign policy than on domestic issues. People know less about foreign affairs, and are more willing, at least initially, to defer to a president's interpretation of a crisis. A number of studies indicate that public opinion shifted in line with presidential policy on the escalation and de-escalation of the Vietnam war, the invasion of Grenada in 1983, and the liberation of Kuwait in 1991. The administration in the White House, thanks to its access to intelligence resources, has an almost unique ability to shape perceptions of foreign policy issues by controlling which information is released and how and when it is released. The political scientist Chaim Kaufmann has shown how the control of information aided the Bush administration in selling the 2003 Iraq War and in influencing evaluations of its likely success.[63]

The political scientists Lawrence Jacobs and Robert Shapiro suggest another strategy that leaders employ to build support: "crafted talk," or simple messages attuned to the particular elements of the favored policy that publics find most appealing. In the American Revolutionary War against Britain, George Washington carefully tailored his public image as a humble citizen soldier. He famously refused any salary for leading the army, simply asking that his expenses be paid. He turned down fully $48,000 for his eight years of military service, symbolizing his willingness to sacrifice for the cause. A detail lost in the adulation was the expense bill Washington eventually submitted—almost $500,000, including $27,000 for visits by Mrs. Washington to his winter headquarters. It seems that not everyone suffered equally at Valley Forge.[64]

According to the political scientist Charles Taber, leaders can "articulate a novel frame for understanding some political object, with the expectation that many citizens will come to view the candidate, issue, or group through that lens," or alternatively, leaders "may increase the accessibility or perceived relevance of some commonly shared frame." For example, leaders can try to lower the metric for success, and thus encourage a positive evaluation, by portraying their aims as being limited. President Bill Clinton threatened Iraq with military strikes in 1998, and the press described his goal as "so modest that [Clinton] will have little trouble declaring it achieved, even if it fails to deal with the larger threat posed by Saddam Hussein." Leaders can also reframe the information used to assess the outcome. President Reagan even made the disastrous explosion of the space shuttle *Challenger* appear heroic when he told the American public: "We will never forget [the crewmembers] nor the last time we saw them—this morning—as they prepared for their journey and waved goodbye, and slipped the surly bonds of earth to touch the face of God."[65]

However, leaders who seek to manipulate perceptions of victory face a dilemma. Focusing on the positive helps them build public support for a mission, but in doing so they heighten expectations about the outcome. Official optimism ultimately encourages observers to employ metrics for victory that are more difficult to achieve. Sooner rather than later the public will expect visible results. The outcome of the Tet offensive was hard for the American public to accept because President Johnson and General Westmoreland had previously been so relentlessly optimistic about the progress of the war in Vietnam. To build support for the invasion of Iraq in 2003, the Bush administration encouraged the belief that U.S. soldiers would be met with flowers as liberators, and that the occupation would be short in duration and limited in cost. This optimistic picture helped make fairly minor battlefield setbacks arouse considerable alarm in the press and the public.[66] In other wars, the fact that the population of the opposing country kept their heads down and largely did not resist an invasion had been taken as a sign of success; in the Iraq War the fact that the invaders were not welcomed with open arms was seen as a sign of failure.

Thus leaders have to perform a balancing act: establishing that the mission is currently, and will be, successful; yet at the same time lowering expectations by stressing that there is a long hard struggle ahead. Some leaders are better than others at achieving this balance. The exemplar might well be Winston Churchill. Asked at a press conference how long World War II would take to win, Churchill replied: "If we manage it well, it will take only half as long as if we manage it badly." Harold Nicholson summarized a speech Churchill made during the dark days of 1941: "Having indicated to us the approaching collapse of India and China, and, in fact, of Europe, Asia and Africa, he somehow leaves us with the impression that we are quite certain to win the war."[67]

When are leaders more likely to alter people's perceptions of victory and defeat? Leaders tend to have more influence under the following circumstances: (1) in nondemocratic regimes (where they have greater control over the flow of information); (2) when they have credibility in the eyes of the public (if they are seen as having been dishonest in past depictions of victory, they will not be believed even when they are telling the truth); (3) when they are popular (people tend to be more receptive to the messages of leaders they approve of); (4) in a dramatic crisis (where the rally phenomenon is strongest); and (5) in a brief crisis (where information is easier to control and the rally effect does not have time to dissipate).

Elite Manipulation. The consensus or lack of it among political elites can also have a significant effect on evaluations of success. When American elites (especially in the administration and in Congress) unite to endorse an outcome, public opinion tends to concur; when elites split, so does the public.[68] Public support for the Vietnam war fell, as did Americans' certainty of victory, after the Fulbright hearings in 1966, which signaled elite disunity about the war. Following the 1968 Tet offensive, as elite unity broke down further, Americans who followed the war closely began to perceive the conflict in more polarized and ideological terms, as either hawks or doves. The political scientist John Zaller wrote: "When elites uphold a clear picture of what should be done, the public tends to see events from that point of view . . . When elites divide, members of the public tend to follow the elites sharing their general ideological or partisan predisposition."[69]

Societal Manipulation. A perception of what everyone else thinks can also be, in itself, a source of social pressure. Undecided observers may be influenced by consensus societal judgments, and may feel pressure to conform to the popular view of the outcome. As Malcolm Gladwell described in *The Tipping Point*, there are a number of social phenomena that can lead to the rapid spread of ideas among a population, especially in situations involving important "connectors" (people who form social links), "mavens" (who pass information along), and "salesmen" (who are skilled at persuasion).[70] In a common pattern, we find that initial debate about victory and defeat is gradually replaced by a single dominant perception in both popular and academic circles.

| Conclusion

Our argument is simple: people can score-keep victory and defeat by measuring gains and losses (Framework 1), or match-fix through the influence of mind-sets, salient events, and social pressures (Framework 2). The relative contributions of the two frameworks vary from case to case.

In the complex clashes that typify international disputes today, match-fixing factors often provide shortcuts to help people process confusing and conflicting information. On an everyday level, these shortcuts can serve useful functions. Indeed, many of them exist precisely because they lent adaptive advantages in our evolutionary past. But in today's very different world, as we will reveal in our case studies, psychological dispositions can foster large discrepancies between fact and perception, presenting significant threats to national interest and democratic ideals. Accomplishments or debacles go unrecognized, and opposing nations and their actions are misunderstood. Policymakers and publics alike must pay attention to these dangers. But to do so, we need to understand the circumstances in which score-keeping and match-fixing occur. To answer this question, we turn to their sources of variation.

4 | SOURCES OF VARIATION

Nothing is more obstinate than a fashionable consensus.

— MARGARET THATCHER

Thus it is that in war the victorious strategist seeks battle only after the victory has been won, whereas he who is destined for defeat first fights and afterwards looks for victory.

— SUN TZU

WE HAVE LAID OUT the argument that people sometimes score-keep and sometimes match-fix when evaluating victory and defeat. But what determines *when* people score-keep and *when* they match-fix? Furthermore, if matches are fixed, what type of country tends to be the beneficiary and what type of country tends to be the victim? In other words, whose performance is judged more favorably than the scorecard suggests, and whose performance is judged more critically? When is a match most likely to be fixed as a victory, and when is it most likely to be fixed as a defeat? In this chapter, we deal with these questions.

Four key variables produce predictions for the likelihood of match-fixing: decisiveness, ambiguity, power, and regime type. These variables are ranked in order of importance below, each one followed by its associated prediction.

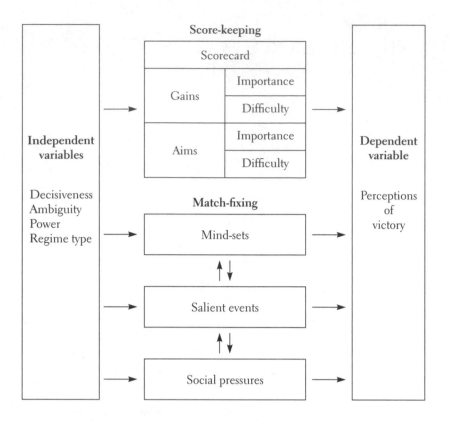

CHART 4.1. Our model of how perceptions of victory are formed. Both score-keeping and match-fixing play a role in shaping perceptions of victory, but their relative influence depends on four sources of variation: decisiveness, ambiguity, power, and regime type.

1. Decisiveness (of the outcome). *Prediction:* people score-keep one-sided outcomes and match-fix draws.
2. Ambiguity (of the dispute). *Prediction:* people match-fix ambiguous events.
3. Power (of the state). *Prediction:* people match-fix against the most powerful side.
4. Regime type (of the state). *Prediction:* people in democracies tend to score-keep, but they are also more likely to match-fix *against themselves.*

With these variables, we can now construct our complete theory, set out in Chart 4.1.

| Predictions

Decisiveness

Prediction: People score-keep one-sided outcomes and match-fix draws. Whether people adopt a score-keeping approach or conjure up an imagined result through match-fixing is often determined by a single key variable: the decisiveness of the outcome on the ground. When the settlement of a crisis or war is very one-sided (like the siege of Tyre in 332 B.C. or World War II), any match-fixing tends to be dominated by the undeniable material triumph of one side. If a material outcome in international relations is sufficiently one-sided, and this is widely known, then even observers of very different beliefs or ideologies will tend to agree on who won, for reasons rooted in material gains and losses. In other words, when results are decisive, people score-keep. There comes a point when even those who are most detached from reality are forced to recognize a crushing defeat. Hitler, for example, killed himself.

Observers' evaluations are therefore not completely arbitrary. Instead, they are anchored, at least in some cases, by a few basic metrics. Such metrics for victory are shared by all people, regardless of individual or cultural differences, but they dominate other potential influences on judgments only in the most extreme outcomes. If one side's territory is occupied, its towns razed, its leader deposed, its citizens killed or enslaved, these circumstances signal defeat the world over. In extreme outcomes, the media and elites have to select from a short list of possible interpretations—all of them very negative for one side. John Buchan, the author of *The Thirty-nine Steps*, commented on his service in the British ministry of propaganda in World War I: "The most active propaganda cannot undo the effect of an enemy victory or explain away an Allied check."[1] This is an important point: even though psychological factors can create imagined victories, such factors pale into insignificance when outcomes are heavily asymmetrical. Subjectivity is often very prevalent in people's judgments, but it is bounded, not limitless. Score-keeping often requires considerable information and quite complex information processing; therefore it tends to be the dominant mode of evaluation only when a clear-cut outcome makes the method easy to apply.

In today's world, the outcomes of wars and crises are typically far from clear-cut. With military annexations now a rarity, international outcomes are marked instead by multiple states and organizations interacting to produce compromise settlements that leave considerable doubt as to which side won and which side lost.[2] In such cases, where there is no decisive victory, match-fixing factors are almost always present in evaluations, and they are often of great consequence. For example, draws offer an opportunity for all countries to claim success. It is natural to laud the achievements of one's own side and to downplay those of the enemy. At the same time, domestic critics of a regime may claim that the draw was actually a defeat. Hence, key groups in different societies are likely to perceive a draw as either a success or a failure.

Consider Thucydides' account of a naval battle between the Corinthians and the Athenians in the fifth century B.C. There was little to choose between the two sides: the Athenians destroyed three ships, but the Corinthians damaged seven Athenian vessels, making them unserviceable. But rather than both sides agreeing that the outcome was a draw, the Athenians erected a victory trophy. They saw themselves as the "masters of the wrecks" because the Corinthi-

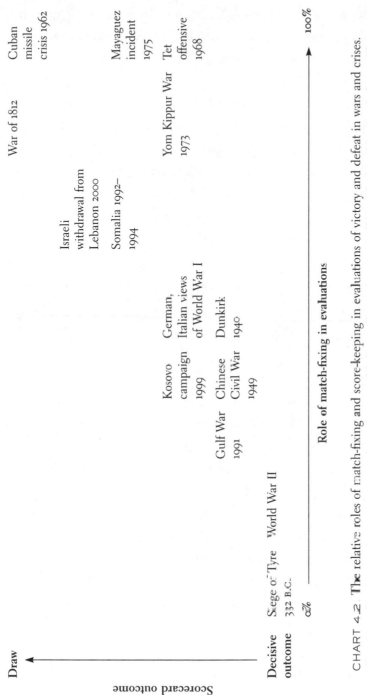

CHART 4.2. The relative roles of match-fixing and score-keeping in evaluations of victory and defeat in wars and crises. The closer the scorecard outcome is to a draw, the more likely it is that judgments will be influenced by match-fixing. The chart includes all of our mini-cases and full cases in which there was a dominant perception of victory (thus excluding Munich and Korea, where perceptions changed over time), and in which the scorecard outcome is reasonably clear (thus excluding the ongoing War on Terror and the Iraq War).

Draw

Scorecard outcome

Decisive outcome

Siege of Tyre 332 B.C.

World War II

0%

Gulf War 1991

Kosovo campaign 1999

Chinese Civil War 1949

German, Italian views of World War I

Dunkirk 1940

Role of match-fixing in evaluations

Israeli withdrawal from Lebanon 2000

Somalia 1992–1994

War of 1812

Yom Kippur War 1973

Cuban missile crisis 1962

Mayaguez incident 1975

Tet offensive 1968

100%

ans had refused to renew the fight. At the same time, the Corinthians also set up a victory trophy, basing this declaration of victory on their one available positive metric: "they had put out of action the greater number of ships."[3]

Chart 4.2 illustrates the relationship between the decisiveness of the scorecard outcome and people's tendency to score-keep or match-fix. Score-keeping dominated evaluations of the decisive World War II outcome. In contrast, match-fixing factors dominated evaluations of the far less decisive Cuban missile crisis. Other cases lie along a continuum between these extremes. There is a positive correlation between decisiveness and the tendency to score-keep, at least in these cases, suggesting that score-keeping is more likely in more decisive outcomes. This prediction is intuitive: indecisive outcomes are much more open to interpretation.

Ambiguity

Prediction: People match-fix ambiguous events. Crises, wars, and day-to-day international relations are inherently cloaked in uncertainty. Perceptions of actors and actions are often skewed by such things as language, history, worldview, and culture. Hardly anyone has a detailed understanding of all the relevant policy concerns. Compared with domestic issues, the tangled web of international relations is hugely complex, difficult to comprehend, and lacking in agreed-upon evaluative standards. But some international events are more ambiguous than others: novel scenarios (which lack historical baselines for comparison); situations where information is limited (putting the onus on subjective judgments and empowering elite manipulation); and multidimensional conflicts (in which numerous aspects of the dispute must be considered).

When outcomes are ambiguous, people are likely to rely even

more heavily on their preexisting beliefs to assess the situation, and to be especially susceptible to interpretive frames constructed by the media or elites. "The more complex and uncertain the environment," writes the political scientist Jerel Rosati, "the more likely individuals will rely on schemas and cognitive heuristics—shortcuts in information processing—to make sense of the world and the situation at hand." Such effects will be greater among observers—the focus of this book—than among decisionmakers, because, according to Rosati, "fragmented, inconsistent, and contradictory beliefs are more likely to exist when individuals have given little thought or have little knowledge and experience."[4]

Power

Prediction: People match-fix against the most powerful side. When one country in a dispute is considerably more powerful than the other (defined as greater material resources), the more powerful side is typically the *victim* of match-fixing. In other words, people are likely to skew their judgments so that the more powerful side is viewed as losing. Of the eleven mini-cases discussed in Chapter 1 where there was a dominant view that one side had won, this prediction holds for eight.

The exceptions are interesting. Italy was perhaps the least powerful of the Great Powers involved in World War I, yet Italians assessed their position at the war's end very critically. Another partial exception is the Cuban missile crisis, in which the less powerful Soviet Union was the victim of match-fixing, and the more powerful United States was the beneficiary. But it is worth noting that the Soviet Union was still extremely powerful, being one of the only two superpowers in the world. Hence many critics were impressed by Soviet power and thought it had failed to live up to expectations. The third exception is the 1975 Mayaguez incident, which Americans match-fixed as a success for the United States despite their country's massive superiority over Cambodia. The existence of some exceptions is not surprising, given the range of factors at work in international affairs. In the other eight cases, however, the victim of match-fixing was the more powerful state in the dispute: Britain in the War of 1812, the United States in the Chinese Civil War, the Tet offensive, and the intervention in Somalia, and Israel in the Yom Kippur War and the 2000 withdrawal from Lebanon. The other two examples are slightly more complex. Many people in Germany (which had been the weaker side in World War I) match-fixed the outcome to conclude that they were undefeated. Many people in Britain (which was the weaker side in 1940) match-fixed the Dunkirk evacuation to conjure up an image of victory.

Why would the performance of the most powerful state tend to be assessed more negatively? Simply put, people expect results from powerful states, and fast. Observers often fail to comprehend the difficulties involved in translating apparently massive material asymmetry into victory in a crisis or a war. When it comes to pitting soldiers or diplomats against one another in far-off lands, local factors may mitigate the material advantages of the more powerful side. In 1812 the British were already at war with France, the most powerful country in the world, when they took on America as well in their own backyard. In 1949 the United States, for all its material power, could not readily defeat the Chinese communists. Similarly, in Vietnam in 1968, many factors, including terrain and the weakness of the South Vietnamese regime, offset U.S. material superiority over communist forces. In Somalia in 1993, the Americans could not have chosen a country less suited for nation building, with virtually no political foundations or even physical infrastructure in place. As for Israel, it was more powerful than the Arab states

in 1973, but the Arabs fought with all the benefits of surprise, attacking at a time, place, and manner of their own choosing. Observers
often expect power differentials to determine outcomes at moments
of crisis and war, and neglect the potentially leveling effect of other
factors.[5]

Regime Type

Prediction: People in democracies tend to score-keep, but they are
also more likely to match-fix *against themselves*. Biases in perception often occur under regimes where the public's access to information is restricted, or where the press is under tight control, since
beliefs are less likely to be corrected by rival sources of information. Nondemocracies typically declare any foreign policy outcome
(even massive blunders) to be a great victory for their side and propagate this verdict through controlled media channels. Democratic
governments have to contend with a much wider range of information sources challenging their presentation of the facts.

But such differences between regime types should not be exaggerated: match-fixing is very prevalent in democracies, as shown in
every one of our case studies. It can sometimes be easier to manipulate opinion in democracies, because in nondemocracies the popu-
lace has greater expectations of manipulation, and is therefore more
psychologically prepared for it. Moreover, democratic societies are
no less (and perhaps are even more) inclined to develop strong ideologies that color people's mind-sets. Americans, for example, were
just as likely as Soviet citizens to believe in their own side's righ-
teousness in the Cold War. Even in countries with copious and divergent sources of information, we can still expect major biases in
perception. In the United States the resistance of some Democrats
to acknowledging any successes by the Bush administration is so

strong that it approximates the heavy-handed match-fixing in a totalitarian state.[6]

If regime type has a qualified effect on the overall tendency to match-fix, it has a substantial effect on a population's tendency to match-fix against *itself*. Match-fixing can take four forms (indicated in Chart 4.3): judgments can be overly positive or overly negative (relative to the scorecard) and can refer to one's own state or to the enemy state. As the chart shows, among our mini-cases, both democratic and nondemocratic states may occupy any of these categories. However, the nearly complete absence of nondemocracies in the bottom left and top right quadrants of the chart suggests that people in democracies are more likely than those in nondemocracies to be *self*-critical — judging their own country's performance more negatively than the scorecard would suggest. Although this is a hotchpotch of cases, this pattern makes intuitive and logical sense.

The media in nondemocracies tends to follow the official line that the country performed *at least* as well in a dispute as the scorecard would indicate. Indeed, nondemocratic regimes regularly present failures as successes, as the Japanese regime did in its account of the battle of Midway in 1942 as a victory for Japan. These regimes are therefore unlikely to allow an overly negative evaluation of their performance to become accepted wisdom in their populations.

In contrast, democratic societies are more pluralistic and open, providing greater opportunities for self-critical match-fixing. It is harder in a democracy to mask a large-scale defeat: the U.S. government could not have kept the outcome of Pearl Harbor secret even if it had wanted to. It is also more likely that democratic successes will go unappreciated at home. Opposition parties, commentators, and lobbying groups have every incentive to disparage the perfor-

Perceptions of

Direction of bias	Own state	Enemy state
Overly positive	• U.S. view of the War of 1812 • German view of WW I • British view of Dunkirk • U.S. view of the Cuban missile crisis • North Vietnamese view of Tet • Arab view of Yom Kippur War • U.S. view of the Mayaguez incident	• USSR view of U.S. in the Cuban missile crisis • U.S. view of North Vietnam in Tet • Israeli view of Arabs in the Yom Kippur War
Overly negative	• Italian view of WW I • U.S. view of the Chinese civil war • USSR view of the Cuban missile crisis • U.S. view of Tet • Israeli view of the Yom Kippur War • U.S. view of Somalia	• Arab view of Israel and the withdrawal from Lebanon • U.S. view of Britain in the War of 1812 • U.S. view of USSR in the Cuban missile crisis • North Vietnamese view of U.S. in Tet • Arab view of Israel in the Yom Kippur War

CHART 4.3. Perceptions of victory can be overly positive or overly negative, and they can refer to one's own state or the enemy state. Observers in democracies (shaded) are more likely to be overly negative about the performance of their own state than observers in nondemocracies (unshaded).

mance of the government. The media in democracies often critically judge their own regime's actions (as indeed is part of their role
in a democracy). The greater openness in democratic systems also
allows other match-fixing factors to negatively shape perceptions.
For example, a symbolic event like the North Vietnamese attack on
the U.S. embassy in the Tet offensive produced critical judgments
because the American media were able to quickly relay the event to
the U.S. public. If a similarly damaging symbolic event had occurred *against* the communists at Tet, the North Vietnamese population might never have heard about it.

As Chart 4.3 shows, there are many examples of democracies
fixing the match against themselves but only one example of a
nondemocracy doing so: the USSR in the Cuban missile crisis. But
this may have been exceptional. Critics of Khrushchev were cir-
cling like vultures before the crisis began, and leapt on the settlement as evidence of his failure. Where a nondemocratic regime is
secure, its population is unlikely to match-fix against it. Such critics
risk their lives.

The four variables outlined above enable us to anticipate match-
fixing in current and future conflicts. *Decisiveness* of outcome has
the strongest effect on whether observers score-keep or match-fix.
Extremely one-sided outcomes can trump every other variable: people would probably score-keep a crushing victory even if that dispute also involved, say, a weak nondemocratic state against a powerful democratic state. *Ambiguity* of a dispute also has a significant
effect; novel situations, for example, are very likely to be judged according to arbitrary metrics based on mind-sets or manipulation by
elites. *Power* is also important; the beneficiary of match-fixing in a
dispute is likely to be the weaker state. *Regime type* is not decisive in
determining whether match-fixing occurs, but it does shape the na-

ture of match-fixing, in particular whether or not a country is *self-critical*.

Decisiveness and ambiguity predict whether there is match-fixing at all, while power and regime type predict whether there is match-fixing and, in addition, predict which side will benefit from it and which will be its victim. These last two factors, in determining the victim of match-fixing, operate independently and can be mutually reinforcing. In the battle of Tet the United States was both the most powerful actor in the dispute and a democracy, increasing the chances that it would be the victim of match-fixing. For the same reasons, in the wars the United States is fighting today, match-fixing is more likely to occur against the United States than against its enemies.

Our four variables are not meant to form an exhaustive list of every factor that can influence whether people match-fix or not. They are typically crucial variables, but other factors may sometimes be important. For example, individuals undoubtedly vary in their propensity to make biased evaluations: some people are better than others at critical thinking, or consult a wider range of sources of information. Some people are aware of political messages (and manipulation), others are not.[7] But in most of the cases of match-fixing outlined in Chapter 1, individuals of all levels of education, intelligence, and awareness subscribed to the dominant perception of which side won. The convergence of opinion about victory suggests that individual variation is not the preeminent factor determining whether match-fixing occurs. Broader forces are at work.

Under what conditions is victory most and least likely to be perceived, and under what conditions is defeat most and least likely to be perceived? Logical inferences from our model suggest that the following conditions will favor perceptions of victory for "State X" (and perceptions of defeat for its opponent):

- State X achieves a decisive material victory.
- State X is weaker than its opponent but the circumstances of the dispute (such as geography or terrain) have an equalizing effect.
- State X has a nondemocratic regime, which bluntly promotes perceptions of victory.
- State X lost the previous dispute, so observers underestimate its chances in the current dispute.
- The leaders of State X are popular before the dispute, and cognitive dissonance ensures that the public views their performance through rose-colored glasses.
- A shocking crisis, and the unwillingness of elites to criticize the leader of State X, produces a pronounced rally phenomenon.
- Observers define the timing of the crisis or war so that it begins with the material nadir for State X, thus maximizing the country's perceived improvement during the dispute.
- The dispute is framed in terms of a stand-off in which State X holds firm and its opponent backs down.
- Symbolic events signify that State X has achieved the key metrics employed by observers.

| The Case Studies

Thus far we have outlined two ways in which people evaluate international disputes (score-keeping and match-fixing), we have outlined some key variables that influence the relative roles of score-keeping and match-fixing, and we have made predictions about which countries tend to be the victims of match-fixing. The logical next step is to explore whether our theory helps to explain real-world cases in which there is a mismatch between victory on the battlefield and victory in the minds of observers.[8]

In each case study, we complete a set of systematic tasks:

1. We set out the prevailing perceptions of who won and who lost, drawing on a wide range of sources (e.g. opinion polls, memoirs, media, secondary sources, and other relevant indicators ranging from popular films to children's art).

2. We test the congruence of these perceptions with the scorecard result, which includes an assessment of the material *gains and losses* incurred by each side (e.g. troops and equipment lost; territory won; key targets captured), adjusting for the difficulty and the importance of each gain or loss; and an assessment of which side achieved its material *aims*, again adjusting for the difficulty and the importance of each aim.

3. We explain the discrepancy between the scorecard result and perceptions of victory through a Framework 2 match-fixing analysis, which tracks the causal chains between mind-sets, salient events, social pressures, and judgments.[9] We use primary and secondary sources, polling data, counterfactuals, and, in our final case, experiments to test the extent to which specific match-fixing factors shape people's evaluations.

Of course, even with archetypal score-keeping—such as evaluations of victory in World War II—members of the public do not entirely agree about the importance or difficulty of particular material gains and losses. As discussed in Chapter 2, people's different preferences would produce somewhat varying scorecards even if they all employed a perfect score-keeping analysis. However, we would expect a population that was score-keeping to generate evaluations that cluster together around the same core material gains and losses. These evaluations may be distinguished from one another by the preferential weighting given to the importance of certain gains and losses and the difficulty of certain aims. There is no single purely objective scorecard, but the variation among bona fide score-keepers is likely to be quite modest. In our own score-keeping we attempt to be as accurate as possible, and although the importance and difficulty we ascribe to gains, and the difficulty we ascribe to aims, are by necessity subjective, we take a commonsense approach, including for example both territorial gains and human costs. But however subjective our score-keeping, most of the case studies involve perceptions that are completely at odds with any reasonable material scorecard; thus the explanation for these perceptions must lie elsewhere.

Perceptions are one of the hardest areas of social science to argue convincingly about. How can we know what other people *really* think? The contents of observers' minds are problematic to define, identify, describe, and measure. An excellent example is that although a leader's aims may objectively exist, in practice these aims are very difficult to discover. However, some of the methodological problems actually represent evidence *for* our overall argument. If a leader's motives are difficult for scholars to discern, then they must be more problematic for observers who have less time and less information. If observers cannot base their evaluations on an accurate understanding of a leader's aims, what exactly is the evaluation based upon?

As with many theories within international relations, especially those related to perceptions, there are issues about whether our argument can be definitively falsified—a sacred standard of scientific theories. We would claim that at the very least, individual aspects of our theory can be falsified, if, for example, (1) a factor we neglect is demonstrated to shape perceptions much more than the factors that we do include; (2) a factor we include is shown to consistently fail to shape perceptions; (3) match-fixing is shown to consistently benefit powerful democratic states; or (4) non-democracies are shown to consistently match-fix against themselves.

5 | THE CUBAN MISSILE CRISIS

*Both sides could . . emerge from the crisis claiming victory, but
there was little doubt as to who the real winners and losers were.*

— JOHN LEWIS GADDIS

IN THIS CHAPTER we examine people's evaluations of the U.S.-Soviet clash over nuclear missiles installed in Cuba in 1962. As one of the most important and best-documented crises of the century, the Cuban missile crisis represents a valuable case for examining our hypotheses about perceptions of victory and defeat. Observers around the world came to view the crisis as a triumph for the United States. The question is, why?

| History

In mid-October 1962 U.S. intelligence discovered that the Soviet Union had installed nuclear missiles on the island of Cuba. The missiles had sufficient range to threaten nearly all major American cities. The secret nature of the installation, in the context of Soviet leader Nikita Khrushchev's earlier assurances that he would not place missiles in Cuba, sparked shock and anger in Washington. President John F. Kennedy convened a committee (dubbed the ExComm) to advise him on the crisis. On 22 October, in a televised speech, Kennedy informed the nation of both the presence of the

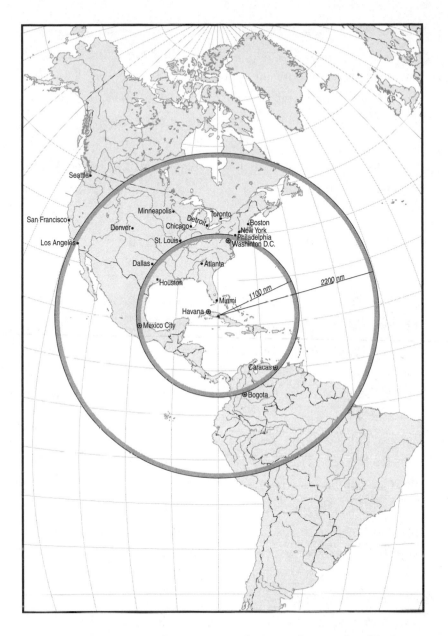

MAP 1. The ranges of Soviet SS-4 and SS-5 nuclear missiles if fired from Cuba. Map by Philip Schwartzberg.

missiles in Cuba and his decision to impose a "quarantine" on ship-
ments of "offensive weapons" to the island. During the next week
the world peered into the abyss of nuclear war. Then on 28 October
Khrushchev announced that he had ordered the weapons to be
dismantled and returned to the Soviet Union. In response, Kennedy
offered a pledge that the United States would not invade Cuba. In
a second pledge, which was not made public, the United States
promised to remove American nuclear missiles from Turkey.[1]

Dominant Perceptions of Victory and Defeat

To a remarkable extent, contemporaries on all sides were convinced
that the United States had emerged victorious from the crisis. Kennedy never claimed victory in public, but his defense secretary, Robert McNamara, later recalled the president's stating privately: "Gentlemen, we won." Kennedy remarked that he had "cut
[Khrushchev's] balls off." The president had no need to declare
victory publicly; others did it for him. According to the historian
Thomas Reeves: "The applause for the President was overwhelming. Congratulations poured into the White House from all over
the world, and Kennedy's popularity at home soared." *Newsweek*
reported that Kennedy's "total victory in the head-on clash with
Khrushchev marked his greatest political triumph." Even Richard
Nixon, Kennedy's defeated electoral opponent from 1960, suggested
that the outcome "demonstrates again that when you stand up to
Communist aggressors, they back down." Kennedy's approval ratings jumped from 61 percent to 74 percent, and the Democrats did
well in the November 1962 elections, gaining four seats in the Senate and losing only four in the House (the party that controls the
White House often loses badly in mid-term elections).[2]

In the wake of the Cuban missile crisis, Americans increasingly based their judgments of Kennedy on foreign policy rather than on domestic issues, and these evaluations were overwhelmingly positive. The months after November 1962 were the only time from 1960 to 1980 when Americans who thought Russian power would decline in the coming year outnumbered those who thought it would increase—a clear indication that the U.S. public believed their country had gained the upper hand in the missile crisis. According to the dominant interpretation of the settlement, Kennedy offered a public pledge not to invade Cuba (which the United States had no intention of doing anyway), thus graciously allowing Khrushchev a fig leaf to hide his retreat and substantive defeat. "Never again," writes the scholar of media and politics Eric Alterman, "would a victory appear quite so unambiguous as the moment when Nikita Khrushchev took to the airwaves to announce his nation's capitulation to American terms." In 1967 a state department publication asserted that "faced with a showdown . . . the Soviet Union didn't dare to respond . . . the U.S. is today the only effective global military power in the world."[3]

It was not only Americans who held this perception. Many important Russians viewed Khrushchev as having lost the crisis, and partly as a result, his political career came to a rapid end. As the political scientists James Blight and Philip Brenner put it: "In the Kremlin, ultimately, the outcome was seen as a U.S. victory and a Soviet humiliation."[4] The Russians announced Khrushchev's removal on 15 October 1964, charging him with "harebrained schemes" and making "rash decisions." A Presidium member, Dmitri Polyansky, attacked Khrushchev: "You insisted that we deploy our missiles on Cuba. This provoked the deepest crisis, carried the world to the brink of nuclear war, and even frightened terribly the organizer of this very danger . . . Not having any other way out

we had to accept every demand and condition dictated by the U.S
. . . This incident damaged the international prestige of our government, our party, our armed forces, while at the same time helping
to raise the authority of the United States."[5]

The Cubans similarly thought that the Soviets had backed down
and been defeated in what they saw as a major loss for both Moscow
and Havana. Fidel Castro was outraged, feeling he had been treated
as a vassal by the Soviets. He called Khrushchev "a son of a bitch
. . . bastard . . . ass-hole." "Cuban leaders," Blight and Brenner note,
"saw the Soviets acquiesce to virtually every U.S. demand without
seriously acknowledging Cuba's [own] perception of the threat it
faced." The Chinese, too, resented the withdrawal of the missiles
and the USSR's apparent weakness in defense of communism, calling the deal "a Soviet Munich." They were dismissive of the Soviet
performance, calling it "adventurism" to place missiles in Cuba in
the first place, but "capitulationism" to withdraw them.[6]

In the years since 1962, these same perceptions of a clear victor and vanquished have endured. American schoolchildren were
grateful to their president for averting war: in a survey of 1,349 children after Kennedy's assassination, almost all of them cited the Cuban missile crisis as part of his legacy. When Americans judge their
leaders in retrospect, Kennedy is the most popular president since
1961, with 83 percent approval. This is in large part due to memories of his handling of the Cuban missile crisis. In 1974, 53 percent
of Americans remembered the crisis as a "proud moment" in U.S.
history, while 18 percent remembered it as a "dark moment." In
1988, 76 percent agreed with Kennedy's decision to blockade Cuba,
and only 10 percent disagreed with it.[7]

For President Kennedy, according to one of his biographers,
"Most American historians have continued the applause." Arthur
Schlesinger Jr., in A Thousand Days, tried to capture the impact of

the Cuban missile crisis: "To the whole world it displayed the ripening of an American leadership unsurpassed in the responsible management of power." As Arthur Stein sees it, "if the United States had capitulated to the Soviet emplacement of missiles in Cuba, the U.S.S.R. would have been the big winner and the United States the big loser. In actuality, the Soviets' decision to retreat in the face of American pressure represented a defeat for them and a victory for the United States."[8] Vladislav Zubok and Constantine Pleshakov argue that "Khrushchev, the gambler of the decade, panicked and capitulated." Robert Service describes Khrushchev as an "old dog" who, "far from intimidating the young pup, had to give way. The ships were turned back and the Soviet regime was humbled in the eyes of the world." Khrushchev removed the missiles and, in the words of William Poundstone, "asked essentially nothing from the United States in return." In their comprehensive study of crises since 1919, Michael Brecher and Jonathan Wilkenfeld find that the crisis had a "definitive" outcome: it was a "victory" for the United States and a "defeat" for the USSR and Cuba.[9]

In contrast, revisionist historians have suggested that the settlement terms of the Cuban missile crisis were more of a compromise deal, rather than an unalloyed U.S. triumph. Richard Lebow and Janice Stein, for example, argue that Kennedy was ultimately as willing to compromise as Khrushchev. There were also a handful of critics of U.S. policy at the time of the crisis. From the left came suggestions that Kennedy had gambled with humankind's future. From the right, General Curtis Le May thought the United States had lost the crisis because it had not invaded Cuba.[10] On several occasions Khrushchev attempted to portray himself as the victor: "In what way have we retreated, one may ask. Socialist Cuba exists. Cuba remains a beacon of Marxist-Leninist ideas in the Western Hemisphere. The impact of her revolutionary example will grow."

Khrushchev also suggested that neither side had really won. "Which side triumphed, who won? In this respect one may say that it was sanity, the cause of peace and security of peoples, that won." In his memoirs, Khrushchev similarly called the settlement a "triumph of common sense," while also claiming: "It was a great victory for us, though, that we had been able to extract from Kennedy a promise that neither America nor any of her allies would invade Cuba."[11]

Yet the voices of discontent, as well as the ambiguous view of victory espoused by Khrushchev, were largely drowned out in the quickly established consensus that 1962 had witnessed a major U.S. triumph. Indeed, the handful of criticisms from hardliners on the left and the right made Kennedy's tough but prudent brand of statesmanship appear even more impressive to most Americans. Lebow notes that even the revisionist writers on the crisis "agree that Kennedy imposed his will on Khrushchev." Khrushchev's Kremlin colleague Pyotr Demichev thought that the Russian leader himself privately "felt it had been a defeat."[12]

| Framework 1: Score-keeping

What factors produced these evaluations of U.S. triumph and Soviet defeat in the Cuban missile crisis? Here we test the extent to which score-keeping, which focuses on the material settlement itself, can explain perceptions of victory and defeat in 1962.

To conduct a score-keeping analysis, following the methods set out at the end of Chapter 4, we first examine the alterations in the relative security positions of the superpowers. This allows us to ascertain the material *gains and losses* that were effectively traded in the final settlement. But in itself, this is not good enough. We must also identify the extent to which each side achieved its material *aims*. This will confirm whether the material gains achieved by each side represented its genuine goals, or whether they were incidental by-products of the outcome (thus deserving less credit). The following analysis suggests that score-keeping does not explain the widespread perception of a major U.S. victory, nor that of a major Soviet defeat, which is to say that many people got the outcome completely wrong.

Sometimes Kennedy is judged to have been the victor in the Cuban missile crisis on the grounds that he displayed resolve or established his credibility. But such psychological effects do not equal victory any more than a football team's demonstration of its resolve on the playing field equals victory. What matters is how these psychological effects translate into tangible gains: points for the football team, material gains and losses for the United States. Psychological effects are merely the means to a tangible end, and it is this tangible end that we measure. A country displaying resolve may or may not be more likely to ultimately win a crisis, but it has not won anything yet. What, then, were the material gains and material aims achieved in 1962?

Material Gains and Losses

In some ways the U.S. security position became stronger as a result of the Cuban missile crisis (see Charts 5.1 and 5.2). Kennedy achieved the removal of the missiles from Cuba, which were much closer to the United States than missiles in the Soviet Union, and therefore would have had shorter flight times and higher accuracy in striking U.S. targets. They were also moveable, and offered the Soviets a more effective second-strike capability (missiles based in the Soviet Union itself were vulnerable because the United States had located their launch pads).[13]

Type of outcome	Event	Material gain or loss?	An aim achieved?	Altering the credit due[a]		
				Importance		Difficulty[c]
				For leader	For observer[b]	
Positive outcomes	Removal of missiles from Cuba	Gain	Achieved	Very high	Moderate/high	Moderate
Negative outcomes	Removal of missiles from Turkey	Loss	Not an aim	Low/moderate	Moderate	Moderate (chance of avoiding)
	Non-invasion pledge	Loss	Not an aim	Low	Moderate	Low/moderate (chance of avoiding)

a. Higher values give *more* credit for positive outcomes and *less* credit for negative outcomes.
b. The importance of a gain or an aim in the minds of observers (in this case the authors) trying to fairly assess its worth.
c. The difficulty of a gain or an aim in the minds of observers (in this case the authors) trying to assess it fairly.

CHART 5.1. Scorecard for the United States in the Cuban missile crisis.

Type of outcome	Event	Material gain or loss?	An aim achieved?	Altering the credit due[a]		
				Importance		Difficulty[c]
				For leader	For observer[b]	
Positive outcomes	Non-invasion pledge	Gain	Achieved	High	Moderate	Low/moderate
	Removal of missiles from Turkey	Gain	Achieved	High	Moderate	Moderate
Negative outcomes	Removal of missiles from Cuba	Loss	Not achieved	High	Moderate/high	Moderate (chance of avoiding)

a. Higher values give *more* credit for positive outcomes and *less* credit for negative outcomes.
b. The importance of a gain or an aim in the minds of observers (in this case the authors) trying to fairly assess its worth.
c. The difficulty of a gain or an aim in the minds of observers (in this case the authors) trying to assess it fairly.

CHART 5.2. Scorecard for the Soviet Union in the Cuban missile crisis.

The overall strategic effect of the missile deployment has been questioned, however, for two reasons. First, a number of nuclear weapons were already available to be launched from Soviet soil, from long-range bombers, and possibly from Soviet submarines. Second, it was understood to be only a matter of time before the Soviets developed a comprehensive arsenal of intercontinental ballistic missiles (ICBMs) in the USSR. Initially, during the crisis, McNamara saw little point in risking war over a nuclear threat that the United States would soon face in any case.[14] Nevertheless, the missiles were removed and Khrushchev accepted that the Soviet Union would never again place nuclear missiles in Cuba. To do so would invite an immediate U.S. military response. One Soviet option thus no longer existed.

In return, the Soviets gained, first of all, a public pledge that the United States would not invade Cuba. At the time, Castro and Khrushchev fully anticipated a second U.S.-backed invasion following the 1961 Bay of Pigs landings by anticommunist Cubans trained by the United States. In the months before the crisis the USSR repeatedly demanded that America not attack Cuba, for example on 11 September 1962. After the Cuban missile crisis, the United States attempted to keep the nature of the non-invasion pledge ambiguous, tying it to Cuban good behavior. Kennedy made clear privately that the pledge did not ban covert action or an economic blockade: "We can't give the impression that Castro is home free."[15] Nevertheless, the evidence suggests that the United States regarded the pledge as a de facto binding agreement, and the political and military costs of a second invasion had been raised considerably. In February 1963 Castro told the Soviets that as a result of the settlement, there was little or no chance of a U.S. attack in the next two years. If Kennedy was reelected, Castro predicted, there would not be another invasion until at least 1969. Overall, the menu of U.S. options for Cuban policy had become more constrained than it had been before Khrushchev sent the missiles to Cuba.[16]

The United States had also agreed to remove nuclear missiles from Turkey. The significance of the Turkish missiles has been downplayed because within the Kennedy administration they were widely seen as being obsolete, and they were due to be replaced in the near future. However, Washington had decided to postpone the missiles' removal for fear Moscow would view it as a sign of weakness, and at the time of the Cuban crisis there was no definite plan for a pullout. In any case, the missiles appeared far from obsolete to the Turks, other NATO allies, and especially those living under their shadow—the Russians. Kennedy was well aware that Turkey was averse to losing the missiles. As it was, Turkey eventually acquiesced in the pullout, but the Cuban settlement meant that even if the Turks had fiercely objected the United States would have had to remove the missiles, potentially weakening U.S.-Turkish relations and the NATO alliance. As Philip Nash has argued, the concern for America's credibility in the eyes of its allies explains why this part of the settlement remained a secret, known only to a small group within the ExComm.[17]

After the crisis ended, McNamara gave orders to dismantle the missiles in Turkey, as well as U.S. missiles in Italy. It has never been proved that the removal of the missiles from Italy was also privately promised to the Russians, but it is quite possible. In his memoirs Khrushchev wrote: "I didn't tell Castro that Kennedy promised to remove the missiles from Turkey and Italy, since that agreement was just between the two of us."[18] If the withdrawal of the missiles from Italy did result from the Cuban missile crisis, this was another gain for Moscow.

To illustrate the point about these changes in the overall balance of material power, imagine for a moment that in this dawn of the space age, an astronaut had gone into space in the summer of 1962 and returned for Christmas without ever hearing about the Cuban missile crisis. On the one hand, there were no nuclear missiles in Cuba when he left, and none when he returned. However, if he paid attention to U.S. policy toward Cuba, he would have noticed a significant change since his departure. After sponsoring an unsuccessful invasion in 1961 and planning a second one, and having never accepted the validity of the communist regime, the United States had now made a public pledge not to invade. If the astronaut also learned of the deal to remove missiles from Turkey, that would have added to his surprise. To suggest to the astronaut that, in his absence, the *Soviets* had been defeated might have appeared baffling. The astronaut's view, based solely on material changes resulting from Khrushchev's decision to send missiles to Cuba, might well have been strikingly different from the perspective of contemporaries on Earth who had lived through the drama of the crisis.

A balance-sheet approach based on material changes resulting from the settlement terms cannot, it seems, explain the virtually unanimous view that the United States won a major victory in 1962. How did the settlement terms, however, correspond to the *aims* of the two sides? Did one side achieve its aims, while the other did not, thus allowing for a legitimate scorecard victory?

Material Aims

Nuclear war was averted in 1962, thus avoiding the shared worst-case scenario. However, while this condition was necessary for any meaningful victory to be achieved, it was not in itself sufficient, because both sides sought goals beyond peace. The Americans focused on removing the missiles from Cuba, and the Soviets had a range of motives, including defending against a U.S. attack on

Cuba, gaining strategic parity with the United States, and bargaining for gains in Europe.[19] The material aims of both sides are considered in detail below (and are noted in Charts 5.1 and 5.2).

Soviet Aims. While a majority of historians see the Soviet decision to place missiles in Cuba as being Khrushchev's personal choice, the Russian leader's aims in the Cuban missile crisis have been widely disputed, and he appears to have acted from a "multiplicity of motives." Certainly Khrushchev did not want a war in the Caribbean, where the Soviets were in no position to fight. There is evidence that he saw the installation of missiles in Cuba as a "cure-all," which would save the Cuban revolution, increase Soviet strategic power, and make any American first strike more problematic. As the crisis escalated, Khrushchev was increasingly fearful that events were getting out of control, and as is clear from his personal cables to Kennedy, it became one of his aims simply to defuse the crisis.[20]

The historian Bruce Kuklick argues that the missiles in Cuba were a gamble intended to resolve the U.S.-Soviet diplomatic deadlock over Germany.[21] However, the fact that Khrushchev barely mentioned Berlin during the crisis (focusing instead on Cuba and Turkey) suggests that pushing the United States out of West Berlin was not his primary rationale. In fact, it is possible that some observers interpret Berlin as the central aim precisely *because* this interpretation fits the story of U.S. victory and Soviet defeat. If the missile deployment was designed to get the United States out of Berlin, it failed; if the aim was to make the United States back off from Cuba, it succeeded. Judging the Cuban missile crisis as a U.S. victory because Khrushchev did not win in Berlin is not entirely unlike Saddam Hussein's judging the first Gulf War as a success because the West did not occupy Iraq. Exaggerating the enemy's supposed aims is a sure way to perceive victory for one's own side.

Khrushchev failed to gain the strategic benefits of a missile deployment in Cuba. He also failed to make wider gains in Berlin (if this was indeed one of his aims). However, the two aims that Khrushchev himself specified during the crisis were both satisfied in the settlement: a U.S. pledge not to invade Cuba, and the removal of the American missiles from Turkey.[22] The United States conceded the first publicly, the second privately. The view that the defense of Cuba was an important reason for the installation of the missiles is not new, and has been corroborated by recent work in the Soviet archives.[23] Khrushchev saw Cuba as a potential model for Third World revolution, as a beacon for the exploited people of Latin America, and as strategically crucial for the advancement of communism in the region. The Soviet leadership was almost certain that the Americans would attempt another attack on the island.[24] It is hard to see how Moscow could have induced the virulently anti-Castro Kennedy administration to pledge not to invade Cuba, except through a superpower crisis.

As for the Turkish missiles, on 26 October Khrushchev wrote to Kennedy: "You are worried over Cuba. You say that it worries you because it lies at a distance of ninety miles across the sea from the shores of the United States. However, Turkey lies next to us."[25] Khrushchev remarked during the crisis that if Moscow could get the removal of the missiles from Turkey as part of the deal, "we would win." On 28 October Khrushchev was in the process of telling the Soviet Presidium that the USSR would have to withdraw the missiles from Cuba in return for the non-invasion pledge, without any reference to Turkey, when a message arrived from the Soviet ambassador in the United States saying that the Americans had also agreed to remove the missiles from Turkey. This concession sealed the deal. The secrecy over the Turkish part of the agreement was not only for Kennedy's benefit. It also helped Khrushchev maintain relations with Castro, who was angered by the prospect that Cuba could be a pawn traded for Soviet gains in Turkey (and was indeed furious when he found out about the arrangement in 1963).[26]

U.S. Aims. Kennedy's core political aim in the crisis was to remove the missiles from Cuba, and this aim was successfully achieved. This is the main basis for the argument that the Americans won, and the literature has focused overwhelmingly on this part of the settlement.

Was it an important aim to keep the invasion option open? It is difficult to say how much of a concession the non-invasion pledge was for the United States, in part because administration officials differed widely on the wisdom of invading Cuba. In his election campaign Kennedy had emphasized the Republican Party's failure to prevent communists from taking power ninety miles off the U.S. coastline. He described the ultimate objective of U.S. policy as being "the overthrow of the Castro regime," and sought throughout his time in office to find an acceptable way to change the government in Havana, including covert operations and the 1961 Bay of Pigs invasion. But he was reluctant to support a second invasion, and in early 1962 he told Cuban exiles that the United States would not provide troops to aid a revolt against Castro. And yet, before the crisis, detailed plans existed for such a contingency, and important figures were in favor of direct military action. On 3 October 1962, with prescient timing, Congress passed a joint resolution sanctioning the use of force against Cuba if it should be required. Kennedy's adviser McGeorge Bundy later recalled: "The president initially resisted a direct assurance against invasion, for he knew that influential forces favored such an invasion. The editors of *Time* among others had been pressing for it even before the crisis."[27]

While a sudden U.S. invasion of Cuba was unlikely even without the missile crisis, the Americans might have used force if Castro had died, or if civil unrest had broken out on the island. Indeed, one operation being actively considered in Washington involved sparking a civil war in Cuba, to be followed by U.S. military intervention. But after the missile crisis, the United States would have been far more constrained in a scenario of civil unrest. The United States sought the removal of Castro, but in the wake of the missile crisis the Cuban communist regime was more secure than ever before. In May 1963 Robert Kennedy told a Soviet diplomat that the missile crisis deal was still in force, including the U.S. pledge not to invade the island. The United States did renew its secret campaign to assassinate Castro, and Kennedy sometimes talked tough, but U.S. policy in regard to Cuba was subsequently much more cautious. For example, the administration authorized a ransom payment of $53 million in food and medicines for the release of those captured during the Bay of Pigs operation. Kennedy even explored a possible modus vivendi with Castro.[28] In any case, the fact that certain U.S. officials did not aim to invade Cuba, and therefore did not rate the non-invasion pledge as a major concession, is balanced by the fact that Khrushchev evidently did value it highly.

There was considerable skepticism within the U.S. administration over the worth of the Turkish missiles. However, the United States agreed to their removal on the strict condition that this part of the deal remain secret, because a public trade would have been considered by elements in the White House (not to mention the department of defense, Turkey, and other NATO allies) as a significant loss.[29] "Any hint of a trade with the Soviets," according to Thomas Reeves, "would prompt Republicans to scream appeasement, rattle NATO allies, and cause fury in the Pentagon and among militant ExCom members." Robert Kennedy was reluctant to write anything down about the missile deal for fear that it would wreck his future political career. Nevertheless, the president was open to a public trade of missiles in Turkey for those in Cuba. Aware that he might face the choice between a missile swap and risky air strikes on the installations in Cuba, he preferred the former. Dean Rusk, Kennedy's secretary of state, recalled later that the president would have been receptive to a public missile trade brokered by the United Nations, but this never became necessary.[30]

To sum up, a Framework 1 score-keeping analysis is insufficient to explain the dominant perceptions of victory and defeat in the Cuban missile crisis. The material *gains and losses* suggest an unclear outcome: "before" and "after" snapshots of the crisis intimate a neutral settlement or even changes favorable to the Soviets. An analysis of material *aims* fails to salvage a scorecard victory for Washington: the United States achieved its core objective of getting rid of the Cuban missiles, while to some extent narrowing its own room for maneuver against the Castro regime and compromising over the missiles in Turkey. Khrushchev's aims in the crisis are disputed, but he achieved both of his publicly stated goals, although he may have failed to realize wider objectives. He would later claim that the preservation of Cuba had cost only the equivalent of the round-trip expenses for the missiles and troops. This is true up to a point, although Khrushchev did not originally intend such a quick entry and exit. Observers did not score-keep the Cuban missile crisis: the scorecard indicates a draw, but the dominant perception was of a U.S. triumph.[31]

| Framework 2: Match-Fixing

A more convincing explanation for perceptions of victory in the Cuban missile crisis is offered by a Framework 2 match-fixing ap-

	Affected aspect of judgment	
Match-fixing factors	Metrics	Information
Mind-sets		
Chinese, Cuban, European beliefs	X	
Russian, U.S. beliefs		X
Salient events		
"Stand-off" image	X	
Time points	X	
Symbolic events		X
Social pressures		
Media and elite manipulation	X	X

CHART 5.3. Key match-fixing factors influencing perceptions of victory and defeat in the Cuban missile crisis.

proach, which incorporates the role of mind-sets, salient events, and social pressures. In the minds of observers, the crisis was fixed so that the Russians would appear to lose, irrespective of the scorecard. Chart 5.3 lists the key match-fixing factors at work in this case, each of which we explore in detail below.

Mind-sets

It is outside the scope of this chapter to offer a comprehensive analysis of the mind-sets of all audiences in 1962, but we can suggest some key prior beliefs that influenced judgments of victory in the Cuban missile crisis.

Mind-sets and Metrics of Success. For several important groups of observers during the Cuban missile crisis, mind-sets produced biased metrics that encouraged perceptions of a Soviet defeat. Kennedy had been viewed as weak in some quarters as a result of his perceived failure at the Bay of Pigs and his perceived poor showing in a meeting with Khrushchev in Vienna. With expectations of Kennedy quite low in 1962, the metric for success became more achievable.[32]

The Chinese, whose view of the crisis was heavily influenced by the developing Sino-Soviet split, tended to measure success by whether the Soviets were selling out to the capitalist states. By 1962 China had become isolated from the Soviet Union. The Soviets refused to back Chinese attempts to resolve the Taiwan issue by force, and China strongly opposed the notion of peaceful coexistence with capitalism. Before the Cuban missile crisis, the Chinese had often accused Moscow of capitulating to imperialism. Thus they saw in Soviet behavior during the crisis what they *expected* to see: the Russians once again backing down and retreating. Mao Zedong interpreted Khrushchev's actions in 1962 as a validation of China's anti-Soviet stance, and the removal of the missiles led to a new low in relations between the two countries.[33]

Castro and members of his regime also approached the crisis with a mind-set that predisposed them toward a critical view of Khrushchev's performance. The Cuban viewpoint in 1962 tended to emphasize several elements: idealistic hopes for an imminent world revolution based on the Cuban model; a belief that Khrushchev had made the protection of Cuba equivalent to the defense of the Soviet motherland; and a view of the expected U.S. invasion of the island as the equivalent of a nuclear holocaust—in the sense that it would have devastated the country—and therefore "more palpably frightening than the abstraction of being a nuclear target." Given this mind-set, the Cuban leaders selected as their key metric for success whether the Soviet Union had stood up to the United States or had sold out Havana in a superpower deal. They were therefore incensed that the Soviets had apparently backed down, that Havana had not even been informed beforehand, and that Moscow had made, in effect, a "cowardly, undignified surrender to the United States at Cuba's expense."[34]

Not all groups of observers, however, were predisposed to select metrics by which Khrushchev failed. Among nonaligned nations the missile withdrawal was initially popular, although many later became critical of the Soviets for having apparently yielded so quickly. The European reaction to the missile crisis strongly reflected Europe's position on the front line of the Cold War. All the major European leaders backed a firm U.S. stance and were deeply skeptical of any missile trade at the expense of European security. Konrad Adenauer, for example, regarded the Russian missiles in Cuba as a major challenge to the West. Charles de Gaulle also strongly supported a military response. Europe's vulnerability did increase concern about a U.S. invasion of Cuba or extensive air strikes to remove the missiles. The Europeans tended overwhelmingly to see the avoidance of general war as the most important metric for judging success, and were therefore less likely to perceive one superpower as the decisive victor and another as defeated. Indeed, their perception that the Soviets had exercised restraint arguably proved beneficial to future European-Soviet relations.[35]

Mind-sets and Information on Success. In addition to the selection of metrics, the information used to judge whether or not these metrics had been achieved exhibited important biases. Within the USSR, mind-sets engendered by the domestic political context tended to shape interpretations of incoming information about the Cuban missile crisis. By 1962 Khrushchev's prestige had fallen among military elites as well as the wider public, and he was suffering from a "crisis of the Kremlin's legitimacy." This stemmed, among other things, from rapid rises in food prices and from rifts with the military over drastic defense cuts. In the spring of 1962 more than twenty demonstrators were killed protesting government policies in the Russian city of Novocherkassk. This context appears to have predisposed many Soviet elites toward a critical evaluation of Khrushchev's performance in 1962.[36]

The U.S. mind-set may have predisposed Americans to interpret information about the crisis as a victory for Kennedy. Americans in 1962 mainly agreed on the basic tenets of Cold War policy, especially the nefarious nature of the Soviet Union and the need for a tough (although not reckless) stance against Moscow. In this context there was likely to be support for a controlled but decisive initiative such as the quarantine of Cuba. Furthermore, the U.S. public was to some extent psychologically prepared for a crisis over Cuba, and therefore incoming information caused less anxiety and unhappiness than it might have. In September 1962 Americans already considered Cuba a major problem facing the United States. Many were aware of the Soviet military buildup in Cuba as well as the possibility that Moscow might be placing missiles on the island. Republicans had claimed that ICBMs were already in Cuba. This preparation (along with Kennedy's image of being in control) may explain why the U.S. public showed no substantial negative psychological effects in the last week of October. According to standardized polls taken periodically in 1962, people professed themselves to have about the same level of anxiety, and to be slightly happier, during the week of the crisis than in the previous spring.[37]

Salient Events

Perceptions of victory and defeat in 1962 were also influenced by a number of salient events, including the image of a standoff, the discovery of the missiles in Cuba, and certain symbolic events such as the dramatic confrontation at the United Nations.

Salient Events and Metrics of Success. Observers of the Cuban missile crisis often use — as an implicit or explicit metric — the notion that whoever backed down lost, and then determine that the Soviet Union backed down and was therefore the loser. The crisis became widely visualized as a standoff, in which one superpower ultimately retreated. Indeed, the crisis is often seen as a game of "chicken." As Soviet ships sailed toward the U.S. naval blockade, one side apparently had to yield or there would be war. After a period of high tension, on 23 October Moscow finally ordered the ships to turn back. As the relief sank in, Secretary of State Rusk commented: "We're eyeball to eyeball and I think the other fellow just blinked."[38]

To the U.S. government and public, the fact that the Soviet ships physically turned around appeared to be categorical evidence that Khrushchev had retreated, and by implication had lost the crisis, a framing effect that was reinforced when the Soviets later pulled out the missiles. Walter Trohan of the *Chicago Tribune* wrote: "For the first time in twenty years, Americans can carry their heads high because the president of the United States has stood up to the premier of Russia and made him back down." The view in *Time* was similar: "The bellicose Premier of the Soviet Union first wavered, then weaseled, and finally backed down." Historians have also tended to evaluate the crisis in these "standoff" terms. According to Lebow and Stein, most Americans believe that the crisis ended because the Soviets retreated. It became very difficult to divorce this mental picture of the crisis as a standoff, with the Soviets blinking first, from the actual terms of the deal, carefully negotiated behind closed doors in Washington and Moscow.[39]

In a counterfactual, suppose the Cuban missile crisis had been settled with the exact same terms, but by way of a negotiated agreement at an international conference. In contrast to the dramatic apparent retreat by the Soviets, had Kennedy and Khrushchev flown to Geneva to hammer out the very same deal, the impression would have been that the settlement was a compromise or a balanced agreement. Observers would then have been much more likely to look back on the settlement terms as a negotiated draw rather than as an American victory.[40]

Salient events also influenced the choice of metrics by affecting the selection of *time points* to define the start and the end of the crisis. Evaluations of victory and defeat require a "before-and-after" comparison to identify who has gained or lost over a particular period. For observers of the Cuban missile crisis, the first time point tends to be October 1962, when the Soviet missile sites were already under preparation (that is, immediately after Kennedy's announcement that the missiles had been discovered). An observer who pairs this starting point with an end point after the crisis, when no Soviet missiles were based in Cuba, naturally inclines toward perceiving a U.S. victory. But why do observers not compare the post-crisis situation with the state of affairs *before* Khrushchev placed missiles in Cuba, say in August 1962? This might be considered the more accurate pre-crisis reference point. A comparison of this starting point with the same post-crisis end point would suggest, instead, that Khrushchev gambled aggressively and won several concessions. The Soviets moved missiles into and then out of Cuba, but not before extracting something in return. Therefore, decisions about which date to use as the first time point are crucial.

The reason for the widespread choice of October 1962 as the starting point of the crisis was the timing of a highly salient event: the discovery of the missiles. If the United States had found the missiles earlier, on Russian ships sailing westward across the Atlantic, the probable U.S. response would have been a quarantine against these ships before they ever reached Cuba, and it is very unlikely that Kennedy would have been willing to offer any concessions in return for the ships' turning around. In reality, with observers' first point of reference in October, at a time when missile sites were already being constructed in Cuba, the missiles' *removal* appeared to be a U.S. *gain.* In the counterfactual, if the first point of reference had been in August, their *placement* on Cuba would be a U.S. *loss.* In the first case, concessions could be seen as acceptable means of achieving a successful outcome, while in the second case, a return to the status quo would demand that the ships turn around without any quid pro quo.

Salient Events and Information on Success. Certain events with strong symbolic meaning strengthened the sense that the United States was in control of the situation and in a commanding moral position, encouraging perceptions of American victory. First, the United States had discovered the missiles, catching the Soviets red-handed doing something widely perceived as wrong. Given the placement of U.S. nuclear missiles and military bases around the globe, it is hard to see what was inherently immoral about the Soviet installations in Cuba, but the secretive and mendacious way in which the missiles were placed on the island caused outrage. Second, there were dramatic events at the United Nations in New York when the United States revealed its information about the missile placement. In a televised exchange, the U.S. ambassador to the United Nations, Adlai Stevenson, theatrically challenged his Soviet counterpart, Valerian Zorin, to confirm or deny the existence of nuclear missiles in Cuba. As Zorin stalled, Stevenson declared that he would wait for an answer until "hell freezes over." Stevenson then produced blown-up aerial photographs clearly showing the missile sites being built. The United States achieved in that exchange a certain moral legitimacy, exposing the Soviets for their secrecy and belligerence. The *Washington Post*, four decades later, ran a story about the episode headlined "The Day Adlai Stevenson Showed 'Em at the UN."[41] In this theater the Soviets were framed as the bad guys. We tend to be more generous about the performance of those we deem to be on the moral side, and more critical about the performance of those we deem to be on the immoral side.

Social Pressures

In the Cuban missile crisis, the Kennedy administration was the key manipulator of perceptions of victory. Once Kennedy announced a national emergency, there was virtually unanimous press compliance, and an acceptance at face value of the administration line. Kennedy's decisionmaking "was praised repeatedly by all newspapers, including the Republican ones." The result was that the media acquiesced in a romanticization of Kennedy's performance.[42]

Social Pressures and Metrics of Success. During the missile crisis, Kennedy successfully established as the metric for judging success whether or not the missiles were removed, and he downplayed the issue of Castro's survival, which had previously so preoccupied the administration. The very fact that the situation came to be known as the "Cuban missile crisis" focused attention on the missiles as the key metric. In contrast, the Russian name for the crisis ("the Caribbean crisis") and the Cuban name ("the October crisis") both tend to make one look beyond the missiles. In addition, Kennedy minimized the importance of the non-invasion pledge by describing it as a mere gesture to allow Khrushchev to save face at home. Framed in this way, the pledge became a politically acceptable means to realize Soviet withdrawal. In another context, the same actions could easily have been branded as appeasement. Consciously or not, the public may have assimilated a way of seeing the crisis that was fed to them by the White House.[43]

Social Pressures and Information on Success. The Kennedy administration also manipulated perceptions of victory and defeat by shaping the information available to the public, either by managing known facts or by keeping certain facts secret. Kennedy had the advantage of making the first move. He chose the time and place to calmly yet firmly announce the discovery of the missiles, couching the crisis in his own terms. By establishing the quarantine, he also created rules for acceptable Soviet behavior. When Moscow ended up conforming to these rules, it appeared that Washington was in control.

The administration carefully spun the image of the president as tough but cool-headed. For example, the tapes of the ExComm meetings reveal that during discussions of how to deal with the crisis Kennedy was comparatively dovish and cautious.[44] However, he and his associates downplayed his dovishness and nurtured the public image of a strong president determined to take whatever action was necessary to remove the missiles from Cuba. One tactic was to label Adlai Stevenson as the appeaser within the U.S. administration. Two of Kennedy's journalist friends, Charles Bartlett and Stewart Alsop, wrote an article for the *Saturday Evening Post* claiming that Stevenson "wanted a Munich," and that he had sought to appease the Soviets with a deal over the missiles in Turkey, which the president had rejected. Stevenson did indeed talk in the ExComm about a possible bargain over the Turkish missiles, but in fact Kennedy made almost exactly the same deal with the Russians in secret. Privately, Kennedy told Stevenson that the article contained "obvious inaccuracies," but Kennedy did not remove the offending statements when asked to correct a draft before publication. Instead, he removed several sentences that served to explain and justify Stevenson's position. In the Kennedy administration's efforts to manipulate public opinion, as the political scientist Graham Allison remarked, Stevenson may have been very usefully "sacrificed to the hawks."[45]

After the crisis, Kennedy used the tactic of combining a major concession with a hard-line ultimatum to give the impression of firm leadership. For example, in November 1962 he ended his demand for on-site inspections of missile sites in Cuba, but combined that concession with an ultimatum that the Soviets remove their IL-28 bombers from Cuba.[46]

Kennedy also shaped the information observers received about the missile crisis by emphasizing that U.S. decisions were the product of a broad and bipartisan group of wise men. Lebow suggests that Kennedy deftly manipulated the ExComm for political ends, giving policymaking responsibility to bipartisan officials in order to engender the strong support he would need for his choice of a risky showdown with Khrushchev. The president remained in control: when Kennedy made the key decisions about trading the Turkey-based missiles, he relied on a carefully selected inner group of the ExComm.[47]

The American concessions in the Cuban missile crisis were deliberately veiled in ambiguity and secrecy, a tactic that minimized their impact on evaluations. The pledge not to invade Cuba was never formalized into the kind of written agreement that would have symbolized a substantive gain for Moscow. Yet, as Robert Kennedy told the Russians in 1963, Washington intended to keep its part of the bargain, as indeed it did.

The second U.S. concession—the removal of the missiles from

Turkey—was kept secret. Even many members of the ExComm were unaware of the trade. The Turkish government, also kept in the dark, offered profuse thanks to the United States for refusing to sacrifice Turkey's interests in a cozy superpower deal. A *New York Times* headline on 29 October pronounced: "Turkey Relieved at U.S. Firmness: Gratified That Bases Were Not Bargained Away." McNamara, despite being aware of the missile trade, assured the Pentagon shortly after the crisis: "There is no Cuba-Turkey deal at present." McGeorge Bundy later admitted: "We misled our colleagues, our countrymen, our successors and our allies," although he justified this deception as necessary "in order to protect Western security."[48]

Khrushchev stuck to his promise not to reveal the agreement despite its potential propaganda value. He apparently wanted to avoid Cuban anger at a Cuba-Turkey missile trade behind Havana's back, and also sought to boost Kennedy's chances of staying in power, which Khrushchev believed would facilitate détente.[49]

Secret contacts between Washington and Moscow were a common Cold War phenomenon, and "the Kennedy administration often used these private channels to promote a more conciliatory approach than was evident in its public policies." In the Cuban missile crisis in particular, Kennedy felt compelled to manipulate the public perception of the outcome. "Apparently obsessed with a need to present a public image of toughness, convinced that it was essential to his political success, Kennedy chose to have the American people believe he had won in a man-to-man showdown with the Soviet premier." The historian Alice George concludes: "Making the missile deal sealed the peace; keeping it secret preserved JFK's career. With no public hint of appeasement, he and his party emerged as winners."[50]

Consider, then, the asymmetry of concessions made by the two sides in terms of their *public salience*. The Russians physically turned their ships away from the blockade and pulled the missiles out of Cuba for the entire world to see. In contrast, the U.S. non-invasion pledge, which Kennedy intended to uphold, was never formalized, and the deal over the missiles in Turkey would not be publicly known for years to come. Former Soviet ambassador to Washington Anatoly Dobrynin recalled in a 1998 interview: "The whole world was under the impression that Khrushchev lost because he had given in to the pressure of a strong president, that he had taken everything out of Cuba and gotten nothing in return. No one knew anything about the agreement regarding the missiles in Turkey."[51]

| Conclusions

The Cuban missile crisis was a draw, with gains and losses on both sides, but it was almost universally perceived as a triumph for the United States. The myth of U.S. success in this crisis has shown remarkable longevity despite the repeated publication of testimony that tells a very different story. Perceptions of victory became entrenched partly because the assassination of Kennedy in 1963 led to his near-deification, undermining any chance of an objective assessment of who won and who lost in 1962.

Score-keeping clearly fails to explain the dominant perception of U.S. success. Kennedy remarked at a National Security Council meeting on 26 October that the United States only had two options remaining for dealing with the missiles: "to trade them out . . . [or] take them out." The Americans and the Russians agreed to trade them out. Moreover, both leaders would apparently have been willing to offer more if pressed, suggesting that neither felt himself to be in a commanding position. Khrushchev was ready to accept a deal that ignored the missiles in Turkey, and it has been suggested that Kennedy would have supported a public trade of the Cuban and Turkish missiles rather than risk ordering air strikes.[52]

Match-fixing is more effective in explaining the almost unanimous perception of U.S. victory. The mind-set of the Cubans, the Chinese, and the Soviets helps to explain why people from these countries tended to agree with observers from their avowed enemy—the United States—that Moscow had lost. The framing of the crisis as a standoff in which the Soviets backed down was a crucial factor: observers, faced with a complex situation, are always tempted to select the simple metric that whoever retreats loses. The Kennedy administration was also skilled at focusing attention on the missiles, and not on the survival of the Cuban regime, and they successfully kept secret a central element in the final settlement—the agreement to withdraw U.S. missiles from Turkey.

Washington established the image that it was in control of events. McGeorge Bundy remarked before the crisis that because of congressional criticism of Kennedy's weakness over Cuba, the president had to offer "a very clear and aggressive explanation" of U.S. policy to show that the Cuban problem was "within our control." When the crisis broke, this is exactly what happened. The United States took several days to draw up a plan, then seized the initiative by announcing the discovery of the missiles and the quarantine on Cuba. Moscow responded to American actions, and the Russians ultimately abided by the rules set out by Kennedy in two respects: no offensive weapons would be allowed through the quarantine, and the missiles had to go. A feeling of having lost control lies behind Dmitri Polyansky's exasperated comment: "Not having any other way out we had to accept every demand and condition dictated by the U.S."[53]

Observers' match-fixing against the Soviet Union's performance runs counter to our predictions in Chapter 4 that people match-fix in *favor* of the less powerful side, and that nondemocracies rarely match-fix against themselves. However, the Cuban missile crisis was an exceptional event. First, the number of domestic critics ready to turn on an already embattled Khrushchev provided a greater potential for criticism of the state than is usual in nondemocratic regimes. Second, despite America's greater power, the protagonists in the crisis were both superpowers of enormous might, so their dispute was not viewed as a case of David versus Goliath, in which observers might have evaluated the Soviet performance more generously.

We can see now that when the crisis began the cards were already stacked against Khrushchev. Unknowingly, he was playing in a match that was fixed. Critics in China, the Soviet Union, and Cuba would be likely to pounce upon any apparent retreat as a dramatic failure. The timing of the discovery of the missiles meant that their removal would be seen as a significant loss. The U.S. quarantine created the image of a standoff, in which it would be difficult to avoid at least a symbolic Soviet retreat without fighting a war in the American backyard. Khrushchev was dealing with a U.S. administration skilled at managing opinion both at home and among its allies. Khrushchev could not even count on the U.S. media to be skeptical toward Washington's foreign policy performance, as would become the norm within the following decade. If Khrushchev had known all this and still sought to avoid losing, he should not have invested his energy in the details of the settlement, but in shaping the way the settlement came about, prioritizing above all the image of a negotiated, balanced agreement.

As perceptions of victory and defeat became sufficiently widespread, they proved to be self-fulfilling. Beliefs about a U.S. victory in 1962, however unrelated to the agreement that had been reached, subsequently influenced international behavior in a way that made a U.S. victory the reality. The balance sheet began to acquire a whole array of negative payoffs for the Soviets that were associated with the crisis. Khrushchev was removed from office, the Sino-Soviet split was exacerbated, and Castro's relations with the USSR were temporarily jeopardized.[54] These effects closed the gap, post hoc, between perception and reality.

At the same time, however, judgments that the United States had been the victor in 1962 turned out to be a double-edged sword, because these perceptions engendered dangerous lessons in the United States. Kennedy was viewed as having won through sheer resolve, the steady escalation of force, and the management of coercive diplomacy. In reality, the crisis ended when both sides made concessions. After Kennedy's death, the Johnson administration applied the logic of coercive diplomacy—thought to be the lesson of Cuba—to Vietnam: unswerving resolve and the steady escalation of air power and then ground troops would once again make the communists retreat. As the historian Barton Bernstein has wondered, if Johnson had known the truth—that Kennedy had cut a deal in 1962—would he have felt able to compromise over Vietnam before coercive diplomacy landed the United States in an unwinnable quagmire?[55]

6 | THE TET OFFENSIVE

*Most of the Saigon-based journalists, stunned and confused at
their first up-close and personal view of combat, quickly declared
the Tet Offensive a Communist victory even before the smoke had
cleared. Cooler, more reasoned appraisals assessed it differently: a
total catastrophe for the Viet Cong. Even General Giap himself
privately conceded that it had been a staggering military defeat.*

—MARK WOODRUFF

*Even though it was a considerable military set-back for the North
Vietnamese and Vietcong out there on the ground, it was, in
effect, a brilliant political victory for them here in the United
States. I'm not sure I fully understand the reasons why that should
have occurred, but it became very clear after the Tet offensive that
many people at the grass roots . . . finally came to the conclusion
that if we could not tell them when this war was going to end, and
we couldn't in any good faith, that we might as well chuck it.*

—DEAN RUSK

On 30 January 1968, at the height of the Vietnam war, communist-
led forces launched a massive military onslaught against hundreds
of major cities, towns, and villages throughout South Vietnam.[1]
The attack achieved considerable surprise, falling during the traditional cease-fire of the Tet holiday. However, U.S. and South Viet-

namese forces pushed back the offensive across the country in a devastating counterattack that left tens of thousands of enemy dead.

Despite this battlefield outcome, the Tet offensive was widely judged in the United States as a massive setback for the U.S. war effort. Just as the battles of Stalingrad and Midway were the turning points in World War II, Tet was the turning point of the Vietnam war. But unlike the Germans at Stalingrad and the Japanese at Midway, the Americans and their South Vietnamese allies actually *won* the battle that set them on the road to defeat.

In the wake of the perceived failure at Tet, the United States curtailed its bombing campaign, sought negotiations with the North, and replaced its field commander, General William C. Westmoreland. To even greater surprise, President Lyndon B. Johnson announced that he would not seek reelection. American perceptions of failure in the Tet offensive contributed significantly to the ultimate withdrawal of U.S. forces from South Vietnam in 1973 and the fall of Saigon to the communists in 1975.

In this chapter we argue that the gap between the U.S. military achievements on the ground in 1968 and the perceived U.S. defeat was the result of match-fixing. Mind-sets, salient events, and social pressures combined in such a way that what happened on the battlefield played only a minor role in evaluations of the outcome. Having been consistently told by their leaders that victory was just around the corner, Americans were shocked by the mere occurrence, let alone the scale, of the Vietcong's offensive. Symbolic events, including the highly publicized attack on the U.S. embassy in Saigon, reinforced the idea that the United States was no longer in control of the war. The enemy decided when and where the fighting occurred, it seemed, and nowhere was safe. According to the military strategist Bernard Brodie, the Tet offensive was "probably unique in that the side that lost completely in the tactical sense came away with an overwhelming psychological and hence political victory."[2] As we show, many of the dynamics that fixed the match in Tet were far from unique, operating in comparable ways in other cases. The Tet offensive is an extreme example, however, of a mismatch between the battlefield outcome and perceptions of victory.

| History

Communist forces in Vietnam fought the French colonial regime to a settlement in 1954, after laying siege to and defeating a French garrison at Dien Bien Phu. The subsequent peace agreement split Vietnam into a communist North and a capitalist South.[3] By the late 1950s an insurgency developed in the South, which aimed to destabilize the regime in Saigon and prepare the way for the unification of Vietnam as an independent communist state. The United States provided assistance to South Vietnam from its foundation. By 1967 this aid had escalated to the provision of hundreds of thousands of combat troops. From the perspective of U.S. officials in Washington, who viewed events through a Cold War prism, if South Vietnam fell, a domino-style collapse of neighboring states could hand all of Southeast Asia over to the communists. Meanwhile, from the perspective of many Vietnamese, U.S. forces were simply the latest in a long line of foreign invaders who had tried to dominate Vietnam over the centuries, including the Chinese, the French, and the Japanese.

Despite the massive U.S. intervention, by 1967 the war had essentially reached a stalemate, with neither side able to quickly defeat the other. Such a situation suited the communists, who were better prepared than the Americans to patiently conduct a war of attrition. At the same time, Johnson and Westmoreland were confidently asserting that the United States was winning the war. With the end supposedly in sight, the troops could soon begin returning home.

It came as a dramatic shock to many Americans, therefore, when

MAP 2. Vietnam in 1968. Map by Philip Schwartzberg.

on 30–31 January 1968 communist-led forces launched the Tet offensive, a countrywide attack of audacious breadth, scope, and synchronization. Some 80,000 personnel from the People's Army of Vietnam (PAVN, or the North Vietnamese regular army) and the National Liberation Front (NLF or southern insurgents, also known as Vietcong/VC) attacked five of the six largest cities and thirty-six of the forty-four provincial capitals in South Vietnam, hitting key targets such as Saigon's air base, radio station, and presidential palace, Westmoreland's command headquarters, and the U.S. embassy.[4]

In bloody fighting, the communist forces were gradually beaten back. In many places, such as the U.S. embassy, the U.S. and the South Vietnamese Army of the Republic of Vietnam (ARVN) forces had the situation under control within a few hours. At other locations, the violence would drag on for several weeks. Some of the heaviest fighting occurred in the old imperial capital Hue, where U.S. marines and South Vietnamese forces had to wrest control of the city back from the enemy house by house. Hue was not retaken until 10 March. The struggle was also bitter at Khe Sanh in the northern part of South Vietnam, where the United States had been fighting long before Tet, but there too the communists withdrew in April. Although the label "Tet offensive" anchors the episode to those early days in February, the communist attacks were prolonged, including a second wave in May 1968 and a third wave in August. Indeed, 1968 was the bloodiest year of the Vietnam war—for both sides.[5] As we will argue, however, in the Tet offensive the U.S. and ARVN troops gained the upper hand in terms of military events on the ground.

Back in the United States, the peace candidate Eugene McCarthy nearly defeated Johnson in the New Hampshire Democratic primary on 12 March, an event described as "an earthquake immeasurable on the political Richter scale."[6] Around the same time, Westmoreland—backed by the chairman of the joint chiefs of staff, General Earle Wheeler—requested 206,000 more troops to push for victory in Vietnam. Civilian leaders in Washington balked at such a figure, which was politically impossible by that time. Johnson agreed to send a few thousand men to fortify gaps in the line, but he publicly declared his desire to de-escalate the war, as well as his decision not to run for reelection.

In Vietnam, therefore, 1968 was the year in which the United States turned the corner from pursuing victory to rescuing some kind of "peace with honor." U.S. forces remained in South Vietnam until 1973, but their numbers were steadily reduced as the war effort was "Vietnamized." President Richard Nixon and Secretary of State Henry Kissinger negotiated a settlement with North Vietnam in 1973 that ended America's eight years of grinding warfare. However, the North soon launched a decisive offensive against the crumbling regime in Saigon, which fell in 1975, with helicopters lifting the last Americans from the rooftops. The events of Tet, seven years before, heralded both the withdrawal of U.S. troops and, as a direct consequence, the almost inevitable defeat of the South.

Dominant Perceptions of Victory and Defeat

In North Vietnam the Tet offensive was perceived as a major defeat for Washington and the South Vietnamese regime. Communist evaluations of Tet suggested that the attack had paralyzed the South Vietnamese government, undermined U.S. efforts to pacify the countryside, and forced the United States to cease the bombing and agree to talks.[7] General Tran Van Tra of North Vietnam accepted that the North had suffered tactical setbacks, but claimed overall that "because of the extraordinary efforts during the three phases of the Offensive by the revolutionary fighters and their supporters in the South, a decisive victory and a strategic turning was achieved." Later communist historians echoed this view, arguing that the key objectives of the offensive had been accomplished, setting the North on the road to victory. Although officials in Hanoi presented the Tet offensive as a clear-cut triumph, insurgents who were actually engaged in the fighting recognized more explicitly that mistakes had been made, and that one of the main aims of the attack—the long-cherished general uprising in the South—had not been realized.[8]

The South Vietnamese elite tended to see the Tet offensive as a defeat for the communists. South Vietnam's ambassador to the United States, Bui Diem, described the mood in Saigon after Tet as "exuberant," and noted that the government had emerged "with more confidence than ever before, and almost doubled its military strength through a general mobilization supported by massive U.S. economic and military aid." Believing that Tet had been a victory for their side, the South Vietnamese elite failed to grasp the possibility that the United States might now withdraw.[9]

Some senior military and administration figures in the United States also viewed Tet as a defeat for the communists. In a news conference on 2 February 1968, Johnson declared: "They say 10,000 [Vietcong] died and we lost 249 and the South Vietnamese lost 500. Now that doesn't look like a Communist victory. I can count." He would hold to this view in later years, writing in his memoirs: "The Tet offensive was, by any standard, a military defeat of massive proportions for the North Vietnamese and the Viet Cong." Westmoreland concurred, arguing in his autobiography that Tet had been "a striking military defeat for the enemy on anybody's terms."[10]

However, despite these positive evaluations, the dominant American perception of Tet in 1968 was that the battle had been a defeat *for the United States.* The offensive came to represent, to the American public, a failure of U.S. intelligence, the puncture of U.S. optimism, the destruction of South Vietnam, the incapacity and illegitimacy of the regime in Saigon, the brutality and immorality of the war, as well as proof of the indefatigable will of the communist forces.[11] Many observers not only saw the Tet offensive as revealing the failure of U.S. strategy in Vietnam; they also thought Tet had been a major loss in itself, worsening the American strategic position on the ground.

The media and public reaction to Tet was strongly negative in tone. A British journalist described the "rancorous, near hysterical atmosphere of the Tet Offensive" in the United States. Within hours, television reports fixated on an image of disaster in Vietnam. The well-respected news anchorman Walter Cronkite, for the first time, openly offered dismal predictions for the U.S. war effort. On 10 March the NBC newsman Frank McGee announced in a special news program: "The war as the Administration has defined it is being lost." The *Wall Street Journal,* in Henry Kissinger's words, also "jumped ship" and became a critic of the war. An editorial in February 1968 suggested that the "whole Vietnam effort may be doomed." The media analyst Daniel Hallin, who compared journalistic accounts of the war before and after Tet, found that before the offensive, when journalists described a battle as a victory or a defeat, they reported 62 percent of battles as U.S. victories, 28 percent as defeats for the United States, and 2 percent as stalemates. After Tet, the figures were 44 percent victories, 32 percent defeats, and 24 percent stalemates. Journalists shifted, therefore, from reporting battles in Vietnam as U.S. victories to reporting them as stalemates. Similarly, editorial comments by television journalists, which had supported the administration's policy in Vietnam by a margin of almost four to one before Tet, ran two to one *against* the administration after Tet.[12]

Opinion polls suggest a complex picture of public attitudes. The Tet offensive did not have a dramatic effect on overall support for the war, which merely continued its slow decline. Some 45 percent of Americans thought intervention in Vietnam was a mistake in December 1967, and 49 percent thought it was a mistake in March 1968. Indeed, in the immediate aftermath of Tet, the public rallied around the president, with a brief spike in support for the war as well as a spike in confidence about the government's military policies.[13]

However, on important dimensions, opinion about the war shifted dramatically after Tet. The number of Americans who believed the United States was making progress in Vietnam fell from 51 percent in November 1967, to 32 percent in February 1968, to just 18 percent in June 1968. Before Tet, 48 percent of Americans thought the war would last two years or less, but after Tet only 35 percent believed this. In March, approval of Johnson's handling of Vietnam collapsed to an all-time low of 26 percent. As Chart 6.1 shows, the number of Americans who saw themselves as "doves" (favoring a reduction of U.S. military efforts in Vietnam) increased from 26 percent of the population in February 1968 to 42 percent in March, while the number of "hawks" (favoring an increase in U.S military efforts in Vietnam) fell from 58 percent in February to 41 percent in March. In a few short weeks, American public opinion had changed from a situation in which there were over twice as many hawks as doves, to a situation in which doves narrowly outnumbered hawks.[14]

General Wheeler compared the mood in Washington after Tet with the mood following the first battle of the American Civil War

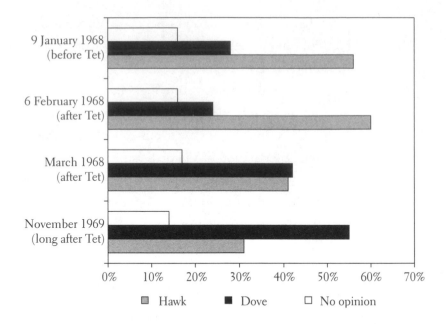

CHART 6.1. Results of Gallup poll, 1968–1969, for the following question: "People are called 'hawks' if they want to step up our military effort in Vietnam. They are called 'doves' if they want to reduce our military effort in Vietnam. How would you describe yourself—as a 'hawk' or a 'dove'?"

at Bull Run in 1861, in which a large crowd from the capital gathered to watch, and looked on with horror as the Union forces lost disastrously to the Confederates. Many members of the Johnson administration and Congress became very pessimistic about Vietnam. According to the historian Marc Jason Gilbert: "Tet had not only demoralized America's political leadership but, as was intended, had shaken the confidence of chairman of the Joint Chiefs of Staff, General Earl Wheeler, and other key figures of the American military establishment." Explanations were demanded. On 11 and 12 March, Secretary of State Dean Rusk testified for eleven hours before the Senate foreign relations committee, an ordeal that Johnson described as the "most prolonged questioning of a Cabinet officer ever broadcast to the American people." These confrontational hearings demonstrated the mounting congressional misgivings about the Vietnam war, which rippled out into wider society. Robert McNamara's replacement as secretary of defense, Clark Clifford, privately warned that "the business community, the press, the churches, professional groups, college presidents, students and most of the intellectual community have turned against the war."[15] The perception of defeat for the United States was confirmed when Johnson appeared on television to announce a shift toward negotiation.

Framework 1: Score-keeping

Despite some dissenting voices, the dominant interpretation in the United States was—and often still is—that the Tet offensive was a triumph for the North and a major setback for the United States and South Vietnam. The official line of the North Vietnamese regime also celebrated a great victory over the imperialist Americans. In conducting a score-keeping analysis we attempt to determine whether or not this verdict reflects the battlefield outcome, by examining the congruence between perceptions of success and failure and the material gains and aims achieved by each side in 1968. Looking—for the moment—at the scorecard alone, was General Tran Van Tra correct in claiming "a decisive victory"?[16]

Material Gains and Losses

The communists made some genuine material gains at Tet. U.S. and ARVN forces were caught off guard, and the communists, having chosen the time and place of the offensive, scored some early successes.[17] Thousands of U.S. and ARVN casualties were incurred.

| Type of outcome | Event | Material gain or loss? | An aim achieved? | Altering the credit due[a] | | Difficulty[c] |
| | | | | Importance | | |
				For leader	For observer[b]	
Positive outcomes	34,000–75,000 communist-led forces killed	Gain	Achieved	Very high	Very high	Moderate
	No territory lost or general uprising	Neither	Achieved	Very high	Very high	Moderate/high
Negative outcomes	4,000–9,000 U.S./ARVN forces killed	Loss	Partially achieved (low casualties)	Moderate	Moderate	Moderate/low (chance of avoiding)

a. Higher values give *more* credit for positive outcomes and *less* credit for negative outcomes.
b. The importance of a gain or an aim in the minds of observers (in this case the authors) trying to fairly assess its worth.
c. The difficulty of a gain or an aim in the minds of observers (in this case the authors) trying to assess it fairly.

CHART 6.2. Scorecard for the United States in the Tet offensive.

Type of outcome	Event	Material gain or loss?	An aim achieved?	Altering the credit due[a]		
				Importance		
				For leader	For observer[b]	Difficulty[c]
Positive outcomes	4,000–9,000 U.S./ARVN forces killed	Gain	Partially achieved	Moderate/high	Moderate	Moderate/low
Negative outcomes	34,000–75,000 communist-led forces killed	Loss	Not achieved	Moderate/high	Very high	Moderate (chance of avoiding)
	No territory gained or general uprising	Neither	Not achieved	Very high	Very high	Moderate/high (chance of avoiding)

a. Higher values give *more* credit for positive outcomes and *less* credit for negative outcomes.
b. The importance of a gain or an aim in the minds of observers (in this case the authors) trying to fairly assess its worth.
c. The difficulty of a gain or an aim in the minds of observers (in this case the authors) trying to assess it fairly.

CHART 6.3. Scorecard for the communists in the Tet offensive.

In a matter of hours, nearly every strategically important town and city in the South had been damaged. The sheer scale of the destruction (much of it caused by U.S. firepower in the counterattack) undermined South Vietnamese society, creating around a million refugees.

However, looking at the wider picture, it was the communist forces that suffered a major defeat on the battlefield. Charts 6.2 and 6.3 show the scorecards for the two sides, which illustrate the massive disparity in key outcomes. Although there were some drawn-out battles, such as those at Hue, Khe Sanh, and certain areas of Saigon, much of the fighting in the Tet offensive lasted only a few days and, ultimately, the communists failed to hold onto a single site in South Vietnam. Later waves of the offensive were costly for the U.S./ARVN forces, but almost always much more costly for the communists. Estimates for U.S./ARVN killed range from 4,000 to 9,000, and estimates of communists killed range from 34,000 to 75,000 or more.[18] From a communist force of some 80,000 fighters involved in the offensive, as many as 40,000 may have been killed in the first month of the fighting. If we take the average of the various estimates, the communists lost 8 fighters for every American/ARVN soldier killed (using the values at either extreme puts this ratio between 4:1 and 18:1). Whatever the actual numbers, it is clear that the U.S./ARVN forces killed far more of their enemies than they lost themselves. As a result of the Tet offensive, the VC was crippled as a fighting force. For the rest of the war, much of the fighting was carried out by regular North Vietnamese Army troops.[19]

There were other U.S./ARVN gains during Tet. For example, the offensive itself, as well as the testimony of prisoners, revealed considerable information about enemy intentions, tactics, and capabilities. Since the U.S./ARVN forces were on the defensive, their actions during Tet did not reveal as much useful information to the North Vietnamese.

Of course, the United States also suffered significant casualties in the fighting. However, as we explained earlier, there is evidence that Americans are far more sensitive to casualties if they think a mission is failing, and far less sensitive if they perceive an operation to be going well. The U.S. casualties in 1968 were not in themselves a major cause of negative perceptions about the Vietnam war among the American public. Rather, the belief that the war effort was failing made the casualty figures far more salient in the public mind. In 1968, according to the political scientists Peter Feaver and Christopher Gelpi, "public perceptions of the likelihood of American success began to change drastically," and in tandem with this, so did the public's tolerance for casualties. Indeed, statistical analyses reveal that after Tet, casualties had about three times as negative an effect on the president's approval ratings as they did before the offensive.[20]

Material Aims

While the material balance sheet clearly favored the United States, did these outcomes accord with the material aims of the combatants?

U.S. Aims. The material aims of the United States during Tet were very simple in comparison with the aims in our other case studies. As the victim of a major attack, it aimed to repel the offensive, kill as many of the communist forces as possible at the lowest cost, hold on to its positions, and thereby preserve the security of South Vietnam. These aims were mainly achieved (see Chart 6.2). Reeling from the initial shock of the attack, U.S. and ARVN forces fought back in a counteroffensive that regained all of the territory previously captured by the communists. ARVN forces proved to be far more effective on the battlefield than many Americans had expected.[21]

In one sense, the U.S./ARVN troops fought in an especially difficult strategic environment. The communists' opportunity for careful planning, combined with the advantage of surprise, allowed the North to maximize its forces at chosen points, sometimes initially outnumbering U.S. and ARVN forces. However, the style of fighting at Tet, which was more conventional than that during much of the Vietnam war, played to U.S. military strengths. The United States could maximize its superior firepower against an enemy that finally came into the open to fight: a battle that the United States and its allies could and did win.

Communist Material Aims. The material aims of the North Vietnamese and the Vietcong in the Tet offensive are still shrouded in secrecy. The latest research shows that the attack was planned in July 1967 as a joint operation between Hanoi and the National Liberation Front, and was intended to strike the enemy where it least expected. The offensive, according to Gilbert, was designed to shift the war from stalemate to strategic victory by delivering a massive assault that would lead to U.S. de-escalation. The "political objective" was to break the "mutually painful deadlock of the war of attrition," and force negotiations; while the "military objective", was "unmanning if not overwhelming U.S. forces" to support the political objective. South Vietnamese citizens, it was hoped, would rise up against the Saigon regime once the offensive was under way. Thus the "General Offensive–General Uprising" would combine a military attack with a popular insurrection, replicating the Vietnamese August Revolution in 1945. Ho Chi Minh would then be welcomed in a triumphal visit to the South. Officials in the North were not under the impression that all these aims would be easy to achieve, but the "minimum objective was to destabilize the situation in the South sufficiently to force the United States to seek negotiations under unfavorable conditions."[22]

The communists did succeed in surprising their enemies. Thousands of troops and weapons were secretly infiltrated into cities and towns. The North's attack on Khe Sanh in 1967 was deliberately intended to divert American attention away from the real focus of the offensive on civilian areas of the country. The diversion worked so well that Westmoreland thought exactly the opposite—that the rest of the offensive was a diversion from the real battle: Khe Sanh as another Dien Bien Phu.[23]

However, once the fighting started, Hanoi failed to achieve its military aims. The communist leaders identified three scenarios for the outcome of the offensive: they might win in Saigon; they might succeed in major cities, but not in Saigon; or they might achieve some victories but not enough to expel the Americans. As it turned out, the communists failed to achieve even their worst-case scenario, because they achieved no battlefield victories at all. In Saigon, the communists had several specific aims to seize government, military, and urban targets. Every objective failed. Perhaps most important, there was no repeat of 1945, no popular uprising to welcome the "liberators." A RAND study found that Saigon citizens offered very little help to the communists during the Tet offensive—their main focus was on self-preservation. Evidently, whatever the people of South Vietnam felt about the regime in Saigon, most of them were not committed to the Vietcong. Furthermore, the damage inflicted on the South Vietnamese infrastructure by the offensive may have been substantial, but it was outweighed by the devastating communist losses.[24]

The tactics of the North were flawed, with the attacks being too dispersed to win decisively in any one location. The North's key assumptions—that the ARVN would collapse, and that the people would join the insurgents—proved mistaken. Hanoi had become overconfident, believing that communist forces were in control of areas in which two-thirds of the South Vietnamese population lived. General Tran Van Tra admitted, rather obliquely, that communist objectives "were beyond our actual strength . . . [and based] in part on an illusion of our subjective desires." The North Vietnamese general Vo Nguyen Giap thought that the attacks were not as well planned, coordinated, and orchestrated as they should have been. The communist commander of the Hue front suggested: "Another mistake was to go into such a large campaign with such large objectives without having reserve forces on the spot and relying instead on reinforcements from the Ministry that never arrived because the battlefield was not properly prepared."[25]

On the ground, Tet altered the strategic environment in ways that were mainly favorable for the United States. The tens of thousands of communist troops who died in the offensive could have been employed more effectively to undermine the South Vietnamese regime. "Perhaps even worse for the Viet Cong" than the numbers of losses, notes the Vietnam war veteran and commentator Mark Woodruff, "was that their secret operatives and spies, a network which had taken years to build, had come out into the open during the attacks. Many of their agents had already been killed during the offensive and those remaining were now exposed and being rigorously pursued by South Vietnam's police and security forces." After Tet, communist insurgents withdrew to the Cambodian border and shifted to a more defensive strategy.[26]

In military terms, the Tet offensive could hardly have turned out worse for the North. The material gains the communists did achieve, such as destroying infrastructure, holding some locations for a few weeks, and killing one enemy soldier for every eight lives of their own, surely represent the minimum that might be expected of a force of 80,000 fighters operating with all the benefits of surprise. An offensive that was intended to reveal the popular yearning for communist rule in the South, or at the very least to decisively win some local battles, achieved none of these objectives. In the end, though, Hanoi made the greater gains from this debacle because, thousands of miles away, observers perceived the Tet offensive as a failure, not for Hanoi, but for the United States. The puzzle is not who won the military confrontation at Tet, but the source of the American perception of defeat.

| Framework 2: Match-Fixing

Some American observers, particularly within the military, did score-keep the material gains and losses for each side, and thus evaluated Tet as a success for the United States. But most Americans were not score-keeping. Instead, they fixed the match so that the communists would be seen to win despite the scorecard. Mind-sets, salient events, and social pressures dominated American judgments of victory in 1968 (as outlined in Chart 6.4).

Mind-sets

The perception of Tet as a communist victory and a U.S. defeat was shaped in part by several beliefs held by Americans prior to Tet.

Mind-sets and Metrics of Success. One of the most important factors biasing metrics for U.S. observers was the overly optimistic expectations about the course of the war held at the start of 1968. Relative

Match-fixing factors	Affected aspect of judgment	
	Metrics	Information
Mind-sets		
Expectations	X	
Beliefs and partisanship		X
Salient events		
Symbolic events		X
Social pressures		

North Vietnamese,
    media, and elite
    manipulation
	X	X

CHART 6.4. Key match-fixing factors influencing perceptions of victory and defeat in the Tet offensive.

to these expectations, Tet looked like a disaster. Such beliefs were partly due to a widespread American confidence about winning wars in general, and partly due to specific assurances by military and civilian leaders that the United States was on the road to victory in Vietnam.

Before Tet, U.S. military supremacy was considered a given. In the American mind, the United States had never lost a war, and expectations about any battle, at any time and place, were very high.[27] "Probably the only people who have the historical sense of inevitable victory," wrote the British historian Denis Brogan "are the Americans." According to the psychologists David Armor and Shelley Taylor, "Americans are widely regarded as the most optimistic people on earth." In 1968 the United States was the most powerful country in the world. With the right planning, organization, and trained troops, so the feeling went, of course the United States would win in Vietnam. There were, after all, half a million Americans fighting what Johnson called a "raggedy-ass little fourth-rate country." The journalist and author David Halberstam wrote that "a remarkable hubris permeated this entire time."[28]

Wider U.S. societal optimism was heavily reinforced in regard to Vietnam by American leaders, who in 1967 repeatedly claimed that victory was imminent. In the autumn of 1967 the Johnson administration coordinated a "progress campaign" to demonstrate that the United States was indeed winning the war. Reporters were shown captured documents indicating the hardships faced by the communist forces; special achievements such as pacified villages were highlighted; the ARVN was painted in a positive light; and statistical analyses produced a glut of data about lowered infiltration rates, reduced enemy troop strength, and increased enemy casualties. Westmoreland remarked in September 1967: "We are now in a position from which the picture of ultimate military success may be viewed with increasing clarity." Johnson declared on 22 December: "All the challenges have been met. The enemy is not beaten but he knows that he has met his master in the field." The military concluded in 1967 that with the United States killing communist soldiers more quickly than they could be replaced, "victory was just around the corner." Senior military and political figures delivered the message convincingly because they believed it was true. Many media commentators accepted it as well: *U.S. News and World Report* ran two articles in November 1967 headlined: "Vietnam: War Tide Turning to U.S.," and "The Coin has Flipped Over to Our Side." Between July and December 1967, according to polling data, the American public became more confident that the United States was finally making progress in Vietnam.[29]

In the context of this earlier optimism, the Tet offensive looked like an enormous defeat. With the American public expecting to turn the corner in Vietnam, the scale and surprise of the attacks sent a shock wave through the American psyche, stripping away illusions about the war. The negative reaction to Tet survived despite later reports indicating just how one-sided the fighting had actually been. Under the shadow of this major reconfiguration of beliefs about Vietnam, many American observers ignored, downplayed, or failed to grasp evidence of their country's success. For these observers, therefore, the metric for U.S. failure at Tet was easily attained. The fact that the communists had staged a coordinated, country-wide attack was, in itself, almost enough for them to place the battle in the defeat column, because the North had been thought incapable of launching such a massive operation. The battlefield outcome of the Tet offensive might have increased U.S. chances of winning the Vietnam war from, say, 5 percent to 10 percent. But to a public that had believed the chance of winning was perhaps 80 percent, the realization that the actual likelihood of a U.S. victory was closer to 10 percent looked like a disastrous collapse in American fortunes. This suggests that a real advance on the ground can be trumped by the disappointment of unmet expectations. In his memoirs, Johnson recognized that his optimistic message had fostered unrealistic expectations: "If I had forecast the possibilities, the American people would have been better prepared for what was to come."[30]

Ambassador Bui Diem later recalled: "Americans were struck by the contrast between the enthusiasm of President Johnson's public relations campaign and the reality of enemy capabilities. Westmoreland and Bunker had been optimistic during their recent tours, but now it seemed as if all the talk about progress and being 'in control' had been either blatantly mistaken or intentionally deceptive." The *New York Times* reported: "These are not the deeds of an enemy whose fighting efficiency has 'progressively declined' and whose morale is 'sinking fast,' as United States military officials put it in November." An *ABC News* commentator suggested that Tet might indeed be the last gamble of the communists, but that nevertheless "it is also the exact opposite of what American leaders have for months been leading us to expect." Dean Rusk observed in a 20

March meeting with Johnson that, whatever the reality, "the element of hope has been taken away by the Tet Offensive."[31]

The chasm between expectations and reality in Vietnam established the idea of a "credibility gap" between the Johnson administration's words and what was really happening. The media and the public, possibly for the first time in U.S. history, began to assume that what their government was telling them about a foreign war was deliberately false. Therefore leaders were not believed even when battles did start going well. In Cronkite's words: "To say that we are closer to victory today is to believe, in the face of the evidence, the optimists who have been wrong in the past. To suggest that we are on the edge of defeat is to yield to unreasonable pessimism. To say that we are mired in stalemate seems the only realistic, yet unsatisfactory conclusion." Cronkite thought the only option was disengagement and negotiation. Johnson's former aide Robert Komer later remembered that, at the end of 1967, "Westmoreland believed, Abrams believed, Bunker believed, and I believed that finally . . . we really were winning. We couldn't quite see clearly how soon, but this wasn't public relations, this wasn't Lyndon Johnson telling us to put a face on it. We genuinely thought we were making it. And then boom, forty towns get attacked, and they didn't believe us anymore."[32]

Mind-sets and Information on Success. The mind-set of U.S. observers also shaped their comprehension of incoming information about the Tet offensive (whatever metrics they may have had). In this sense the timing of the war was important: it occurred in the 1960s during the greatest cultural, social, and political upheaval in U.S. history. The war became a lightning rod for the wider civil rights and anti-establishment movements, which provided fertile ground for negative appraisals of U.S. performance. Americans who opposed the war tended to view information about Tet as evidence corroborating their view that U.S. intervention in Vietnam had been mistaken all along.[33] Hawks, by contrast, tended to perceive the same information as evidence that the United States should take the initiative and escalate the war. As is common in such perceptions, members of each group picked out pieces of information about events that confirmed their core beliefs.

In the 1960s, as their views on foreign policy became more divided along partisan lines, Americans increasingly followed party cues in their judgments about international affairs. Information about the foreign policy actions of a favored politician was applauded, while information about the actions of a disfavored politician tended to be criticized. For example, immediately after Tet, during the Paris peace talks in 1968, Democrats were more likely than Republicans to state that the talks were going well. But after Nixon became president in 1969, Republicans were suddenly more likely to think the talks were going well. There was a similar switch in confidence along partisan lines about how soon the war would end.[34]

Salient Events

The perception of Tet as a victory for the communists and a defeat for the United States was reinforced by salient events during the offensive.

Salient Events and Information on Success. The nature of the Tet offensive as a dramatic surprise attack encouraged negative American evaluations. A few Americans did see the attacks coming. Days before the offensive, Lt. General Frederick Weyand reinforced the Saigon area, anticipating some form of enemy action. Furthermore, some of the communists attacked a day early, in confusion over the start of the lunar calendar, prompting U.S. and ARVN units to go on alert.[35]

However, these events barely reduced the general psychological effect of the surprise attack. Nguyen Cao Ky, South Vietnam's prime minister from 1965 to 1967 and then vice president until 1971, wrote that Tet was "savage, brilliantly executed, it caught us all off balance." Robert Komer recalled: "It was the Tet shock to the American psyche that made me first think we might lose." According to Clark Clifford: "Despite their retrospective claims to the contrary, at the time of the initial attacks the reaction of some of our most senior military leaders approached panic."[36] Americans, many of whom used security as their key metric for judging success in South Vietnam, were bombarded with pictures of terror and mayhem across the country. Mundane facts were naturally drowned out or ignored in the spectacle, including evidence about how ineffective the attacks had actually been in substantive terms. We can conjecture that if the same battlefield gains and losses had occurred through a different process, say a gradual buildup of attacks at Khe Sanh, Hue, and elsewhere, they would not have generated the same acute sense of impending doom, panic, and betrayed beliefs.

The impact of the surprise attack on evaluations was exacerbated by a series of striking symbolic images that achieved wide prominence in the United States. People tend to generalize from specific events to universal conclusions, and many Americans accepted these symbolic images as key pieces of information by which to judge metrics.

In attacking the U.S. embassy in Saigon, the communists struck the major symbol of the American presence in South Vietnam. The attack was one of the smallest-scale actions of the entire offensive, but it dominated press coverage. The embassy happened to be close to the hotels where many journalists were based, so in a matter of minutes practically every foreign news station had a correspondent on the scene. The high wall around the embassy compound both protected journalists from gunfire and blinded them to the reality of what was happening inside. This led to "confused and often out-landishly fabricated dispatches and reports . . . flashing across the airwaves worldwide." NBC incorrectly told viewers that VC snipers had fired down on rescuers in the embassy courtyard. One UPI re-porter claimed that VC fighters had occupied the embassy building for several hours. In fact, all of the attackers were soon lying dead in the courtyard, never having made it into the main building at all (they did breach a separate building, and reporters may not have distinguished between the two). The *New York Times* incorrectly stated as late as 2 February that guerrillas had penetrated at least as far as the first floor of the embassy.[37]

When Westmoreland told journalists on 31 January that Tet would allow the United States to gain the initiative in the war, he chose to deliver this message from the blood-spattered lawn of the em-bassy, with dead Vietcong being carried away behind him. Re-porters could scarcely believe what they were hearing. One re-called: "Westmoreland was standing in the ruins and saying everything was great."[38] It was a simple mental leap from seeing the embassy attacked to concluding that no part of South Vietnam was safe, and therefore that America's stated goal of providing security for the country had failed.

The other widely discussed image that emblazoned Tet in peo-ple's memories, and symbolized chaos and desperation, was a photo taken by the Associated Press photographer Eddie Adams. It showed General Nguyen Ngoc Loan, the chief of South Vietnam's national police, executing a VC captive by shooting him in the head in the streets of Saigon. The image won Adams the Pulitzer Prize for photography.

After Loan fired the shot, he said to the reporters present: "They killed many Americans and many of my men. Buddha will understand. Do you?" But many news agencies let the image speak for itself—and it spoke powerfully about the brutality and moral degradation of the war.[39]

Elsewhere in the country, examples of apparent folly and futility caught the attention of the press, including the infamous comment alleged to have been made by a U.S officer at Ben Tre: "It became necessary to destroy the town in order to save it." This remark came to symbolize the pointless destruction of the war. But there is some debate over who, if anyone, actually delivered the line. Meanwhile, after the United States declared victory at Khe Sanh, American commanders decided to abandon the marine base there. This made sense in military terms—the United States had inflicted huge casualties until the enemy forces withdrew, and now there was little point in staying. But the move had a negative symbolic effect. Americans had been told for months, while Khe Sanh was under siege, that the base had to be defended at any price: it could not be allowed to become another Dien Bien Phu. The U.S. withdrawal, after the enormous effort to hold out, looked like a retreat.[40]

It is hard to know how many people altered their view of Tet or Vietnam on the basis of the embassy coverage, Eddie Adams's photo, the alleged comment at Ben Tre, or the decision to leave Khe Sanh. Twenty million Americans watched the film of the shooting by General Loan on NBC, but only ninety people wrote to the network about it, with the vast majority complaining that the film was in bad taste, or that children could have seen it.[41] Privately some Americans might have applauded this kind of summary justice. Yet, as we shall see, these salient images and events served to frame the wider societal debate about Vietnam. Almost forty years later, these symbolic actions remain very well known, much more so than the details of the battles and the casualties. For many observers, these images *became* the Tet offensive.

Social Pressures

Social pressures from three main sources influenced American judgments about Tet: the North Vietnamese regime, the American media, and U.S. elites. In each case, these pressures tended to bias metrics and information in the same direction, promoting negative evaluations of U.S. performance.

North Vietnamese Manipulation. U.S. public opinion was not the key focus of the Tet offensive. Hanoi's primary psychological targets were the South Vietnamese regime, which they intended to shock and cripple through a sudden and vast attack, and the South Vietnamese people, whom they hoped to inspire to revolution. Indeed, the North Vietnamese general Tran Do remarked: "As for making an impact in the United States, it had not been our intention—but it turned out to be a fortunate result."[42] Nevertheless, after Tet, leaders such as Giap were quick to claim that the advantageous shifts in American public opinion and the subsequent political outcomes had been deliberately orchestrated, or at least encouraged, by Hanoi. North Vietnamese leaders probably recognized that the attack would have a psychological impact in the United States whatever happened on the ground. Well aware of growing American opposition to the war, General Giap sought to exploit U.S. overextension, domestic economic problems, and tensions in the alliance with South Vietnam. He chose to take the war to the cities, precisely the areas that Americans considered safe. A grand attack would destroy American confidence and force the United States to negotiate.[43] The choice of highly symbolic targets in Saigon suggests an overtly psychological motive. However, even though American perceptions shifted in a direction that favored Hanoi, this process may have been largely beyond the communists' control, or indeed, their expectations. The North Vietnamese believed that political gains in the United States would follow from victories on the battlefield, but in the end, they achieved these political gains in spite of losing militarily.

Media Manipulation. Some Americans have criticized the media for contributing to the U.S. failure in Vietnam, but those who blame the press for the defeat often miss the complexity of the relationship between reporters and the war. Throughout the conflict, and especially between 1965 and 1967, coverage was actually quite favorable. Even after 1968 the media never truly turned against the war: the Americans were still usually portrayed as the good guys, although the war was less often described as "our war" and more often as "the war," and U.S. casualties were more explicitly discussed.[44]

Nevertheless, during the Tet offensive, the media do appear to have influenced people's interpretation of events as a defeat, although in a more subtle way than is often claimed. While the attackers were being beaten back on the ground, in the words of the former war correspondent Erik Durschmied, "the Vietcong were scoring big on American TV." Before 1968 few reporters had been exposed to combat, but suddenly the whole press corps in Saigon found themselves in a war zone, with their attention focused on the battle at the embassy. Westmoreland and Johnson's official optimism had established such great expectations that the media's reaction to Tet was increasingly to doubt everything they had been told. Contrary to administration claims, there was, it seemed, no light at the end of the tunnel after all.[45]

There is certainly evidence of media bias during Tet, both in the selection of what to report (information about success) and in discussion of whether these events signaled gains or losses (metrics for success). According to the historian George Herring, the media often portrayed the Tet battles in "highly unfavorable and sometimes distorted terms," with many premature reports of communist victories. The main themes about Tet conveyed in the media were the omnipresent enemy, the U.S. military destroying South Vietnam, the communists gaining the initiative, the impressive performance of the insurgent forces, and the wily leadership of General Giap. The overall picture was one of U.S. failure. Journalists were very critical about the performance of the South Vietnamese regime and military, even though the ARVN fought far more effectively than almost anyone expected. Indeed, it is not clear whether a single newspaper in the United States ever ran a positive story about the fighting performance of the ARVN.[46]

In any case, reporters tended to depict the military result as irrelevant, in favor of the view that the communists were obviously dominant among the wider population and the offensive had provoked the United States into the wholesale destruction of cities and towns. "It was a convenient thesis," notes the journalist and author Peter Braestrup; "it required no analysis of the battlefield, assumed average South Vietnamese reactions were those of American commentators, and conveyed the notion that the foe's chief goal was to provoke air attacks by the allies on Hanoi's own forces in urban areas." By focusing on Saigon and Hue, the media gave the impression that the battlefield outcome was in doubt well into March—but in fact the outcome of the offensive had been decided within a few days. Media coverage increased the power of symbolic and emotional fragments of knowledge without always providing the necessary context. While General Loan's execution of the VC captive was widely covered, massacres by communist forces, such as the killing of several thousand civilians in Hue, tended to be underreported. Robert Elegant, a former editor of *Newsweek*, argued in 1981 that the press had "consistently magnified the allies' deficiencies, and displayed almost saintly tolerance of those misdeeds of Hanoi it could neither disregard nor deny."[47]

"Rarely," according to Braestrup, "has contemporary crisis-journalism turned out, in retrospect, to have veered so widely from reality. Essentially, the dominant themes of the words and film from Vietnam (rebroadcast in commentary, editorials, and much political rhetoric at home) added up to a portrait of defeat for the allies . . . To have portrayed such a setback for one side as a defeat for the other—in a major crisis abroad—cannot be counted as a triumph for American journalism." Unsurprisingly, public challenges to the government's views were more evident in the democratic United States than in North Vietnam. As a stark contrast with the American media's relationship with the Johnson administration in 1968, prior to Tet Hanoi arrested more than two hundred officials who argued for negotiation with Washington rather than an offensive, and many of them were imprisoned or executed.[48]

Elite Manipulation. In the United States, by the time of the Tet offensive, senior elements of the Democratic Party were in open revolt against the Vietnam war. About a quarter of the House of Representatives opposed the continuation of the conflict, together with a few senators. Such critics tended to emphasize the negative aspects of Tet, and provided an alternative interpretation of events to the one offered by the White House. Senator Robert Kennedy, for

example, on 8 February 1968 described Tet as having "finally shattered the mask of official illusion with which we have concealed
our true circumstances, even from ourselves."[49]

Elite attitudes may have shaped different racial responses to Tet
and the war. While blacks and whites were similar in their opinions
about Vietnam until March 1968, after that point blacks were significantly less likely than whites to approve of the war. This may
have been because, as the political scientist Scott Gartner suggests,
"white leaders were divided on the war in the first Nixon administration, while black leaders were more uniformly against it."[50] By the
time of the Tet offensive Martin Luther King Jr. had transformed
the civil rights campaign into a broader antiwar movement.

Part of the reason for growing divisions between Congress and
the White House were the different metrics they employed to judge
success in Vietnam. "Congress," according to Gartner, "assessed
success through minimizing U.S. casualties, the army evaluated
performance through maximizing the number of enemy dead and
enemy weapons captured, and the Johnson Administration based
its assessments of U.S. effectiveness largely on U.S. and communist casualties. These measures, however, led to fundamentally different assessments of performance, particularly when the fighting
dramatically increased during the Tet offensive."[51] What looked like
a success to the U.S. military because ratios of enemy to U.S. casualties had spiked was a failure for many congressmen because U.S.
casualties had shot up without any obvious progress toward overall
victory.

The White House tried to counter antiwar critics by making the
case that Tet was a success after all. In March 1968, discussing Khe
Sanh, Johnson told reporters: "Make no mistake about it. I don't
want a man in here to go back home thinking otherwise. We are going to win!" But such efforts were strikingly unsuccessful in coun-

teracting the emerging and solidifying perception of a U.S. defeat. Johnson's credibility had been bankrupted by the unwarranted optimism of 1967. His administration's words jarred against the daily images and stories indicating that the United States had lost control of the war. Furthermore, efforts to convince Americans that their side had won the Tet offensive were hampered by the fact that many administration and military figures themselves were shocked by events, and at least partially accepted the argument that the battle favored the communists. Johnson was privately stunned by the attack. At a press conference on 2 February, despite some upbeat words, he radiated weariness and indecision, not confidence.[52]

Manipulation by elites took an unusual turn when a group of hawks in the U.S. military decided to deliberately focus on the negative aspects of Tet. General Wheeler wrote a deeply pessimistic report about the progress of the war, describing Tet as a near disaster for the United States. "By presenting a gloomy assessment," according to Herring, "he hoped to stampede the administration into providing [more] troops." Wheeler encouraged Westmoreland to request 206,000 additional men to win the war, knowing that the request would absolve the military from responsibility if the president refused to send more troops and then the United States lost. Someone in the Johnson White House leaked the proposal to the press, and the story broke in the *New York Times* on 10 March 1968. The American media portrayed this request as a call for reinforcements following a battlefield defeat for the United States. Johnson was shaken by Wheeler's negative appraisal of Tet, and instead of ordering reinforcements he turned to his civilian advisors for a reevaluation of the overall situation.[53]

In a decisive move, a majority of Johnson's most trusted civilian advisors now turned against the war. The so-called Wise Men, among them Dean Acheson, Abe Fortas, Maxwell Taylor, George

Ball, and Omar Bradley, met in Washington on 18 March. Most of these eminent figures felt that the war could not be won and argued against further escalation. Instead, they recommended that the United States focus on building up South Vietnamese forces and seeking a negotiated settlement. Johnson was shocked: these were the same men who had almost unanimously pushed for continued military efforts the previous autumn. Their advice was hugely important in Johnson's decision to recall Westmoreland, and for Johnson's famous speech on 31 March, in which he announced a partial bombing halt, accepted negotiations, and said he would not run for reelection. Johnson's speech helped to entrench the perception that the Tet offensive had been a defeat for the United States. His decision to withdraw from the presidential race signaled that he had failed. "Precisely two months after the initial enemy attacks," in the words of the diplomatic historian Robert Buzzanco, "Lyndon Johnson had become the latest and best known casualty of the Tet Offensive."[54]

| Conclusions

The outcome of the Tet offensive was fixed in the minds of observers, with most Americans sure they had lost the battle, if not the war. In the aftermath of Tet, an NBC television producer proposed a documentary program to set the record straight on the U.S. victory. His idea was rejected because, as a senior producer put it to him, Tet was seen "in the public's mind as a defeat, and therefore it was an American defeat."[55]

The dominant interpretation of Tet as a major American setback cannot have been the product of score-keeping because perceptions of victory and defeat were so divorced from the material gains and aims achieved in 1968. The United States reversed the offensive

and killed tens of thousands of enemy troops, and thereby amelio-
rated South Vietnam's strategic position—however doomed this
position may have been in the longer term. The North and the
Vietcong suffered unambiguous defeat on the battlefield, failing to
accomplish any of their military objectives. The communists had
believed that local victories on the ground, or at least the killing of
large numbers of U.S./ARVN combatants, would be a prerequisite
for achieving any subsequent political aims, such as a halt to the
bombing. According to General Van Tra: "There was never such a
thing as snatching political victory from the jaws of military defeat
or gaining diplomatic success without blood having been spilled
and bones scattered across the battlefield."[56]

The communists were wrong. Match-fixing factors meant that in
1968 the North merely had to attack in sufficient depth, and especially breadth, to be well on the way to a victory in the minds of
most Americans. Perceptions of U.S. defeat, and the political and
social pressure these perceptions exerted on the Johnson administration, led to U.S. de-escalation and—in a kind of self-fulfilling
prophecy—a real victory for the communist forces. Without match-
fixing factors, the disastrous battlefield outcome could never have
translated into substantive communist gains.

Among Americans, the perception of defeat arose primarily because of overoptimistic expectations before the offensive, the psychological effect of the surprise attack, and media and elite responses. Tet awakened the U.S. public to a more realistic view of
the progress of the Vietnam war. But this view so clashed with the
earlier months of official optimism that the Tet offensive itself could
scarcely be interpreted as anything other than a defeat.

Match-fixing factors operating in 1968 all tended to reinforce
one another. Overoptimistic U.S. expectations before Tet (mind-
set) provided fertile ground for critics of the war to exploit (social

pressure). The North Vietnamese (social pressure) at least partially engineered the psychological impact on Americans by deliberately attacking symbolic targets (salient events). Congressional debates (social pressure) were often explicitly about television and photographic images or news stories (salient events, social pressure).[57]

Crucial to this case was the perception of *control*. Had U.S. forces themselves launched an offensive—as they often had in the past—then the American public would have both expected and tolerated high numbers of casualties. As it was, the enemy was in control of the location and timing of violence. U.S./ARVN units, winning or not, were merely reacting to communist forces that had taken the initiative. Ambassador Bui Diem recalled: "It seemed to many of us that during those last years events were out of our hands. They occurred out of our control. Tet made this so. Maybe it should not have but it did."[58]

The communists were likely to lose any direct military confrontation they fought against the United States in 1968, since conventional fighting favored the American superiority in firepower. However, it was also likely that the communists would come to be perceived as victors even if their attack failed. Indeed, it is hard to see how the United States could have been seen as the victor in any large-scale communist offensive in 1968, whatever the events on the ground. By choosing to attack in limited strength but at a large number of locations across South Vietnam, the communists, knowingly or unknowingly, decreased their chances of a battlefield victory but increased their chances of a perceived victory.

We can discern the causal processes by which decisiveness, ambiguity, power, and regime type encouraged match-fixing in 1968. Tet, although very one-sided, did not display the sort of *decisive outcome* that trumps perceptual biases. The communist forces were killed in great numbers, but the United States did not take the offensive and capture new territory. Tet was also unusually *ambiguous*. Judging progress in counterinsurgencies is inherently difficult because the underlying strength of the insurgents is typically unknown or unclear. In addition, for U.S. observers, there were few, if any, precedents for battling such a huge surprise offensive by insurgents, and the picture of events on the ground was highly confusing. Meanwhile, the great *asymmetry in power* between U.S. and communist forces created expectations of rapid U.S. results that tended to ignore the difficulties of the environment in Vietnam. Finally, the *democratic* nature of the United States allowed for self-critical match-fixing, including a skeptical response by the media and elites. In the end, by virtue of a familiar set of match-fixing factors, a battle that could not have proceeded more favorably for the United States proved to be its greatest defeat in Vietnam.

7 | THE YOM KIPPUR WAR

*[Sadat] crushed the defeat lying deep within us all when he
resolved upon the crossing . . . The crossing is deliverance.*

—YUSSEF IDRIS

*I cannot fight the United States or accept the responsibility before
history for the destruction of our armed forces for a second time . . .
My heart bleeds to tell you this, but I feel that my office compels
me to take this decision.*

—SADAT TO ASSAD

OPERATION BADR, named after the first victory of the Prophet Muhammad, was a coordinated surprise attack launched by Egypt and
Syria against Israel on the afternoon of 6 October 1973. The day was
Yom Kippur, the holiest day in the Jewish calendar. The Arabs
achieved considerable strategic surprise, and the thinly spread Israeli defenders initially lost territory in both the Sinai on the southern front and the Golan Heights on the northern front. Within a
couple of weeks, however, Israel's mobilized reserves had counterat-
tacked and attained substantial military victories over both Egypt
and Syria, encircling the Egyptian Third Army and threatening
both Cairo and Damascus.

What was in many ways a great success for Israel became a
source of enormous disillusionment in the country. In the Arab
states, by contrast, and especially in Egypt, a war that started well

and then progressively deteriorated was viewed as a great victory. This conflict, known variously as the Yom Kippur War, the Ramadan War, and the October War, changed the face of the Middle East and proved instrumental in shaping the Israeli-Egyptian peace settlement reached between 1975 and 1979. In this chapter we focus on the Israeli and Arab (especially Egyptian) reactions to this critical war, showing how mind-sets, salient events, and social pressures combined to produce perceptions of victory that bore only a loose relationship to the military events on the ground, fixing the match so that Israel would be seen to lose.

| History

The immediate roots of the Yom Kippur War lay in the previous Israeli victory in the 1967 Six-Day War. In 1967, fearing imminent attack, Israel carried out a preemptive strike against Egypt, destroying much of its air force while the planes were still on the ground. In response, Syria and Jordan moved against Israel, but both suffered similar rapid destruction of their air forces. Within a few days Israel captured the Sinai Peninsula, the Golan Heights, the West Bank of the Jordan River, and East Jerusalem. In a stunning triumph, Israel gained land which tripled the size of its original territory. However, the immediate outcome was yet more conflict. In an effort to force Israel to return the Sinai, Egypt began the War of Attrition across the Suez Canal in March 1969, which ended in stalemate a year and a half later. In 1970 new leadership arose in Syria, when Hafez al-Assad seized power, and in Egypt, with the emergence of Anwar el-Sadat. Both leaders considered the status quo to be intolerable. The two nations' capacity to fight Israel was enhanced by substantial Soviet military aid, including massive infusions of equipment and advisors.

On 6 October 1973 Israel was surprised by a two-front attack by Egypt and Syria, later supported by forces from much of the Arab world. Egypt crossed the Suez Canal and quickly captured much of the Bar Lev Line, a series of Israeli fortifications along the east bank of the canal. For a few days Israeli forces were also pushed back by a massive Syrian armored assault on the Golan Heights. The war soon acquired the characteristics of a proxy superpower conflict, with the United States airlifting supplies to Israel and the Soviet Union providing even greater support for Egypt and Syria. The course of the war shifted significantly after the first week, when Israeli forces advanced into Syria and crossed the Suez Canal into Egypt, surrounding the stranded Egyptian Third Army on the east bank. On 17 October the Arab oil-producing states initiated an oil embargo against countries that supported Israel.

As their position deteriorated, Arab forces, backed diplomatically by the USSR, pushed for a cease-fire, which was declared by the United Nations Security Council on 22 October. The fighting continued even after a second cease-fire resolution on 23 October, and Israel completed the encirclement of Egypt's Third Army. Moscow issued a threat to intervene, a move that sparked a superpower crisis. However, Israel and the Arab states finally agreed to observe a cease-fire under the supervision of UN observers.

The disengagement agreement between Israel and Egypt specified that Israeli forces would pull back a few miles from the canal, the canal would reopen, and the towns in the Canal Zone would be repopulated. The outcome of the Yom Kippur War played a key role in the 1975–1979 peace negotiations between Israel and Egypt. The Sinai was returned to Egypt in exchange for full peace between the two countries, including Egypt's recognition of the state of Israel. There was no parallel peace process between Israel and Syria, although an agreement was reached to pull back to approxi-

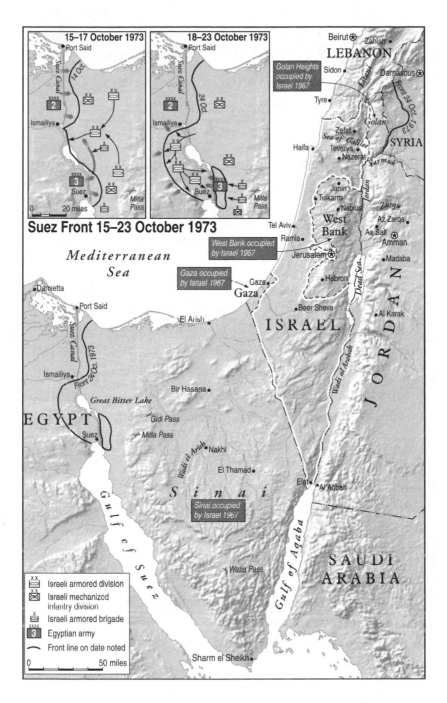

MAP 3. The 1973 Yom Kippur War. Map by Philip Schwartzberg.

mately the lines held before the Yom Kippur War, with the insertion of a force of UN observers between the two sides.

Dominant Perceptions of Victory and Defeat

Israelis typically see the Yom Kippur War as the most traumatic event in the history of their country. The conflict and its perceived outcome deeply shook Israeli society, culture, and politics. The 2,688 Israelis who died were a significant loss in a country of only 3.3 million people. Labels often used to describe the war in Israel include "earthquake," "thunderstorm," and "flood." Most often used is the word *mehdal*, meaning omission or shortcoming: a failure short of a catastrophe, which carries a strong connotation of negligence. Indeed, the surprise attack, and the initial defeats for Israel, discredited the country's entire establishment. There was great bitterness against the government and the military for not foreseeing or being prepared for the war. Ya'acov Hisdai, a reserve colonel in Israel's army, commented: "The Israeli self-confidence, the optimism, the feeling of the justice of the cause, all that fell apart on Yom Kippur."[1] In a collection of Israeli children's art from the period, we find depictions of dragons rising from the Nile and monsters from Syria, typifying the "tragedy of this war in contrast to the relative optimism of the Six-Day War and previous wars." The sense of depression after the war was compounded by the fear that Israel would now have to face never-ending conflict with its Arab neighbors. According to Israeli military commentators, the Yom Kippur War had transformed Israel from a state which in 1967 "had won the most brilliant victory in the history of modern warfare" to a "country living under the shadow of extermination."[2]

Prime Minister Golda Meir stated in her memoirs that Israel had "won the Yom Kippur War," but nevertheless her recollections were marked by loss and anguish. The war had been a "near disaster, a nightmare that I myself experienced and which will always be with me." She declared in November 1973: "There is no Jew in Israel who can say that he is the same today as he was on Yom Kippur eve. I don't believe I will ever be the same." Meir reportedly carried suicide pills around with her as the attacks intensified, and she authorized preparations for the launch of nuclear weapons. She recounted a postwar meeting with the British politician Richard Crossman, who could not understand the atmosphere of gloom and despondency in Israel. The British had suffered similar military crises, Crossman said, but "didn't take things in such an intense way." In her memoirs Meir could only conclude: "We are different I suppose." She added: "the word 'trauma' that was on everyone's lips all that winter most accurately describes the national sense of loss and injury that Crossman thought was so excessive."[3]

Israeli perceptions of the Yom Kippur War are partly captured in survey data collected between 1967 and 1978 by the Israel Institute of Applied Social Research. Before the 1973 war, about 60–70 percent of Israelis saw their country's overall situation as favorable. During the war this figure fell to 10–15 percent. In the subsequent years, apart from a brief spike after Sadat visited Israel in 1977, the number of Israelis who saw the situation as favorable never recovered to prewar levels. Furthermore, in the six years before 1973, about 35–45 percent of Israelis claimed that their mood was "almost always good" or "mostly good." This figure fell dramatically following the outbreak of the Yom Kippur War, and continued to fall even after the cease-fire. In November 1973 only 16 percent of Israelis reported a positive mood.[4]

The complex Israeli response to the Yom Kippur War combined feelings of grief, anguish, defeat and anger. Army veterans initiated a protest movement against the government. Crowds demonstrated against the failure to anticipate the war and the perceived high number of Israeli casualties. Many senior politicians lost much of their popularity. The defense minister, Moshe Dayan, was the most popular leader in Israel in 1970, but a month after the Yom Kippur War only 36 percent favored his continuation in office. Jews around the world displayed greater worries about living in Israel. Far fewer people immigrated to Israel in the first half of 1974 (16,800) than in the first half of 1973 (24,300), and there is evidence that more Israelis seriously considered emigrating.[5]

In April 1974 the Agranat Commission, headed by the president of the Israeli Supreme Court and formed to investigate the circumstances that had led to the war, reported that many government errors had cost lives, with culpability in the highest ranks of the army and the intelligence service. Although Golda Meir was personally cleared of responsibility, she resigned a week after the report was issued, as did her entire cabinet. In the long run, the Yom Kippur War helped to produce the end of the Labor Alignment as the governing party of Israel. This process culminated in the 1977 victory for the right-wing alliance led by Menachem Begin's Likud Party. The war also widened divisions in the Israeli polity, typified by the parallel rise of the Gush Emunim movement to settle the occupied territories and Peace Now, which argued for returning land to the Arabs in exchange for peace.[6]

The view of the Yom Kippur War in Egypt in many ways mirrored that in Israel. Following the conflict, many Egyptians were gripped by a mood of triumphant success and elation. Writers in Cairo exulted that their country was living in "times of victory."[7] Sadat talked of "the most glorious days in our history." Field Marshal Ahmad Isma'il argued that the world had seen that Egypt was "capable of fighting, capable of victory." King Faisal of Saudi Arabia pressed Arabs to "consolidate our victories." Field Marshal El-Gamasy also depicted the war as a victory for Egypt, praising its successful crossing of the Suez Canal. Sadat, on his way to address the People's Assembly in Cairo on 16 October 1973, was cheered by thousands of Egyptians, some carrying banners declaring him "the Hero of the Crossing." The Museum of the Ramadan War in Cairo presented the conflict as one of the great military triumphs of all time. According to many Arab observers, the attack had removed the stain of 1967's defeat, and was directly responsible for the later withdrawal of Israel from the Sinai. After returning from his dramatic visit to Jerusalem in 1977, Sadat was feted as a hero, both of war and of peace.[8]

The war continues to be viewed favorably in Egypt, remembered on "Victory Day." In 1998 Egypt's president, Hosni Mubarak, called the war a victory for peace and "a lightning point in Egypt's modern military history." According to the political scientist Kirk Beattie: "The average Egyptian, to this day, remains convinced that [in 1973] victory was Egypt's." On the thirtieth anniversary of the war in 2003, the weekly *Sabah Al-Kheir* described the conflict as "the dearest and greatest victory."[9]

Within this general picture of Israeli perceptions of failure and Arab perceptions of success, there are some important exceptions. Many Palestinians, for example, argued that Sadat had betrayed their cause by entering into a bilateral peace process with Israel without insisting on a resolution of the Palestinian issue. Iraq refused to participate in disengagement or peace talks after the Yom Kippur War, protesting the Egyptian and Syrian willingness to negotiate with Israel. In Syria the war tends to be seen positively, but in more muted terms than in Egypt. The Syrian commemoration of the anniversary of the conflict in 1998 involved war planes flying in formation and official statements that Syria would continue its efforts to liberate the Golan Heights.[10]

In addition, Israelis tend to see aspects of the war as positive, especially the heroism of ordinary soldiers, and the efforts of the Israeli people to stop a near-debacle caused by the mistakes of their leaders. A few individual Israelis came out of the conflict perceived as victors. General Ariel Sharon gained prestige as the man who initiated the Israeli crossing of the Suez Canal. Israeli generals have repeatedly portrayed the war as an overall success. Chaim Herzog, for example, depicted the conflict as the most striking victory in Israel's history, and dismissed the view that the Arab countries had won as "imaginary."[11]

However, such opinions had little effect on the Israeli public's collective memory. The anniversary of the Yom Kippur War is quite unlike that of any other event in Israeli history, and the conflict is depicted largely in negative terms, with a focus on the surprise attack, Israeli deaths, intelligence failures, and initial battlefield reverses. To sum up, the dominant interpretation of the Yom Kippur War in both Israel and the Arab world is one of Egyptian or Arab victory or success, and Israeli defeat or failure. Why did these perceptions emerge?

| Framework 1: Score-keeping

Were observers of the Yom Kippur War score-keeping—as they ideally should have been—or did their judgments result from a biased process of match-fixing? To discover whether people were score-keeping or not, we analyze the congruence between the perceptions of victory discussed above and the material changes in the war and the achievement of leaders' aims (see Charts 7.1 and 7.2). In general, since it was a military conflict over contested territory, each side's gains were the other side's losses.

Material Gains and Losses

In several respects the war was costly for Israel. Intelligence failures contributed to the success of the surprise attacks.[12] The Egyptians defied expectations by moving 100,000 men and 1,000 tanks across the Suez Canal in twenty-four hours, at the cost of just a few hundred casualties, and quickly captured the eastern bank of the canal and 1,200 square kilometers of the Sinai. Israel suffered another clear battlefield reverse when it launched expensive and ineffective tank assaults against Egyptian troops armed with Russian antitank weaponry. Furthermore, Egyptian surface-to-air missiles shot whole squadrons of Israeli planes out of the sky. By the end of the war, about 8,000–10,000 Israelis had been killed or injured. Diplomatically, Israel found itself virtually isolated. Many developing states broke off relations with Israel at the time of the war, partly because of the Arabs' use of oil as a bargaining chip. European states also tended to take a critical position on Israel, with many countries refusing to grant landing rights to U.S. planes flying aid to Tel Aviv.

However, in material terms the Israelis won a clear victory in the Yom Kippur War. Their country's diplomatic isolation was a long-term process that was highlighted, but not caused, by the war. Its real causes included Arab oil diplomacy and Israel's perceived reluctance to return land occupied in 1967. Months before the war, in July 1973, a UN Security Council resolution condemning the continued Israeli occupation of Arab lands was only averted by a U.S. veto. European opinion of Israel had evolved since 1967, toward a perception that Israel was now victimizing rather than being the victim.[13] Also, if the 1973 conflict highlighted Israel's diplomatic

Type of outcome	Event	Material gain or loss?	An aim achieved?	Altering the credit due[a] Importance For leader	For observer[b]	Difficulty[c]
Positive outcomes	Gained 1,600 km² on west bank of Suez Canal and 500 km² in Syria	Gain	Achieved	Very high	Very high	Moderate/high
	40,000–50,000 Arabs killed or injured	Gain	Achieved	Very high	Very high	Moderate
	2,250 Arab tanks, 430–500 aircraft, 19–34 naval vessels destroyed; 8,800 POWs captured	Gain	Achieved	Very high	Very high	Moderate/high
Negative outcomes	Lost 1,200 km² on east bank of Suez Canal	Loss	Not achieved	Very high	High	Moderate (chance of avoiding)
	8,000–10,000 Israelis killed or injured	Loss	Not achieved	High	Moderate/high	Moderate (chance of avoiding)
	400 Israeli tanks, 102 aircraft destroyed; 294 Israelis captured	Loss	Not achieved	Moderate/high	Moderate	Moderate (chance of avoiding)

a. Higher values give *more* credit for positive outcomes and *less* credit for negative outcomes.
b. The importance of a gain or an aim in the minds of observers (in this case the authors) trying to fairly assess its worth.
c. The difficulty of a gain or an aim in the minds of observers (in this case the authors) trying to assess it fairly.

CHART 7.1. Scorecard for Israel in the Yom Kippur War.

Type of outcome	Event	Material gain or loss?	An aim achieved?	Importance		Altering the credit due[a] Difficulty[c]
				For leader	For observer[b]	
Positive outcomes	Gained 1,200 km² on the east bank of Suez Canal	Gain	Partially achieved	Very high	High	Moderate
	8,000–10,000 Israelis killed or injured	Gain	Achieved	Very high	Moderate/high	Moderate
	400 Israeli tanks, 102 aircraft destroyed; 294 POWs captured	Gain	Achieved	High	Moderate	Moderate
Negative outcomes	Lost 1,600 km² on west bank of Suez Canal and 500 km² in Syria	Loss	Not achieved	Very high	Very high	Moderate/high (chance of avoiding)
	40,000–50,000 Arabs killed or injured	Loss	Not achieved	Moderate/high	Very high	Moderate (chance of avoiding)
	2,250 Arab tanks; 430–500 aircraft; 19–34 naval vessels destroyed; 8,800 POWs captured	Loss	Not achieved	High	Very high	Moderate/high (chance of avoiding)

a. Higher values give *more* credit for positive outcomes and *less* credit for negative outcomes.
b. The importance of a gain or an aim in the minds of observers (in this case the authors) trying to fairly assess its worth.
c. The difficulty of a gain or an aim in the minds of observers (in this case the authors) trying to assess it fairly.

CHART 7.2. Scorecard for the Arab nations in the Yom Kippur War.

isolation, it also demonstrated Israel's close strategic relationship with the United States.

The Israeli performance was more impressive in the Yom Kippur War than in the 1967 Six-Day War, because in 1973 Israel fought in more difficult circumstances. Rather than launching a surprise attack and dictating the course of the conflict, Israel was itself caught by surprise. In 1973 there were over 1,200,000 Egyptian troops (including reserves) and 600,000 Syrian soldiers (although only some of these were committed to battle), as well as 100,000 troops from other Arab states. Israel's army was 375,000 strong. Israel had 2,100 tanks against 2,200 Egyptian tanks, 1,650 Syrian tanks, 500 Iraqi tanks, and 170 Jordanian tanks. Israel's 359 warplanes faced 400 Egyptian and 280 Syrian warplanes (and these were airborne, not sitting on the ground as in the Six-Day War).[14] The Arab forces were also much better trained and equipped than they had been in 1967, thanks to extensive Soviet aid, and they were backed diplomatically by Moscow.

Despite this difficult strategic environment, for Israel the end of the Yom Kippur War displayed many of the traditional characteristics of an outright military victory. Israel inflicted four or five casualties for every one incurred; destroyed five tanks for every tank lost; shot down four or five aircraft for every one lost; and won a total, if relatively unimportant, naval victory. Israeli tactics and improvisational ability were generally far superior to those of Egypt and Syria. In Egypt, Israel broke through the center of the Egyptian lines, captured 1,600 square kilometers of territory, and encircled the 30,000-strong Third Army in the Sinai desert. By this stage, thousands of Egyptian troops were surrendering. Indeed, had the fighting lasted a few more days, the Egyptian Third Army would probably have been battered into submission. Israel forced Syrian troops off the Golan Heights in a dramatic armored battle and pushed into Syrian territory. According to the intelligence analyst Kenneth Pollack: "The Syrians paid a horrendous price for the successes they did achieve . . . Although the Syrians outnumbered the Israelis in all relevant categories of combat power throughout the war . . . Israeli tactical skills were so far superior to those of Syria that a numerical advantage of only three or four to one was inadequate for the Syrians . . . Syrian tactical capabilities were so poor that they took good Soviet tactics and made them bad and took bad Soviet tactics and made them worse." Much of Syria's infrastructure was also damaged by air raids. Israel had never held more territory than it did at the end of the Yom Kippur War—a war it had supposedly lost. At the cease-fire, Israeli troops were only fifty miles from Cairo and thirty miles from Damascus. The Soviet ambassador to Egypt, Aleksei Kosygin, saw the situation in Cairo at the end of the war as a "catastrophe." He declared: "We must have a cease-fire, because, otherwise, everything will collapse."[15]

In important respects, the Yom Kippur War improved Israel's strategic position. Before the war, Israel's security was worsening as Soviet aid to the Arab states increased and the diplomatic balance of power shifted against Tel Aviv. Although Israelis were not fully cognizant of the reality, their country was constantly at risk of a surprise attack. In contrast, the disengagement provisions in the Yom Kippur War settlement enhanced Israel's security because there could be no more surprise attacks similar to that of October 1973. The Syrians agreed to a UN observer force and limitations on troop deployments, and the Egyptians agreed to reopen the Suez Canal and repopulate the nearby cities. Israel withdrew its forces from the west bank of the canal as well as from a strip of territory adjacent to the east bank—but any Egyptian military presence on the east bank was to be strictly limited. Furthermore, although the disengagement negotiations after the war produced small territorial gains for the Arab states, Israel made diplomatic gains. The war led to the first direct negotiations between Israel and an Arab nation, when the Egyptian and Israeli generals met and shook hands.[16]

Critics of Israel's performance in the 1973 war usually point to high casualties as the basis for their negative judgment. The 2,688 Israeli deaths in 1973 were viewed in Israel as a dramatically greater burden than the 776 deaths incurred in the triumphant war of 1967. However, it should be noted that the Yom Kippur War lasted much longer: eighteen days rather than six days. Also, around 6,000 Israelis were killed in the 1948–1949 War of Independence, when Israel had a fraction of the population it had in 1973. In fact, relative to the war's duration and the Israeli population at the time, the 1967 war was more costly in terms of Israeli lives than the wars of either 1948–1949 or 1973.[17] This suggests that the cost in lives is not the primary reason why Israelis perceive the Yom Kippur War as a failure. If they were most worried by the total loss of life, they would feel more negatively about the war of 1948–1949; and if they were most concerned about the intensity of casualties, they would feel more negatively about 1967's Six-Day War. Israeli casualty sensitivity depended upon whether the soldiers were seen as having died in a winning or a losing cause. Israelis are far more sensitive to the losses in 1973 than in previous wars because of the way this war is popularly viewed.

If we include the later peace process in our calculation of the material gains of the Yom Kippur War, then Israel returned territory to Egypt. But in return Israel gained a peace settlement and full diplomatic relations with its strongest and most threatening enemy. Sadat settled for a separate Israeli-Egyptian deal that left unaddressed issues such as Palestinian rights, the West Bank, the Golan Heights, and Jerusalem. After the war, Syria's Assad also effectively abandoned the use of force in favor of diplomatic means, and proved more amenable to a comprehensive peace settlement with Israel based on a return of the lands captured in 1967 and a solution to the Palestinian issue.[18]

Material Aims

Evaluating which side achieved more of its material aims is quite difficult. Along with the usual problems in accurately comprehending motives, the aims of participants also tended to shift: from pre-war aims, to more limited aims after battlefield defeat, to expanded aims after battlefield victory.

Israeli Aims. Israel's aims before and during the war tended to be military in nature: to protect its security; to defeat once again its neighbors in war at minimal cost; and to deter the Arab states from fighting it again. Israel was a status quo state. It did not seek additional territory; rather it wanted to keep what it had, or to negotiate an exchange of some of the territory it had won in 1967 for peace and security.[19]

Within this broad framework, the exact nature of Israeli aims had shifted since 1967. In the aftermath of the Six-Day War, Israel had offered to withdraw from the Sinai and the Golan Heights, with minor modifications, in return for peace and recognition. After the Arabs rejected this offer, Israel rescinded it. By 1971, partly because of perceived implacable Arab hostility, partly because of greater domestic confidence about its own bargaining position, Israel's position had hardened, and it sought unspecified territorial adjustments in any peace deal. Most of the occupied Egyptian and Syrian land would be returned, but Israel insisted on defensible borders, often said to include the strategic Sinai town of Sharm el-Sheikh. In the spring of 1971 Golda Meir rejected a proposal that Israel withdraw from the Suez Canal so that it could be reopened, insisting instead on a full peace treaty with Egypt. Following the surprise attack in 1973, some senior Israelis narrowed their aims and argued for an immediate cease-fire even at the cost of losing territory to Egypt. After the military tide turned in Israel's favor, however, aims tended to shift upward. Israel now wanted to capture Syrian territory in the north, and preferably also territory in Egypt, before any cease-fire, to offset territorial losses on the east bank of the canal.[20]

Not all of these Israeli aims were achieved in 1973. Israel incurred fairly high casualties, and ultimately withdrew from a small part of the Sinai. If the cost in lives was considerable, Israel had nevertheless achieved its core military objectives, winning a clear battlefield victory and destroying much of the invading Arab armies. Israel therefore accomplished its major strategic aims: to deny the enemy the military advantage. The terms of the disengagement agreements with Egypt and Syria made Israel, in many respects, more secure from attack after the war than it had been before. At the time Israelis feared that the conflict would be followed by further major wars with Egypt and Syria, but this never happened. The 1979 peace settlement with Egypt fulfilled one of the goals of Israel's foreign policy since its foundation, and it was achieved without concessions on the other territories occupied in 1967. This deal was an enormous gain for Israel, and a move that was hugely popular in the country.

Would Israel have accepted the terms of 1975–1979 without the Yom Kippur War? This is a difficult question to answer. On the one hand, opinion polls showed that 96 percent of Israelis before and during the Yom Kippur War opposed returning Sharm el-Sheikh, yet in the end this town was given back to Egypt. In this sense the war led Israel to abandon what it had once clung to. However, the

Israelis' hostility to giving up Sharm el-Sheikh was partly due to a widespread belief that the Arab states had no genuine peaceful intentions toward Israel: in November 1973 only 5 percent of the Israeli population believed that the Arab states were ready to discuss a real peace with Israel.[21] It is at least plausible that most Israelis would have accepted the terms of 1975–1979 without the Yom Kippur War, if, crucially, they had been confident that these terms would produce a lasting peace. In contrast, it is almost impossible to imagine Egypt having accepted the terms of 1975–1979 without the Yom Kippur War. This is striking because after a war it is usually the losing side that offers the greatest concessions in political bargaining.

Egyptian Aims. Egypt in 1973 was a revisionist state. Sadat's major material aim was to change the status quo and end Israel's occupation of Arab lands it had captured in 1967, especially the Sinai. There was consistency in Egypt's prewar diplomacy, with Sadat unwilling to shift from his position that Israel must make a total withdrawal from the territories captured in 1967, and resolve the issue of Palestinian refugees, before any agreement could be reached.[22] In 1973 Sadat sought to accelerate the political process by deliberately creating an international crisis that would force the superpowers to pressure Israel into returning to the 1967 borders. The war, he thought, would cause heavy casualties for Israel and undermine its national morale.[23]

In deciding on war, Sadat aimed for a short, sharp, but limited blow to initiate a peace process. The great Egyptian fear was that, over time, Israeli occupation of the Arab lands would become an unchangeable fact on the ground. Without action, détente between the superpowers might serve to freeze the status quo. Meanwhile,

Soviet weapons gave Egypt an opportunity to attack with a reasonable chance of holding its initial gains in the Sinai.[24]

Once the war began, Sadat described his strategic goal as the exhaustion of Israel, his territorial goal as the Gidi and Mitla Passes in Sinai, and his political goal as a peaceful settlement of the Middle East conflict. With the war initially proceeding favorably, on 16 October Sadat demanded a guaranteed withdrawal from all Israeli-occupied territory before any cease-fire occurred. After Israeli victories, Sadat's aims narrowed dramatically, and he requested that Moscow call for an immediate cease-fire at the United Nations.[25]

Egypt had mixed success in achieving its aims. In military terms, the canal crossing proceeded more smoothly than Sadat expected, and 1,200 square kilometers of territory were captured. However, Egypt failed to gain the Gidi and Mitla passes, and it suffered major defeats in the final days of the war. General Shazli, Egypt's chief of staff, toured the front on 19 October and returned to headquarters convinced that the whole war was lost. When Sadat requested a cease-fire, Assad was disheartened and wanted to keep fighting: "Although the enemy has as a result of an accident been able to break our front this does not mean that they will be able to achieve victory."[26] In the end, Egypt accepted cease-fire terms much less favorable than those demanded on 16 October.

Sadat shattered the complacency of Israelis and kick-started a political process that eventually returned the entire Sinai to Egypt. However, this process involved abandoning some traditional positions: no direct negotiations with Israel, and no deal unless all the Arab territories were returned. Pursuing a separate peace left Egypt isolated in the Arab world, although its relations with the United States improved. Israel certainly made concessions after 1973, but Egypt shifted its position to an equal or greater extent by accepting a peace agreement that did not address wider Arab grievances.

Syrian Aims. While Egypt could point to the achievement of some of its aims, Syria in 1973 achieved almost none of its aims. Assad primarily wanted to regain the Golan Heights, lost in 1967, but also talked of restoring Palestinian rights. Syria's war was to be limited: take and defend the Golan Heights, then protect these gains with a Soviet-sponsored cease-fire at the United Nations. The Syrian defense minister later wrote: "We sought to liberate the conquered Arab lands, while Egypt sought to cross the Canal and remain on [both] its banks . . . out of a desire to push things forward on the international plane."[27]

The war left Syria without the Golan, except for a tiny strip of territory. Syria also agreed to limitations on forward troop deployment that left Israeli control of the Golan Heights more secure than ever. Syria made no progress on the aim of Palestinian rights.[28] Efforts to achieve Arab unity were partially successful. Egypt and Syria effectively coordinated the surprise attack; several Arab states dispatched troops to front-line service; and the collective use of oil as a weapon was a striking move. However, these developments must be balanced by Egypt's unilateral pursuit of a cease-fire, which left Assad astonished and angry. At the subsequent Geneva talks, Israel was faced by an Egyptian and Jordanian delegation, not by a united Arab world. In 1979, in response to Egypt's peace process with Israel, Egypt's membership of the Arab League was suspended. Ultimately, the Yom Kippur War engendered almost as much disunity as it did unity among Arab states.

There is a striking gap between the perceptions of Arab victory and Israeli defeat in 1973 and the material outcome viewed through a Framework 1 score-keeping analysis. The material gains and aims achieved in the war suggest a moderate Israeli victory, partial success and partial failure for Egypt, and a substantial failure for Syria.

| Framework 2: Match-Fixing

Score-keeping clearly fails to explain perceptions of victory and defeat in the Yom Kippur War. Perceptions can be much better accounted for by a Framework 2 match-fixing approach, which analyzes how Arab and Israeli judgments were shaped by mind-sets, salient events, and social pressures. These factors in effect fixed the result in favor of the Arab states in the minds of observers on all sides. Chart 7.3 summarizes the key factors at work in this case.

Mind-sets

The perception of the Yom Kippur War as an Arab victory and an Israeli defeat was influenced in part by several key beliefs held by Israelis and Arabs prior to the war.

Mind-sets and Metrics of Success. For both Israelis and Arabs, perceptions of the Yom Kippur War were strongly influenced by expectations arising out of the Six-Day War in 1967. For many Israelis the 1967 war established a metric for measuring victory in future wars that was extremely hard to achieve. In 1967 Israel launched a spectacularly successful surprise attack and captured territory of strategic and religious significance. The Six-Day War encouraged the expectation that Israel would be secure, self-sufficient, and prosperous—that it could control its own destiny. The fears that preceded the 1967 war in Israeli society amplified the subsequent feelings of relief and success, because the outcome far exceeded expectations. In contrast, after the 1973 war began, prewar confidence was replaced by a general feeling of victimization, shock, and insecurity that cast Israeli military reverses in a dramatically negative light.[29]

Match-fixing factors	Affected aspect of judgment	
	Metrics	Information
Mind-sets		
Expectations	X	
Arab honor	X	
Israeli beliefs		X
Salient events		
Time points	X	
Symbolic events		X
Social pressures		
Media and elite		
manipulation	X	X

CHART 7.3. Key match-fixing factors influencing perceptions of victory and defeat in the Yom Kippur War.

In effect, the 1967 war created an Israeli mind-set built on a series of illusions, the shattering of which in October 1973 was sufficiently painful that many Israelis ignored or downplayed clear evidence of their country's military victory. "How could this have happened?" was their dominant concern. In October 1973 Israeli military supremacy was considered a given and expectations of victory in any future conflict with the Arabs were extremely high. Israel had enjoyed a series of successes since 1948: the War of Independence; the Sinai campaign in 1956; massive immigration; a strong economy; and the triumph of 1967. These events, and above all the Six-Day War, created confident assumptions. Ariel Sharon proclaimed, "Israel is now a military superpower . . . We can conquer in one week the area from Khartoum to Baghdad and Algeria." In March 1973 Yitzhak Rabin found that Israel had a "self-confident, almost smug aura to it, as befits a country far removed from the possibility of war."[30]

The Arabs were widely seen by Israelis as uneducated and unsophisticated, and the Arab states were viewed as deeply divided. According to the journalist and author Abraham Rabinovich: "An attitude of disdain for Arab military capability had etched itself insidiously into the [Israeli] national psyche." This was not simply a belief that Arab tactics had failed in 1967, but faith that a deep cultural, social, and educational gulf existed between Israel and the Arab states and gave Israel a huge advantage in war. There was an element of the so-called groupthink phenomenon: a shared set of beliefs among leaders in Israel that reinforced one another and encouraged an underestimation of Arab potential.[31] With remarkable ease, dissonant facts were made to fit the prevailing view. The scornful attitude toward Arab forces created a governmental preconception that any attack could be quickly held and then defeated in two or three days. General Elazar remarked in 1973 about the front with Syria: "We'll have one hundred tanks against their eight hundred. That ought to be enough." Elazar claimed that the air force would "finish off Syria in half a day." Moshe Dayan commented on a potential Egyptian attack across the Suez Canal: "We'll step on them, I will crush them, let them come." One Israeli recalled having been in synagogue on Yom Kippur when the siren went off: "A man sitting next to me said smiling: The war will be over by nightfall; the Arabs must have been crazy to start with us again."[32]

Israelis saw the Six-Day War as a model for future wars and largely ignored developments indicating that the next conflict might be different. Increased Soviet backing for Egypt and Syria included the provision of antitank weaponry as well as SAM missile batteries that would challenge the Israeli defense force's previous dominance. Arab solidarity had also increased and included plans to use the oil weapon against states that supported Israel. In 1973 Israelis set the metric for success at close to total triumph, rather than pursuing a more realistic assessment of what might be expected by a country of three million against one hundred million Arabs backed by the Soviet Union.

It was a traumatic experience for many Israelis to have their deeply established views suddenly proved incorrect. According to Rabinovich: "Viewing the Arabs through the spectrum of the Six-Day War, the Israelis in 1973 were startled by the daring the Arabs displayed, and by the way they held their ground." As Sharon recalled, Israelis were shaken: "These were soldiers who had been brought up on victories . . . It was a generation that had never lost. Now they were in a state of shock." Moshe Dayan shifted from extreme confidence to extreme depression as news from the front came in. On the first day of the war, Golda Meir and her staff "acted as if they were already in mourning."[33]

Dayan's overconfidence and his subsequent depression were both misplaced. Although the Arab forces were better equipped and used improved tactics in the Yom Kippur War, the performance of the two sides in 1967 and 1973 was more similar than many Israeli observers believed. The 1967 rout had given a falsely negative impression of the Arab armies, because this rout had resulted from poor decisionmaking rather than from a fundamental inability to fight. The Israelis had also fought in 1967 with the advantages of surprise against enemies who were largely unprepared and uncoordinated. In being forced to shake off overconfident misconceptions resulting from the 1967 war, the Israelis lurched to the other extreme in their perceptions of the Yom Kippur War, exaggerating the Arab states' capability and the extent of their success. In 1973 Egypt, Syria, and their allies had fought under optimal conditions—gaining surprise, outnumbering Israeli forces at times by 10:1 or more, using the oil weapon, benefiting from Israeli intelligence failures—*and they had still lost.* After eighteen days of fighting, Israel had recaptured from Syria all the land lost in the north, and had advanced to within artillery range of Damascus. Israel had broken through the Egyptian lines and surrounded much of Egypt's army in the Sinai. In both wars the Arabs fought resiliently on the defensive, but the Israelis' tactics, their coordination with close air support, the improvisation of their commanders, their tank gunnery, and the quality of their aircraft were all consistently superior to those of their enemies.[34] For example, the fighting in the Sinai on 14 October 1973, the second-largest tank battle in history (after the 1943 battle of Kursk in Russia), was similar to events in 1967, with heavy Arab losses attributable to poor offensive ability, weak leadership, and unimaginative tactics.

In Arab countries, too, the outcome of the Yom Kippur War was viewed with a mind-set heavily influenced by the Six-Day War. In 1967 there had been considerable prewar confidence in Egypt, which was then followed by anguish and hopelessness. The war engendered strong feelings of insecurity and humiliation in the Arab world. The Israelis were not weak and inferior, as they had been told, but stronger than their Arab neighbors. A literature emerged in the Arab states of despair and the need for spiritual resurrection. The trauma of defeat weakened the legitimacy of some Arab rulers, although it did not immediately lead to their ousting. The political scientist John Waterbury wrote that the Six-Day War "led to the disgrace of the Egyptian Army, the suicide of its leader, Field Marshal Hakim Amer, and treason trials for its senior officers." Fears about a repeat of the 1967 rout amplified the psychological effect of unexpected Egyptian and Syrian successes in 1973. Arab commentaries on the 1973 war self-consciously compared the situation with 1967, emphasizing the contrast by depicting the earlier events in much starker negative language than they had originally used in 1967. The period before the 1973 war was also one in which paranoia had gripped the Arab world about an imminent Israeli-U.S. attack, but these fears and anxieties were suddenly replaced with news of victory.[35]

Minimal Arab metrics for victory in 1973 were also derived from a focus in Arab culture and society on the maintenance of dignity and honor as an important factor in judging success and failure. Sa'ad al-Din Shadhili told the Arab chiefs of staff conference in 1971: "So let us together regain the glory of Arabism and prove to the whole world that we are men of war, who either live proudly or die honorably." El-Gamasy argued that the 1973 war was "a battle of honor for Egypt," which would "erase the shame of 1967." The war might be costly in material terms—the Arab states might even lose on the battlefield—but if the war was perceived as honorable, it was unlikely to be viewed as a defeat. The Pakistani newspaper *Dawn*, for example, ran the headline on 23 October 1973: "Arabs regain honor." In 1973, simply daring to fight Israel was almost enough to create the perception of victory. Egyptian observers tended to downplay the actual battlefield events of the war, which they saw as secondary to the bigger picture of psychological and political gains. "As far as the Arabs were concerned," Chaim Herzog wrote, "the mere fact of initiating the attack was in itself a major move forward and constituted an important political change."[36]

Mind-sets and Information on Success. Israeli mind-sets also shaped the interpretation of information about whether the selected metrics for victory had been achieved in the Yom Kippur War. For many Israelis, the sudden refutation of assumptions, expectations, and myths built on the 1967 conflict was shocking in itself, and it also evoked underlying fears in Israeli society, which had existed since the birth of the state and indeed, throughout Jewish history. The war apparently reaffirmed a consistent theme in Jewish tradition and teaching: that the Jew is an object of hatred for the Gentiles. The metaphor often used was that of the Jewish lamb in a world of wolves. The war reinforced the perception that it was the Jews' destiny to be outcasts. That Israel had failed to arouse sympathy even when it became the victim of aggression in 1973 was, in the words of the political scientist Daniel Elazar, "a hard truth, one that has struck the Israelis with great ferocity." "One of the harshest lessons of the Yom Kippur War," noted the *Jerusalem Post*, "is that we won't manage to win people's sympathy and understanding even by being beaten." The ultra-orthodox Haredim were especially likely to perceive the war as an affirmation of the age-old experience of the Jewish people: the primary cause of the war was the eternal hatred of Gentiles toward Jews. Israel was a ghetto among the nations.[37]

The war in 1973 was also taken as confirmation of the Jewish view of Arabs as implacable opponents, insatiable in their quest to destroy Israel. The *Jerusalem Post* reported on 19 October 1973 that Sadat's aim was the "dismemberment of Israel." Golda Meir declared that the true aim of the Arab states was "the total destruction of the state of Israel." Israel was apparently destined to fight war after war with no peace in sight. The 1973 conflict reinforced fears about the survival of Israel and the Zionist project. Despite the reality of limited Arab aims in the war, the conflict challenged the core idea that Israel was a safe haven for the Jews. Elie Wiesel said in an address entitled "Against Despair" in December 1973: "Like Job we sat in mourning and like Job we felt alone—abandoned by our allies and friends. Forsaken, betrayed. So—how can one not be sad today? How can one be Jewish in this Gentile world of ours and not succumb to despair?" He added: "If we won in '67, it was because the terms of reference were those of the Holocaust. In 1973 it was different: the terms of reference were those of '67." And he concluded: "Judaism teaches man to overcome despair."[38]

There was an apocalyptic tone in Israeli discourse, which included repeated references to the Holocaust. An Arab victory was seen as likely to mean the end of Israel and perhaps the destruction of its people. Many Israelis in 1973 were either Holocaust survivors or descendents of Holocaust survivors. According to the Yiddish newspaper *Morgen Freiheit:* "For the Jewish people, the eruption of the war evoked the specter of a new holocaust. It looked like an attempt to wipe out the Jewish state once and for all—through a war on all sides." The Israeli commander responsible for preparing the demolition of bridges over the River Jordan in anticipation of a Syrian advance later told the Agranat Commission: "The feeling was that there was going to be a holocaust." According to some reports, Moshe Dayan stated that the Third Temple—Israel—was in danger. He advocated the use of nuclear weapons if things got worse, and discussed arming every man and boy in Israel's cities with anti-tank weapons.[39]

Furthermore, the mentality of the average Israeli in 1973 was very different from that in 1948. In the late 1940s Israelis were hardened veterans of World War II and the Holocaust, pioneers building a new society in a hostile land. By 1973 Israelis were more affluent and more confident, living in an increasingly westernized society. It is likely, although difficult to prove, that because of their changing mind-sets Israelis were more sensitive to casualties in 1973 than they had been in 1948. Therefore, the timing of the Yom Kippur War was important: if a similar conflict had occurred twenty years earlier, the reaction of Israelis might have been quite different.

Salient Events

The particular way in which the Yom Kippur War unfolded, and the salience of certain events, also shaped perceptions of success on both sides.

Salient Events and Metrics of Success. Both Israelis and Arabs used comparisons of "before" and "after" time points to decide which side had emerged victorious. However, in the Yom Kippur War the choice of time points was not obvious, and different combinations had a major effect on perceptions of victory. Any of the following "before" time points could be utilized: pre-1967 war, pre-1973 war, or the Arab breakthrough following the successful surprise attack. And the "after" time point could be the Arab breakthrough, the cease-fire, or the 1979 Camp David accords.

Different pairs of time points encouraged different evaluations of which side won. Although there are eight possible pairs of time points (as set out in the numbered cells in Chart 7.4), in reality certain combinations tend to be chosen rather than others, and these pairs favor perceptions of Arab success. Scenarios 1, 2, and 3, which use the situation before the 1967 war as the "before" comparison point, would point strongly toward an Israeli victory—but they are rarely, if ever, employed. One reason these scenarios are not used is the changes of leadership in Egypt and Syria in 1970. Egypt's president, Gamal Abdel Nasser, had been seen as responsible for his country's defeat in 1967. Therefore, for Nasser to regain part or all of the Sinai while Israel retained the other territories it had gained in the 1967 war would have looked like an acceptance of defeat. Sadat's presidency, however, represented a new "before" time point: any territory wrested from Israel was compared with the situation before the 1973 war, and was therefore considered a gain.

The pairs of time points that are usually employed are those in cells 4 and 6 of the chart, which use the situation before the 1973 war as a starting point and focus on the gains made in the initial Arab breakthrough and the eventual return of the Sinai to Egypt. The frequency with which these scenarios are used is due partly to the powerful salience of the Arab surprise attack. The scenario indicated in cell 5, which examines the whole period of the Yom Kippur War, is surprisingly rarely employed, and Moshe Dayan was ex-

"Before" time point	"After" time point		
	Arab breakthrough	Cease-fire	Camp David
Pre-1967 war	1. Israel gains land, but some gains reversed	2. Israel gains land	3. Israel gains land and peace
Pre-1973 war	4. Egyptian and Syrian military victory	5. Israeli military victory	6. Israeli and Egyptian victory (land for peace)
Arab breakthrough	Not applicable	7. Israel recovers and wins militarily	8. Israel recovers and wins militarily, then gains peace

CHART 7.4. Effect of time-point selection on evaluations of victory in the Yom Kippur War. The unshaded cells indicate combinations of time points that suggest an Israeli victory, cell 4 indicates an Arab victory, and cell 6 is an ambiguous outcome.

ceptional in using the scenario in cell 7, which focuses on the recovery of Israel's position after its initial reverses: "A war that began with us being pushed back from the eastern bank of the Suez Canal and ends with us sitting on the west bank is a tremendous victory."[40]

Salient Events and Information on Success. Several events in the Yom Kippur War came to symbolize defeat for Israel, out of all proportion to their actual impact on the battlefield. For example, the conflict tended to be framed in terms of the Arabs' surprise attack, particularly the successful crossing of the Suez Canal by Egyptian forces. According to the psychologist and historian Baylis Thomas: "For Egypt to cross the Suez Canal to establish a beachhead on the east bank was considered impossible by all military observers." Surprise was maintained by an effective plan of deception, with the Arabs making peace overtures until the eve of the war. The crossing was logistically impressive, with the use of high-power water cannons to create gaps in the Israeli earthwork emplacements. Egyptian commandos crossed in rubber boats, overcame the Israeli defenses, built bridges, and quickly transported thousands of troops and tanks across the canal. General El-Gamasy's memoirs focus on this first phase of the war, depicting the canal as a "daunting and unique obstruction" defended by the "invincible Israeli army." Sadat thought he might lose 10,000–20,000 troops in the crossing. Soviet officials in Moscow predicted that 40 percent of Egypt's aircraft would be lost in the initial attack. Seen from this perspective, the crossing defied expectations, with Egypt only losing 208 soldiers. The attack enabled the Arabs to seize the initiative and to rehabilitate their forces' pride and prestige. According to the political scientists Richard Lebow and Janice Stein: "The unexpectedly easy crossing gave President Sadat an enormous psychological and political victory in the Arab Middle East."[41]

The surprise attack became one of the central images of the war. There was huge symbolic power in images of thousands of soldiers crossing the canal in boats shouting in unison "Allahu Akbar," and of assault units planting Egyptian flags along the length of the east bank. One Egyptian army captain recalled: "As soon as the troops saw their flag floating over the east bank, they surged forward sweeping all obstacles in their path. The cry 'God is Great' had a magical effect." The dean of Egyptian letters, Tawfiq al-Hakim, described the crossing of the canal as "not merely a military victory or a material crossing, as much as it is a spiritual crossing to a new stage in our history." "In most Egyptians' eyes," Kirk Beattie notes, "it seemed that after years of bitterness and despair following the catastrophic June 1967 defeat, God had finally bestowed His blessing on Egypt's soldiers and guided their incredible crossing of the Canal. After all, some soldiers had even seen angels riding on the shoulders of their comrades as the miraculous canal crossing unfolded." The journalist and author Howard Blum suggests: "Regardless of the final battles, this war had already been won. History had been rewritten. Egypt's armies had crossed the impregnable canal, caught

Israeli by surprise, and now held the Sinai shore. Arab honor had been restored."[42]

In Israel, too, perceptions of victory and defeat were shaped by the surprise attack. Given prewar beliefs and assumptions, the crossing of the canal represented a psychological *Blitzkrieg*. Only at the last minute did the Israeli government realize that war was imminent. Because of Israeli preconceptions, Arab deception, and previous false alarms, the intelligence service did not manage to separate true danger signals from the background noise. The common Israeli belief was that Sadat would not fight until he had long-range fighter-bombers to use against Israeli air bases and Scud missiles to deter air attacks inside Egypt. These assumptions came to be known as "the Concept," which, Blum notes, "became an article of faith throughout the nation's military and political establishment." Therefore a large number of warnings that war was coming were ignored, including one directly from King Hussein of Jordan. Hussein's "facts were undermined and rationalized until, finally, they meshed with the prevailing assumptions. The Concept remained impregnable."[43]

The fact that the surprise attack occurred on Yom Kippur, the Jewish Day of Atonement, also helped to frame the war in negative terms. It was shocking for many Israelis to be attacked on the holiest day in their calendar. Yom Kippur is a day of fasting and prayer when most Jews spend their time in a synagogue: a day to be cleansed from sin.[44]

The framing effect of the surprise attack proved highly resilient even as military fortunes shifted. In contrast to 1967, there was no period of anticipatory fear in Israel to ease the shock of battle; instead, assumptions and beliefs were suddenly destroyed. On the afternoon of 6 October, Israeli radio announcers described how Egyptians had crossed the canal and Syrians were attacking the

Golan. Residents of Israel were told to black out their windows and prepare for bombing raids. The Israeli commentator Mark Geffen observed that ordinary Israelis were stunned by the early successes of the surprise attack. The first two days of fear and doubt seemed more like two months. When Henry Kissinger, the U.S. secretary of state, visited Israel after the cease-fire, he was moved by the sense of national trauma and exhaustion.[45]

The perception of the Egyptian crossing of the canal as an incredible military feat was overblown. Egypt did overcome considerable logistical hurdles, not least in getting troops and tanks across the 200-yard-wide canal. However, Israel's Bar Lev line in the Sinai was not the French Maginot Line of the 1930s. On the eve of the war, 100,000 Egyptian troops and 1,350 tanks were lined up against an Israeli force of 450 troops and 3 tanks along the canal plus about 90 tanks in the Canal Zone. Another 200 Israeli tanks stood in reserve in the Sinai, but were too far away to prevent the crossing. As Kenneth Pollack observes: "Given the enormous advantages the Egyptians enjoyed in force ratios and strategic surprise, they should have been expected to do far better than they did in their initial offensive." More impressive was Egypt's later defense of its gains on 6–8 October, when Israel's counterattacks were defeated by the careful deployment of Egyptian infantry using antitank weapons. Also more impressive was Israel's crossing to the west bank of the canal on 15–16 October, when the Israelis attacked at the junction between two large enemy forces in an operation that was hastily planned and improvised. However, what mattered were perceptions. Golda Meir told Kissinger that Sadat would survive the end of the war: "He is the hero. He dared."[46]

The focus on the Arabs' surprise attack in evaluations of victory in the Yom Kippur War produced an unusual emphasis on the first battles in determinations of who had won. In most wars we look for victory by examining the situation at the end; the winner is not the side that strikes the initial successful blow. We do not judge the outcome of the 1991 Gulf War, or the war in the Pacific in World War II, in terms of the success of Iraq's and Japan's surprise attacks, but in terms of their later defeats. This standard tends not to be applied to the Arab nations' performance in 1973.

The view of the Yom Kippur War as a defeat for Israel also results from the way the war came to be symbolized in terms of superpower manipulation. The role of the U.S. airlift in the final days of the war created an image of Israeli dependence on the United States for military support. The U.S. airlifted some 22,000 tons of matériel, and 33,000 tons of U.S. aid arrived by sea after 15 November. The war cost Israel the equivalent of one year's GNP, thus making U.S. aid even more important and, according to some observers, turning the country into a client state of Washington. The U.S. and the USSR, to a large extent, determined the timing of the end of hostilities, so that the war ended before Israel could fully consummate its victory. These events suggested Israeli weakness and subjectivity to political constraints, undermining the perception of Israel as victorious.

There are several reasons to be critical of this dominant image of Israeli dependence on the United States. First, superpower intervention tended to balance itself out. Moscow extensively backed the Arab states, both militarily and diplomatically. The Soviets were estimated to have airlifted 15,000 tons of equipment to Syria and Egypt, in addition to 85,000 tons that arrived by sea.[17] Second, by the time U.S. planes landed on 14 October, the course of the war had already shifted in Israel's favor. Most of the U.S. supplies were not used in the war, although the Israelis' knowledge of their future arrival did allow a more liberal use of Israel's own supplies. Third, far from being the client states of the superpowers, Israel and the

Arab countries exercised considerable independence. Georgi Arbatov, an advisor to Soviet premier Leonid Brezhnev, commented: "What could we do? We had to deal with an Egyptian leadership that played its own game. Israel played its own game. It was a lesson for everyone." Moscow had actually opposed the war, fearing its outcome. The KGB head Yuri Andropov argued: "We tried to hold the Arabs back from starting military operations, but they didn't listen."[48] Israeli strategic decisions were influenced, but not determined, by Washington. Fourth, in any case, the U.S. involvement in the conflict could have been interpreted very differently by Israelis: as evidence that the most powerful country in the world was committed to Israel's security. The war strengthened the relationship between the two nations. Fifth, in 1973 many Israelis, in fact, condemned the United States for delaying the transfer of military equipment and for not standing by Israel as the Soviet Union had stood by the Arab states. Israel was apparently damned if it was a client state and damned if it was not.

Social Pressures

The view that the 1973 war was an Arab victory also resulted from social pressures emanating from the leaders and media in the Arab states and in Israel. These pressures tended to shape metrics and information in parallel.

Arab governments in 1973 were extremely concerned about the images they projected to their own people, and nothing was more important than projecting an image of honor and victory in war. Their overwhelming defeat in 1967 was officially presented as "the setback," caused not by the Israelis but by alleged U.S. intervention. Nasser was reluctant to admit the scale of the military losses even to his allies. "The Jordanians," according to King Hussein, "had to wait 48 hours to learn what had really happened in Egypt at the start of the conflict which determined the war's outcome." Hussein too sought to shift the metric for victory downward, writing of the Six-Day War: "We are not defeated. A defeated man is one whose morale has been broken. Our morale has not been weakened." Arab leaders have a significant capacity to shape perceptions given their control of the press. There are limits, however: despite leaders' attempts at manipulation in 1967, their populations recognized that the war had been a catastrophe. El-Gamasy noted in his memoirs that many Egyptians thought the 1967 defeat was worse than had been officially admitted.[49]

The outcome of the 1973 war was altogether more ambiguous, and this gave Arab regimes considerable room to shape perceptions of victory and defeat. During the early part of the war, the media in the Arab states presented a fairly accurate view of the fighting. However, this accuracy faded as the Arab military situation deteriorated. According to the military analyst Edgar O'Ballance: "Many facts were kept from the people, such as the extent of the reverses on the Syrian front, the Israeli penetration of the west bank of the canal, that the Third Army was surrounded, or the extent of Soviet help."[50]

In a sense, Sadat's whole strategy was based on shaping perceptions, and at this task he succeeded to a large extent. Sadat made a bold military move to restore Egyptian pride and achieve a degree of psychological equality before any peace talks began. According to Kissinger, the U.S. administration "did not take seriously the notion of starting an unwinnable war to restore self-respect." Sadat's face-saving reason for accepting the cease-fire was the claim that Egypt was now fighting the United States.[51] Egyptian leaders made great efforts to persuade their own public that they had won the 1973 war, pointing to the opening of the Suez Canal to traffic and the regaining of parts of the east bank. General Isma'il argued in

December 1973 that Egypt had won because it had stormed the Bar Lev Line. Without mentioning that only 450 Israeli soldiers had been stationed along the line to defend the fortifications, Isma'il quoted unnamed foreign generals who, he claimed, had told him that only "an atomic bomb" could overcome the Bar Lev Line. Sadat, in his memoirs, attempted to make the postwar settlement accord with his earlier objectives by altering what his earlier objectives had been. He wrote that in a 1971 speech he had offered a peace agreement based on a staged Israeli withdrawal from the Sinai. However, in the original speech he had described a partial Israeli pullout from the Sinai as a first step in a timetable of full Israeli withdrawal from all the territories captured in 1967, and in any case he had not offered a peace agreement.[52]

In Syria after the war, Assad went to imaginative lengths to explain away the Israeli breakthrough into Syrian territory. These small incursions, he claimed, had occurred because of "continuous supplies from the United States," and had been blocked by brave soldiers who fought to the last man. Furthermore, at the time of the cease-fire, Syria had been preparing a counteroffensive to destroy an enemy "weakened to the point of collapse." Thus a Syrian triumph of historic proportions had been prevented by the Egyptian decision to end the war prematurely.[53]

The United States, and especially Kissinger, also sought to manipulate events and perceptions in the war, but in this case the aim was to prevent a decisive victory, or a perceived decisive victory, by either side. To aid the subsequent peace process, Kissinger wanted the Arab states to achieve a restored sense of honor, preferably accompanied by a limited Israeli military victory. Kissinger told the U.S. secretary of defense, James Schlesinger: "The best result would be if Israel comes out a little ahead but got bloodied in the process, and if the U.S. stayed clean."[54] In this delicate balancing act, Kissinger worked both to defend Israel's security and later to prevent Israel from destroying the Egyptian Third Army, by exerting enormous pressure on Israel to permit the passage of nonmilitary supplies to the surrounded Egyptian troops.

Social pressures on perceptions of victory were also rife in Israel. The Israeli press was routinely censored in military matters. However, the government's manipulation failed to shift perceptions of victory, and may, in fact, have been counterproductive. Media censorship contributed to the exaggerated picture of Israel's military superiority on the eve of the war. As Moshe Jaque of the newspaper *Ma'ariv* commented: "Even when we knew of all sorts of defects, we always submitted to the will of the censor." The editor of *Ha'aretz*, Gershom Shoken, suggested that if the Israeli press had been free to report on security matters "it would have given a warning of the dangers inherent in the buildup of Arab forces, in advance, while expressing doubts in our secure victory."[55] During the first days of the war Israel deliberately suppressed information about how bad the situation was, a move that helped to maintain Israeli morale in the short term. The fall of the Israeli position at Mount Hermon in the Golan Heights, known as "the eyes of the state of Israel," was concealed from the public, although its later recapture was announced. However, news of military reverses arrived through foreign press sources, as well as from soldiers returning from the front lines, creating a damaging credibility gap for the Israeli leadership in the eyes of the public.

| Conclusions

The dominant interpretation of the Yom Kippur War as a victory for the Arab states and a defeat for Israel is substantially divorced from the reality of material gains and aims achieved. A Framework 1 score-keeping analysis suggests that the biggest loser in 1973 was Syria, a state that was defeated on the battlefield and failed to accomplish any of its major material aims. Egypt had a much better war. The timing of the cease-fire meant that Egypt could plausibly show that it had won territory on the east bank; the canal was reopened; and (if we include this as a result of the Yom Kippur War) eventually the Sinai was returned. However, the war was militarily costly, and Egypt won concessions by pursuing a unilateral diplomatic policy with Israel that split the Arab world and left unaddressed such issues as the West Bank, the Golan Heights, and Palestinian rights. In Pollack's words: "Although the Egyptians continue to tout the October War as a great victory, in truth their successes were modest and their failures equal or greater than their achievements."[56]

Many of Egypt's psychological gains, such as a restored sense of national honor, prestige for Sadat, and disillusionment in Israel, resulted from the dominant perceptions of victory, which bore little resemblance to the state of the armies at the end of the conflict. Israel destroyed more tanks, troops, naval vessels, and aircraft than its enemies; captured more land; gained a degree of recognition from Egypt; split the Arab world; and later negotiated a peace treaty that at a stroke removed the principal threat to its survival. Yet in Israel the war is seen as a defeat or a failure.

Many of the features of the 1973 war that were perceived as negative had also been evident in earlier Israeli wars; yet those wars were widely seen as victories. In 1948–1949, for example, Jewish forces were initially driven back and then went on to win, as in 1973, but in the first case, this was viewed as a heroic recovery. Israel's intervention in the Sinai in 1956, like the Yom Kippur War, was curtailed by superpower pressure, but events in 1956 were not seen as a tragedy. Israelis also tended to view the 1969–1970 War of Attrition as a victory because Israel had stood firm in a long war and had resisted international pressure to withdraw from the Sinai without political concessions from Egypt.[57] These same metrics for victory could have been, but were not, applied to the 1973 war. Israelis were far more sensitive to casualties in 1973 than in earlier wars, even though the daily proportion of the population killed was higher in 1967 and overall casualties were higher in 1948–1949. Evidently Israeli tolerance for casualties differed substantially, depending on whether the war in question was viewed as a victory or a defeat.

In 1972 Sadat argued: "We cannot go to war unless victory is guaranteed. The country cannot take another defeat."[58] And yet Egypt and Syria went to war in 1973, when circumstances meant that they were likely to lose any military conflict with Israel. The Israeli forces were better equipped and better led, and displayed far greater offensive and improvisational ability. Conditions at the time also meant, however (as predicted in Chapter 4), that the Arab states were likely to be perceived as victors in almost any outcome, apart from a humiliating rout. In the minds of observers the match had already been fixed. Israel's power encouraged expectations of a rapid victory in any war with its neighbors. Meanwhile, Israel's democratic system allowed for pronounced criticism of the government's performance. Finally, the cease-fire foreclosed any decisive military triumph.

The Arab and Israeli biases in 1967 were almost mirror images of those in 1973. In 1967 Israeli prewar fears and anxiety heightened the exhilaration at the favorable outcome of the Six-Day War, while Arab prewar confidence deepened the sense of defeat. In 1973 it was the Israelis who were confident and thereby shocked by initial setbacks, and the Arab states whose prewar anxieties were replaced by overblown feelings of triumph.

The Yom Kippur War was a psychological conflict: a Framework 2 war. The Israeli defense force won a major military victory on the battlefield, and was poised to strike both of its enemies' capitals. Israel was arguably in a stronger strategic position after the war than it had been immediately before it. Yet few people appreciated this at the time. Match-fixing factors produced a perception of Israeli defeat in both Israel and the Arab states. It was Sadat, therefore, and not Golda Meir, who gained many of the fruits of perceived victory. This was due to the mind-sets of observers, the effects of symbolic events, and successful efforts by Sadat and other Arab leaders to shape perceptions of victory.

In the longer term, match-fixing may have played a positive role because the perceived Israeli defeat facilitated peace negotiations between Egypt and Israel. After the war the Israeli government displayed greater readiness to compromise and return all of the Sinai in exchange for peace. Meanwhile, Sadat's perceived victory gave him the political capital, and Egypt the self-confidence, to recognize Israel. After the Yom Kippur War, partly because of perceptions, the two major combatants were primed for peace. Israel had to perceive itself to lose in 1973, and Egypt had to perceive itself to win, in order for both to achieve the greater prize.

8 | THE U.S. INTERVENTION IN SOMALIA

It would require quite remarkable ignorance to consider all this a UN success.

—IOAN LEWIS AND JAMES MAYALL

Judging by the Somali death toll of 1992, one could reasonably estimate that upwards of a quarter of a million Somali lives were saved. Some failure.

—CHESTER CROCKER

A TRAGIC CASE of match-fixing in international relations concerned the U.S. intervention in Somalia in 1992–1994. It was tragic because perceptions that the intervention had failed would have dramatic and negative consequences for future international responses to humanitarian emergencies, especially in Rwanda in 1994. The U.S. involvement in Somalia produced a number of substantial successes, including saving the lives of tens if not hundreds of thousands of Somalis. Despite these accomplishments, in the minds of observers the outcome became fixed as a debacle for the United States. In particular, the infamous October 1993 firefight in the Somali capital, Mogadishu, in which eighteen U.S. soldiers died, became Exhibit A in the case that America should avoid peacekeeping or nation-building missions. According to the political scientist Robert DiPrizio, perceptions of the events in

Mogadishu, more than anything else, "turned Americans against humanitarian interventions and spawned catch phrases such as *crossing the Mogadishu line.*"[1] Here we examine the process by which a complex and multifaceted operation, with several remarkable successes along with some undoubted mistakes and costs, came to be viewed by Americans as an ignominious failure.

| History

Following its independence in 1960, the East African state of Somalia was first a Soviet and then a U.S. client. Siad Barre seized control of Somalia in 1969 and ruled as dictator for over twenty years. But after the end of the Cold War, Barre was overwhelmed by the uprisings of numerous Somali clans, and was finally ejected from the presidential palace in 1991. Civil conflict spread further after his ousting, as warlords quarreled over the succession. Somalia quickly destabilized from its already fragile condition and became the archetypal failed state. As anarchy spread and Somalia succumbed to drought, the country's agriculture collapsed, relief efforts stalled, and starvation became rife. "The same drought that devastated Somalia also devastated neighbouring Ethiopia and northern Kenya, but only Somalia suffered massive casualties because chaos made it impossible to deliver relief."[2]

In July 1992 the International Committee of the Red Cross warned that 95 percent of Somalia's population was malnourished and 70 percent in imminent danger of starvation. By the end of 1992, out of a population of 6 million, 1,000–3,000 Somalis were starving to death every day, and over the course of the year about 300,000–350,000 had died. UN and NGO programs already in place in Somalia were ineffective. Aid workers and humanitarian convoys were routinely attacked, and international organizations were trapped

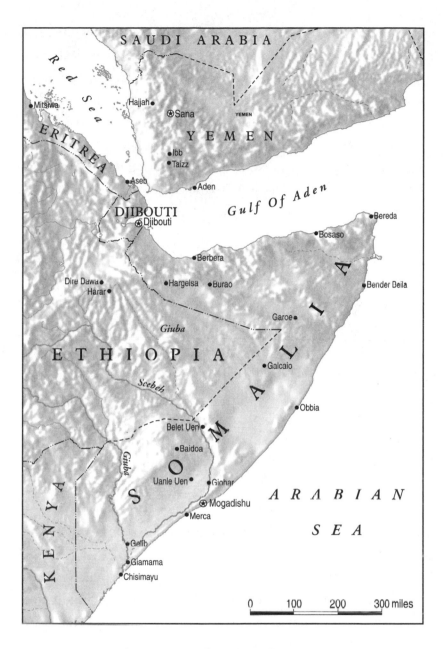

MAP 4. Somalia. Map by Philip Schwartzberg.

into bribing militias for protection, effectively subsidizing their war effort. In August 1992 the United States launched what it dubbed Operation Provide Relief to airlift aid into Somalia, but, without secure ground transportation, the supplies were often appropriated by militias and did not reach many of the most needy civilians. Five hundred UN peacekeepers arrived in September to reinforce the existing UN operation (UNOSOM I), but owing to a lack of manpower and equipment they were restricted to Mogadishu and acted as little more than observers of the anarchy and starvation ravaging the country.[3]

There were two main stages to the U.S. military intervention. Stage 1 began in November 1992, when President George H. W. Bush offered American military and logistical leadership for a UN-sponsored intervention to dramatically improve the delivery of aid to Somalia. Operation Restore Hope involved 28,000 U.S. troops, who began to arrive in Somalia in December 1992, plus 10,000 troops from other countries (together forming the multinational United Task Force—UNITAF). The force had a limited mission: to create secure conditions so that humanitarian aid could get through to desperate civilians, especially in famine-stricken southern Somalia.

Stage 2 of the U.S. intervention began on 4 May 1993, when, as had always been intended, UNITAF was replaced by UNOSOM II. The new mission was given a much broader mandate: not only to establish and maintain security throughout Somalia but also to end the interclan fighting and restore the country's political institutions. Although the Clinton administration largely wrote the expansive UN Resolution 814 for UNOSOM II, the role of the American military was to be far smaller than during the UNITAF phase. U.S. forces were limited to logistical support and a quick-reaction force under U.S. command. However, violence mounted in Somalia, and one warlord in particular—General Mohammed Farah Aidid—was blamed for attacks on UN forces, and a new UN Security Council Resolution (837) called for the arrest of those responsible.

This manhunt led to the infamous battle in Mogadishu on 3 October 1993. What was expected to be a routine mission by a team of Delta Force and U.S. Rangers to capture several of Aidid's high-level associates, turned into a protracted overnight firefight after two U.S. Black Hawk helicopters were shot down. During the ensuing battle, 18 U.S. soldiers were killed (and 80 wounded), along with hundreds of Somalis. A large contingent of armored UN troops was eventually called in to extricate the surviving Americans. In the wake of this battle, on 7 October, President Clinton announced a new policy, which distanced the United States from nation-building efforts in Somalia and led to the withdrawal of all U.S. personnel from the country by March 1994. UNOSOM II pulled out of Somalia in 1995. A decade later, Somalia's transitional government resided in Kenya because it was unsafe to rule from Mogadishu.[4]

Although the United States was somewhat involved in UNOSOM I before December 1992 (for example, flying in food supplies), and although U.S. troops stayed in Somalia until March 1994 (in a very limited capacity), the phase of active U.S. military intervention in the country was from December 1992 to October 1993, and it is on this critical ten-month period that we focus.

Dominant Perceptions of Victory and Defeat

The U.S. intervention in Somalia is usually summarized in one word: "failure." The intervention, according to the media expert Robert Entman, was "framed prominently and resonantly as a disastrous failure." DiPrizio noted that efforts to stabilize the country were "regarded by most as an abominable failure." Mark Bowden, in his bestselling book about the battle in Mogadishu, *Black Hawk Down*, wrote that the mission "was perceived outside the special operations community as a failure." John Hirsch, an advisor to UNITAF, and Robert Oakley, who served as U.S. special envoy to Somalia under both Bush and Clinton, lamented the post-Mogadishu publicity suggesting that "peacekeeping operations and the combined use of force, humanitarian relief, and political involvement in Somalia have been a huge failure." The perceived "lessons" of Somalia are usually negative, referring to the dangers of misguided internationalism and the inadequacies of the United Nations.[5]

When Bush announced the U.S. military operation on 4 December 1992, it was, according to one insider, "a decision generally popular with the public and with the majority in Congress—and also one immediately endorsed by President-elect Clinton." Colin Powell, the chairman of the joint chiefs of staff, was eager to ensure that everything was done to "sell the operation to the American public," including labeling it "Operation Restore Hope to ensure widespread support." In the early stages of UNITAF, 70–80 percent of Americans expressed approval for the president's handling of Somalia. As late as April 1993, 77 percent thought the United States was doing "a good job" rather than "a poor job" of helping the United Nations in Somalia.[6]

However, support for the mission began to wane in the late spring and early summer of 1993, after UNITAF was replaced by the more ambitious UNOSOM II. Approval for U.S. policy in Somalia fell to 51 percent in June and to 41 percent in September. Indeed, by September a narrow majority wanted U.S. forces to leave Somalia rather than stay to preserve the peace.[7]

The battle in Mogadishu on 3 October led to a storm of criticism of the Somalia mission and an additional fall in support. According to a *Time*/CNN poll on 7 October, 60 percent of Americans agreed that: "Nothing the US could accomplish in Somalia is worth the death of even one more US soldier." Approval of President Clinton's handling of Somalia fell to around 30 percent in October.[8]

After Mogadishu, a congressional report blamed the president and the secretary of defense, Les Aspin, for mistakes leading up to the battle. The main issue was Aspin's earlier rejection of a request for armored vehicles, equipment that might have reduced the number of U.S. casualties. Aspin soon resigned, corroborating the perception of failure.

From October to December 1993, most Americans considered the intervention to be "right," but the country was split on whether it had been worth the cost. At the same time a small majority thought the mission had been "a mistake." The one poll that directly asked about success found, two days after the Mogadishu battle, that only 25 percent viewed the intervention "to provide humanitarian relief" as successful and 66 percent saw it as unsuccessful.[9]

Not all Americans judged the Somalia intervention as a failure. A few diplomats such as Oakley have argued that the intervention produced much that was positive. Bowden reported that the U.S. Special Forces who carried out the raid in Mogadishu were "proud of successfully completing their mission," and were annoyed by Clinton's decision to abandon the intervention. The picture among soldiers more generally was mixed.[10]

But overall, it became accepted wisdom that Somalia was a failure. When *Time* and CNN conducted a poll about a possible U.S. intervention in Haiti in 1994, they revealingly asked people if they thought such an action would be "a fairly quick but unsuccessful effort, like the U.S. intervention in Somalia."[11]

| Framework 1: Score-keeping

Were people score-keeping in forming their judgments about the Somalia mission, or were their evaluations biased by match-fixing factors? Because the United States did not face a clear enemy in Somalia, we focus only on U.S. gains and losses and U.S. aims achieved and not achieved, rather than comparing them with those of an enemy.

Material Gains and Losses

We consider the material gains and losses ensuing from each of the two main stages of the U.S. intervention in Somalia: the UNITAF stage and the UNOSOM II stage. Since a fair judgment ultimately rests on the overall gains and losses from both stages, Chart 8.1 summarizes the material changes as a whole from 1992–1994.

The gains and losses of the U.S. mission (as well as the achievement of aims, which we will come to shortly) need to be considered in the light of the inherent difficulties involved in an intervention in Somalia. The United States and the United Nations could not have chosen a country less suitable for creating stable political and economic structures. By 1992 there was open civil war between clan-based warlords, with no peace for the UN peacekeepers to keep. In many other civil wars of the era, such as those in Bosnia and Angola, the combatants were organized into a few large, coherent factions, so the key to peace involved negotiating with two or three main players. Somalia, by contrast, had a dozen or so major factions and many lesser groups. Indeed, the political and so-

| Type of outcome | Event | Material gain or loss? | An aim achieved? | Altering the credit due[a] | | Difficulty[c] |
| | | | | Importance | | |
				For leader	For observer[b]	
Positive outcomes	25,000–1 million Somalis saved	Gain	Achieved	High	Very high	Moderate
	Halving of refugees from 1.5 million to 750,000	Gain	Achieved	High	Very high	Moderate
	Improvements in infrastructure	Gain	Partially achieved	Moderate	Moderate	Moderate
	Capture of Aidid's associates	Gain	Achieved	Moderate	Moderate/low	Moderate
Negative outcomes	43 U.S. dead (about 150 UN fatalities)	Loss	Not achieved	Very high	Moderate/high	Moderate (chance of avoiding)
	1600 Somali fatalities	Loss	Not achieved	Moderate	High	Low (chance of avoiding)
	$2.2 billion cost for U.S.	Loss	Not an aim	Low	Low	Very low (chance of avoiding)
	Failure to capture Aidid	Neither	Not achieved	High	Moderate/high	Moderate/low (chance of achieving)

a. Higher values give *more* credit for positive outcomes and *less* credit for negative outcomes.
b. The importance of a gain or an aim in the minds of observers (in this case the authors) trying to fairly assess its worth.
c. The difficulty of a gain or an aim in the minds of observers (in this case the authors) trying to assess it fairly.

CHART 8.1. U.S. scorecard for the intervention in Somalia (covering both UNITAF and UNOSOM II missions).

cial fabric had unraveled to such an extent that complete stability was an impossible goal for the time being, while moderate improvements in security, together with the alleviation of suffering, were the only realistic objectives. Furthermore, in 1992–1994 the United Nations was engaged in unprecedented peacekeeping efforts around the world, with thousands of personnel in Cambodia, Croatia, and elsewhere. The organization's resources were therefore stretched thin, and now it was intervening in a country that presented a worst-case scenario for delivering aid, let alone for nation-building.[12] Somalia is typically seen as an example of asymmetric warfare, with the powerful United States arrayed against weak Somali insurgents. But in reality it was asymmetric warfare in the opposite sense. On one side there was the David of a few thousand foreign troops, and on the other side the Goliath of Somalia's social, political, and economic decay.

UNITAF/Operation Restore Hope. The first stage in the U.S. military intervention, UNITAF, produced several substantial gains. By the autumn of 1992 Washington's assessment of existing international efforts in Somalia was that "the UN emergency intervention had essentially failed . . . and it was obvious that—whatever the longer-term possibilities—the UN offered no immediate solutions to Somalia's crisis."[13]

In contrast, by the end of the UNITAF operation in May 1993, the humanitarian catastrophe had been substantially alleviated. Areas critical to the relief effort had been secured, and humanitarian organizations were able to distribute aid far more effectively than before. Estimates of the number of Somalis whose lives were saved from violence or famine range from the tens of thousands to more than one million.[14] During this same period, December 1992 to May 1993, the United States suffered only around a dozen casualties, most of them accidental.[15] In other words, for every U.S. soldier *deployed* the lives of between one and forty Somalis may have been saved; for every U.S. soldier *killed*, thousands of Somalis were saved.

Many of those who had fled to refugee camps were able to return home and plant crops. The number of refugees halved from 1.5 million to around 750,000 from 1992 to 1994. Somalia's infrastructure was also repaired or constructed, including roads, schools, bridges, and sanitation, and some 3,500 police were trained (tasks that went beyond the original UN mandate). UNITAF enforced a cease-fire in the worst-hit areas and responded forcefully to attacks. There was some political progress, with warlords signing a far-reaching agreement for national reconciliation at Addis Ababa in March 1993. In contrast to the generally unconcerned and lethargic international responses to humanitarian disasters in the early 1990s, here the international community acted, and to great effect. The UNITAF operation cost the United States about $700 million. The political scientist John Mueller concluded: "Never before, perhaps, has so much been done for so many at such little cost."[16]

UNOSOM II. The second stage in the U.S. military intervention in Somalia, UNOSOM II, produced a rather more mixed picture of gains and losses. Its shortcomings have been copiously documented: incompetence, overstretching of resources, poor diplomacy, as well as weaknesses in command and control.[17] The difficulties of coordinating a multinational force made up primarily of troops from developing nations left a post-UNITAF vacuum in which the militias could reorganize.

Yet at the same time, continuing the work of UNITAF, there were some further material improvements, including infrastructure development, judicial reform, food aid, and the combating of disease. At the very least, as Chester Crocker, a former assistant secretary of state for African affairs, suggested, the intervention "knocked a hideously costly, stalemated clan war off dead center and opened the field for local initiatives." Major warlords agreed to form a national government. The fact that these accords broke down was hardly surprising given the country's previous warfare, and does not remove the fact that the possibility of peace had improved, albeit modestly. In any case, attempts to improve the material situation on the ground were soon overshadowed by the decision to hunt down one particular warlord—Aidid.[18]

This manhunt, and the October battle in Mogadishu, also produced a mixed picture of gains and losses. The battle was far more costly than anticipated, and 18 U.S. soldiers died with dozens more wounded. An unknown number of civilians were also caught in the crossfire. Yet at the same time, between 500 and 1,000 or more members of Aidid's forces were killed—in purely military terms, a remarkable asymmetry in favor of the United States. The raid also captured two of Aidid's key associates—the targets of the mission. Mark Bowden suggests: "By most indications, Aidid's supporters were decimated and demoralized the day after the Battle of Mogadishu. Some, appalled by the indecency of their countrymen, were certain the United States would violently respond to such an insult and challenge. They contacted UN authorities offering to negotiate, or simply packed their things and fled. These are the ones who miscalculated. Instead the United States did nothing, effectively abandoning the field to Aidid and his henchmen."[19]

Material Aims

Material gains and losses evidently do not, in themselves, account for the dominant perception of U.S. failure in Somalia. Next we consider whether these perceptions can be accounted for by the achievement of U.S. material aims.

UNITAF/Operation Restore Hope. UNITAF was authorized by UN Security Council Resolution 794 to "use all necessary means to establish as soon as possible a secure environment for humanitarian relief operations in Somalia." The major motivation for U.S. intervention was humanitarian. President Bush publicly stated that this was his aim, and he seems to have been sincere. At the end of 1992, with reports of starvation in Somalia on television, Bush told Colin Powell and Secretary of Defense Dick Cheney: "I—we—can't watch this anymore. You've got to do something." Bush saw a disaster developing which he could ameliorate at a limited cost to the United States. Brent Scowcroft, his national security advisor, believed that an intervention in Somalia could show other developing nations that the United States was not indifferent to their plight, strengthening the U.S. position as a world leader.[20]

There may, of course, have been other aims as well, such as deflecting the incoming Clinton administration from intervening in Bosnia. In some ways the mission was a parting gesture from an outgoing president eager to make his mark on history. The media were not the primary factor driving the decision to intervene; instead, heightened media interest followed administration announcements. Television pictures helped propel the administration further in the interventionist direction in which it was already moving.[21]

UNITAF therefore had a restricted objective: to improve the humanitarian situation by providing a secure environment for the delivery of food. From the start, the United States intended to quickly hand over operations to the United Nations. In a public address, Bush stressed the limited objectives and declared that the United

States would "not stay one day longer than is absolutely necessary." America sought to treat some of the worst symptoms of Somali anarchy, and to leave efforts to tackle the underlying disease to the United Nations.[22]

Overall, in pursuing its aims, UNITAF was a spectacular success. As William Durch, an expert on peacekeeping, concluded: "In general UNITAF performed its assigned tasks in an exemplary manner." Within a few weeks the intervention had achieved almost all of its goals, stabilizing the region, enforcing a cease-fire, building infrastructure, and delivering food. The operation proceeded well ahead of schedule, finishing its task in 146 days rather than the official target of 240 days. Of course, this success partly reflected the limited scope of its aims.[23]

UNOSOM II. UNOSOM II, which took over from UNITAF on 3 May 1993, was given a far broader mandate: to end the civil war in Somalia and build a democratic polity. UN Resolution 814 instructed UNOSOM II "to provide humanitarian and other assistance to the people of Somalia in rehabilitating their political institutions and economy and promoting political settlement and national reconciliation." UNOSOM II aimed to promote and monitor a cease-fire, seize small arms, restrict the movement of heavy weapons, protect international personnel and humanitarian deliveries, de-mine affected areas, and repatriate refugees. The U.S. ambassador to the United Nations, Madeleine Albright, called it "an unprecedented enterprise aimed at nothing less than the restoration of an entire country as a functioning member of the community of nations."[24]

Clearly, in the spring and summer of 1993, UNOSOM II did not come close to satisfying its full mandate. The civil war continued, and no democratic polity was formed. The transition from UNITAF to UNOSOM II was poorly handled. There were also numerous, and partly avoidable, problems of command and control, largely because, unlike UNITAF, UNOSOM II had no single dominant contingent to provide effective leadership.[25]

However, in assessing UNOSOM II we should ask whether it made reasonable progress toward the goals mandated in Resolution 814, given UNOSOM II's capabilities and its operating environment. On a strict reading of the resolution, the UN Security Council had gifted UNOSOM II with mission impossible. If UNOSOM II had created political stability in Somalia, it would have been an extraordinary success—probably the greatest achievement in the history of the United Nations. Theoretically, UNOSOM II had 20,000 troops, 8,000 logistical staff, and 2,800 civilian staff, plus 1,300 U.S. quick-reaction troops, but many of these forces were never deployed. UNOSOM II's capabilities were qualitatively far inferior to the U.S.-dominated UNITAF. There was also no peace for UNOSOM II to keep, and it was a tough assignment simply keeping the lid on the violence in Mogadishu. Nevertheless, UNOSOM II achieved some success under horrendous circumstances. After all, Resolution 814 authorized the operation for "an initial period through 31 October 1993," by which time the United Nations would review its "progress toward accomplishing the purposes of the present resolution."[26] In that time, as mentioned earlier, there were some signs of tangible success.

Our focus in this chapter is mainly on U.S. success or failure, not UN success or failure (although obviously they overlap to a considerable extent). It is not clear exactly what the United States aimed to achieve under the auspices of UNOSOM II. On the one hand, Clinton's staff was instrumental in writing the ambitious language in the new UN resolution. On the other hand, the United States greatly reduced its involvement compared with UNITAF.[27] UNOSOM II provided an exit strategy for the bulk of U.S. forces. It is not clear whether the United States intended UNOSOM II to completely transform the situation in Somalia, or more likely, whether it was designed to facilitate a moderate degree of political progress.

After attacks on UN troops, the goals of UNOSOM II shifted toward hunting for Aidid, as mandated by a new UN Resolution (837). Whether it was wise to go after Aidid is debatable. What we do know is that Washington spurred the process and offered Special Forces for the task. The October battle in Mogadishu did not, of course, go as intended. After two U.S. Black Hawk helicopters were shot down, U.S. forces had to reach the crash sites on foot, and then defend against a militia onslaught while a rescue mission was arranged. Some of the U.S. casualties may have resulted from tactical mistakes and hasty improvisation. The soldiers were not as well equipped as they might have been, lacking armored vehicles and night-vision goggles (the raid had been expected to take only about thirty minutes). However, the primary objective of the Mogadishu raid, to capture two of Aidid's associates, was achieved, and Aidid's forces suffered heavy losses. As the policy analysts Daniel Byman and Matthew Waxman sum it up: "Aidid's rag-tag militia forced the United States to back down, even though [the militia] 'lost' the battle of Mogadishu, suffering perhaps a 50-to-1 casualty ratio."[28]

If we assess the overall material gains and losses resulting from the U.S. intervention in Somalia, while taking into account the achievement of U.S. material aims, the intervention can be viewed as a partial success. UNITAF was not only moral in intention, it was also extremely effective, saving thousands, perhaps hundreds of thousands, of lives and achieving the goals set for it by President Bush ahead of schedule.

In contrast, UNOSOM II never achieved anything close to its full mandate, because of problems inherent to the difficult environment, the scale of the task it was set, a lack of troops and resources, and operational mistakes. But its net effect was probably moderately positive — marginal progress in the face of unfavorable odds. The U.S. raid on 3 October went badly wrong, and yet even this episode was a victory by traditional standards of battle: the main mission objective was achieved and vastly more enemy combatants than Americans were killed. Most of the U.S. efforts in Somalia were successful; indeed, it was when the United States was absent that UNOSOM II was less effective. Of all the countries involved in Somalia in 1992–1994, the United States had the most reason to feel pride in its performance.

In comparing the dominant perceptions of success and failure with a score-keeping analysis, we can see that events on the battlefield did have some impact on people's evaluations. American support for the mission declined in the summer of 1993, as Aidid kept slipping away, and declined further after the casualties in Mogadishu.[29] Overall, however, there is a striking gap between perceptions and the tangible gains and aims achieved. A mission with several substantial successes became viewed in simple black-and-white terms as a failure. Material outcomes in Somalia were evidently not the main factors driving U.S. perceptions of victory and defeat.

| Framework 2: Match-Fixing

Perceptions of success in 1992–1994 can be better explained by Framework 2 match-fixing factors (see Chart 8.2). Because of a

Match-fixing factors	Affected aspect of judgment	
	Metric	Information
Mind-sets		
Demographics and partisanship	X	X
Timing and nature of the intervention	X	
Casualty aversion	X	
Expectations	X	
Aversion to nation-building		X
Salient events		
The hunt for Aideed	X	
The battle in Mogadishu		X
Social pressures		
Media and elite manipulation	X	X

CHART 8.2. Key match-fixing factors influencing perceptions of victory and defeat in Somalia.

combination of mind-sets, salient events, and social pressures, people imagined that the U.S. performance in Somalia was an outright failure. They were wrong. It was, at worst, a qualified success.

Mind-sets

Mind-sets and Metrics and Information on Success. Polling data suggest that there are significant demographic differences in perceptions of success in the U.S. intervention in Somalia, but this information does not allow us to determine whether judgments resulted from biased metrics or biased information. So we consider these broader demographic factors first. Initial opinion polls in January 1993 showed strong support for the mission across race. But over time a significant racial gap developed: by November, blacks approved of Clinton's policy by 48 percent to 47 percent, while whites disapproved by 57 percent to 34 percent. Greater black support for the intervention partly reflected the fact that most black voters were Democrats. Although there were few strong partisan effects in judgments about Somalia until elite criticism increased in October 1993, Republicans were somewhat less supportive than Democrats. By November, following fierce partisan attacks in Congress, Democrats disapproved of Clinton's Somalia policy by 47 percent to 45 percent, but Republicans disapproved by 71 percent to 20 percent.[30]

However, black support for the mission went beyond partisanship: it also reflected a greater tendency for black Americans to favor interventionist efforts in Africa. Blacks, for example, stated that the events in Somalia made them more rather than less willing to support the use of force for humanitarian relief by 32 percent to 4 percent. For whites the figures were reversed: only 11 percent were more supportive of the use of force for humanitarian efforts because of Somalia, and 48 percent were less supportive. In this same poll, Democrats and Republicans offered similar views about whether Somalia had made them more or less inclined to support humanitarian operations.[31]

Gender differences were sometimes apparent in judgments about Somalia. Men tended to support the mission more than women, both before the battle in October (68 to 61 percent on average) and after (46 to 35 percent on average). This is similar to previous conflicts, such as the 1991 Gulf War, for which support was consistently higher among men than among women. Men were also more attracted to the Wild West–style hunt for Aidid (there was even a reward poster, offering $25,000 for information leading to his capture). In June 1993, after attacks on UN personnel, 76 percent of men but only 58 percent of women thought it was a good idea to capture Aidid, even at the risk of becoming involved in Somalia's civil war.[32]

Mind-sets and Metrics of Success. Other elements of observers' mind-sets specifically shaped the metrics employed to judge success in Somalia. If we compare Americans' perceptions of Somalia with their perceptions of other situations in which the United States has used force since 1945, we can see that both the timing and the humanitarian nature of the mission in Somalia influenced judgments. If the Mogadishu battle had occurred during the Vietnam war, the metric for success would have been very different: the deaths of eighteen soldiers would barely have been noticed, the high enemy casualties would have been lauded, and the battle might well have been viewed as a success. Instead the battle shocked the American public because it occurred in 1993, when it was "the bloodiest single combat episode involving U.S. casualties since Vietnam — worse than anything in the Gulf War."[33] Furthermore, the fact that the intervention was humanitarian reduced the tendency to see enemy casualties as being, in any sense, a sign of success. Americans were meant to be saving Somalis, not killing them, and Somalis were meant to be throwing flowers at Americans, not shooting them.

Were Americans especially averse to U.S. casualties in the 1990s? Many writers have suggested that negative reactions to Somalia were based on such an aversion. According to John Mueller: "Despite the enormous number of lives the international mission appears to have saved, U.S. policy there has been labeled a failure in large part because a few Americans were killed in the process. In essence, when Americans asked themselves how many American lives peace in Somalia was worth, the answer came out rather close to zero."[34]

There is some truth to this, but we need to carefully qualify the

idea that aversion to casualties was the primary explanation for perceptions of failure in Somalia. The political psychologist Steven
Kull has found that the U.S. public is not averse to casualties as
such, even in peacekeeping missions. Often casualties elicit the opposite response: a desire to reinforce U.S. troops or to retaliate. At
the start of the intervention in Somalia, Americans appeared to be
willing to tolerate some casualties: support for the mission fell only
1 percent if casualties were mentioned in polling questions.[35] The
intervention was still very popular in April 1993, after four American deaths. Evaluations took a downturn during the early summer
of 1993, when there were still only a few U.S. casualties, implying
that other processes had more effect on public perceptions of success. Furthermore, earlier U.S. interventions in Panama and Grenada resulted in similar levels of American casualties, but support
remained high for these missions. What was the difference? Following a pattern seen in most of our case studies, observers were especially sensitive to U.S. casualties in Somalia because the soldiers
were seen as having died in a futile and losing exercise. It seems
that perceptions of victory drove tolerance for casualties, rather than
the other way around.

Mind-sets also influenced the metric for success because of expectations formed in the first few days of the operation. The intervention occurred during a period of heightened confidence about
UN activism, resulting from the end of the Cold War and the
success of the 1991 Gulf War. Somalia was to be a demonstration of
the new world order promised by the first President Bush in 1991.
Although many Americans recognized that Somali militias would
target U.S. forces (and therefore expected some fighting), the public understood the intervention to be narrowly humanitarian and of
short duration, as Bush had promised. In the early days of UNITAF,
51 percent thought U.S. involvement would be over within six

months. Americans were confident and expected success: 77 percent thought the United States would achieve its objectives, and only 17 percent felt it would withdraw without having achieved its objectives.[36]

Early success with UNITAF set a high bar for subsequent months. The press was ready and waiting for the U.S. marines when they stormed ashore in Somalia on 9 December 1992, in time for the evening news back home. For many people, this was the last memorable image before the dreadful scenes of October 1993, and it was an image of hope and of the United States acting as a Good Samaritan. In preceding weeks the media had strongly played up the suffering of the Somali population, and the developing impression was one of decisive U.S. force being employed to solve the problem. The United States had stepped in where the United Nations had failed. When President Bush arrived in Somalia in December 1992, he was greeted by adoring crowds; when UN Secretary General Boutros Boutros-Ghali arrived a few days later, his motorcade was pelted with stones and fruit. As Crocker comments: "Perhaps, ironically, the impressive leadership, coherence, and dramatic success of the U.S.-led UNITAF phase made it look too easy, facilitating the 'mission creep' that produced UNOSOM II's vast nation-building mandate." Hirsch and Oakley sound a similar tune: Operation Restore Hope "raised unrealistic expectations" of the UN. When UNOSOM II took over, the only way to go was down. Clinton did little to explain the new mission's objectives, and as a result, it was "unsurprising that the October 3 events generated an immediate political explosion."[37]

U.S. observers tended to set daunting metrics for success for UNOSOM II's political, social, and economic work in Somalia. In a war between separate states, the standard for success is reasonably clear—defeat the enemy army in battle or capture a certain strategic target—but in internal conflicts like the one in Somalia, the standard for success is much less obvious. Americans sometimes based their metrics for success on their own values, ideals, and democratic standards. Success would require resolving the conflict between warring Somali factions and building a stable political system. More reasonable observers might instead have asked whether UNOSOM II had a positive impact relative to the goals of its creators, its capabilities, and the limitations of the environment. Indeed, the very phrase "nation-building" establishes an extremely high metric for success. It is not clear how a few thousand UN troops of mixed quality were meant to turn an anarchical society into a "nation." Either UNOSOM II would create domestic stability in Somalia (in which case it would be, by some margin, the greatest success in UN history) or the intervention would probably be seen as a failure.

Mind-sets and Information on Success. With Somalia, Americans not only tended to employ harsh metrics when judging nation-building efforts, they also tended to perceive incoming information about the success of nation-building in a critical light. Americans simply do not like nation-building. Polls suggest that Americans are quite favorable to the use of force to restrain the aggressive foreign policies of other states. They are also sympathetic to the use of force for strictly humanitarian operations. However, as the political scientist Bruce Jentleson argues, the U.S. public has little stomach for engendering internal political change. From the start in Somalia, Americans were reluctant to go beyond the delivery of aid to create a working government, and this reluctance influenced the way the mission, especially UNOSOM II, was perceived and evaluated.[38]

In part this aversion to nation-building results from the lack of clear-cut feedback about success in such conflicts compared with fighting against states on traditional battlefields. It may, additionally, reflect a perception that it is more legitimate to use force to restrain states in the international arena than to intervene in their domestic affairs. Opposition to nation-building is also influenced by memories of Vietnam. Such memories revived buried fears about getting bogged down in an unwinnable war against a shadowy enemy in civilian clothes. The analogy with Vietnam seemed to signal that the United States could not win in the long run: it could only sink deeper into the Somalia quagmire. Polling questions that evoked Vietnam by using the phrase "bogged down" produced more critical responses than similar questions without the evocative phrase. In December 1992, 30 percent of Americans thought the United States would get "bogged down" in Somalia and 62 percent thought it would quickly achieve its goals there. At that same time, another poll (which did not evoke Vietnam) found that 77 percent of Americans thought the United States would achieve its goals in Somalia.[39]

After the Mogadishu raid but before Clinton announced his withdrawal plan, 56 percent of Americans said they thought there was "a real danger" that Somalia would become "another Vietnam." At this time, the United States had lost a few dozen soldiers in Somalia as compared with tens of thousands in Vietnam. Even after Clinton had declared the plan for U.S. withdrawal, between 22 and 26 October 1993, 62 percent thought U.S. intervention in Somalia "could turn into another Vietnam."[40]

Therefore, once the Somalia mission shifted to nation-building, bringing analogies with Vietnam more sharply into focus, it was likely that U.S. observers would judge incoming information more critically and show greater sensitivity to costs, almost regardless of what occurred on the ground. Indeed, as we saw earlier, there was a sharp drop-off in public support soon after the UNITAF humanitarian operation switched to the broader objectives of UNOSOM II in May 1993.[41]

Salient Events

Particular events in the Somalia intervention influenced American perceptions of success out of all proportion to their importance on the ground, and almost invariably in a negative direction.

Salient Events and Metrics of Success. By deciding to go after Aidid, thus personalizing the operation in Somalia into a Wild West–style manhunt, the United States created a clear-cut metric for success: whether Aidid was captured or not. Other humanitarian and political operations were proceeding in the background, but in the U.S. media, and therefore in the minds of a sporadically attentive American public, the intervention boiled down to finding one man.

There followed a series of attacks and counterattacks in which a number of UN troops and members of Aidid's militia were killed. Aidid himself remained elusive, a state of affairs that began to color perceptions of the whole mission. With the United States having framed the objective in these terms, as one analysis put it, the "failure to capture him was seen as a failure of the entire U.N. operation and has cast a long shadow on forceful humanitarian efforts—the powerlessness of the 'Somalia syndrome,' which is the post-Cold War equivalent of the Vietnam syndrome."[42]

Salient Events and Information on Success. The phrase "Black Hawk Down" still encapsulates the disbelief and shock with which Americans reacted to the unfolding chaos in Mogadishu, on 3 October 1993. Certain events in the firefight took on such enormous symbolic power that they became many people's primary source of information with which to judge the whole operation in Somalia.

The battle did not turn an enthusiastic public against the mission—most Americans were already skeptical by September—but the images did strongly entrench critical appraisals of the intervention. For opponents and fence-sitters, worst-case fears seemed to have been confirmed. For many former supporters, things had now gone irretrievably wrong.

In the battle, Somali fighters captured Michael Durant, the surviving pilot of one of the two downed helicopters. The image of Durant as a prisoner plastered the cover of *Time, Newsweek,* and *U.S. News and World Report.* It was hard to avoid an emotional reaction. In another infamous event, the bodies of dead Americans were paraded through Mogadishu, stripped and mutilated—images that were widely broadcast on American television. In one such image, as the media analyst Cori Dauber describes it, "an American body, face obscured, is shown from the waist up, stripped, being pulled through the streets by a group of Somalis with their backs to the body who appear fairly nonchalant about the entire affair. In the other image that received wide play, a body, clearly American only because it is stripped and therefore obviously white, is hogtied, surrounded by celebrating Somalis." Mark Bowden argues that the display of American bodies was very deliberate: "It has a clear intent: to insult, to challenge and to frighten the enemy, and to excite and enlist allies . . . Paul Watson, a white Canadian journalist, moved unharmed with his [camera] through the angry mobs in Mogadishu on October 4, 1993. The idea is to spread the image."[43]

The battle in Mogadishu, the capture of Durant, and the desecration of American corpses were the lead story on all the major networks from 5 October until 9 October. The tag line for reports was often America's "humiliation." A large majority of Americans said they had seen the images. Two days after the raid 59 percent had seen the pictures; by mid-October, 84 percent had seen them. The footage, as Entman notes, "activated the anti-interventionist, quagmire schema" among those watching back home. What mattered was not just the deaths themselves but also the particular manner of the deaths, the images that were produced, and the media's handling of the issue. The two corpses had more impact than the other sixteen dead Americans. Polls suggest that Americans who saw the images were somewhat more inclined to support an immediate pullout than those who did not see them (although majorities of both groups favored withdrawal). As soon as the images were shown, the White House and Congress were inundated with messages and phone calls—many demanding that U.S. troops be immediately brought home. Congressmen referred to the images in angry speeches insisting on withdrawal. On 13 October, *Time* ran a story headlined: "Anatomy of the Disaster in Somalia." *Newsweek*, having supported the intervention in preceding months, adopted an alarmist tone with its 18 October headline: "Trapped in Somalia."[44]

In a double-whammy effect, the Mogadishu battle had particular power as a source of *information* because of the *metrics* that Americans were employing to judge success. One of these metrics was whether or not Aidid had been captured, and after 3 October he was still very plainly at large. The battle also had a shocking effect because it was used to judge metrics constructed in the heady early days of the intervention. Observers would often compare what happened in October with the Somalis' enthusiastic reaction to the arrival of the marines back in December. Now Somalis were shooting at Americans. Indeed, rather than fairly assessing the complex dynamics of the U.S. mission over time, observers contrasted snapshots from December and October and largely ignored or missed what had happened in the months in between.

This effect was due in part to the varying attention paid by most Americans to events in Somalia. Attention was high immediately after the two salient and widely covered events (the landing of the marines in December 1992 and the Mogadishu battle in October 1993), but between these two periods Somalia dropped off the media and public radar. In January 1993, 52 percent of Americans claimed to be closely following events in Somalia; by June the figure was between 7 and 16 percent; then it leapt back above 50 percent after the Mogadishu raid. In other words, a large majority of those who ever paid close attention to Somalia did so only during two short periods of time—and the sharp contrast between those periods came to dominate their evaluations. The first event was carefully orchestrated and highly successful; the second was unexpected and seemingly disastrous. The media and polling organizations, too, displayed varying levels of interest in Somalia: almost 80 percent of the opinion polls about the intervention were conducted either in the first two months of the operation or in the month after the Mogadishu battle.[45] From April to October, a public inherently skeptical about the shift toward nation-building, and at the same time largely unaware of what was occurring on the ground, began to become more negative about the mission. When they turned on their televisions in October to discover carnage in Mogadishu, Americans had a clear memory of U.S. soldiers arriving to hand out food, but only a vague notion about the trials and tribulations that had occurred since.

With just these two data points being contrasted, the impression was one of U.S. troops going to help Somalis, but later being killed and mutilated for their efforts. The journalist and former aid worker Michael Maren commented: "A cartoon by Oliphant seemed to sum it up for most Americans. In frame one, a soldier is feeding a hungry Somali child. In frame two the child shoots the soldier. Copies of that cartoon hung in the offices and barracks of the American military." Senator Phil Gramm reportedly remarked that those dragging the bodies around "don't look very hungry to the people of Texas."[46]

The initial phase of the mission, UNITAF, had been all but forgotten. When Americans said they wanted to avoid "another Somalia" they meant "another Mogadishu."[47] Later, Hollywood helped to entrench the notion that the Mogadishu battle *was* the Somalia mission. The highly popular 2001 film *Black Hawk Down* focused almost solely on the forty-eight hours of that battle, and largely ignored the previous ten months of U.S. intervention.

Social Pressures

The perception of the mission to Somalia as a failure for the United States also resulted from the manipulation of opinion by the media and from counterproductive strategies employed by U.S. leaders, which tended to shape both metrics and information in parallel.

Media Manipulation. There is evidence of bias in both *when* and *what* the U.S. media chose to report about Somalia. First, the media contributed to the declining interest in Somalia between January and October 1993 by drastically reducing coverage during that period (whether the media were setting the agenda or simply responding to lower public demand, they underreported the ongoing events).

Second, the content of media reports shaped perceptions of the Somalia mission. After the October raid, the media focused on U.S. casualties and ungrateful Somalis, while tending to ignore the large *pro*-American demonstrations in Somalia. This selective presentation of the views of ordinary Somalis mattered: in mid-October 1993, 88 percent of Americans supported withdrawal if the Somalis wanted the United States to leave, but 54 percent said they would "definitely" or "probably" support staying if a "substantial majority" of Somalis wanted the United States to remain. Crucially, 58 percent of Americans thought that most Somalis wanted the United States to leave. Outside Mogadishu the mission had restored a good deal of order, but media coverage concentrated overwhelmingly on the capital. For example, a review of *New York Times* articles in October 1993 found that rural areas—where success in delivering food and in improving infrastructure was most marked—received almost no mention. Congressman Richard Gephardt told reporters on 5 October: "There is a great success story here that the television pictures don't always show."[48]

The media first built up and then undermined the Somalia mission. The initial weeks of the intervention were portrayed in laudatory terms, as a low-cost mission of mercy. The media thereafter tended to ignore the difficult realities on the ground and the likelihood of costs, including casualties, creating an overly rosy view of the situation. Thus the events in early October produced a sharp reversal in media treatment. According to the media analysts Andrew Kohut and Robert Toth, the coverage of Somalia "illustrates the capacity of the media to be almost embarrassingly enthusiastic for a mission, then turn abruptly against it when pictures of the human cost begin to appear in American homes." "U.S. policy," notes Richard Haass, a former state department policy planner, "risks being unduly influenced by the domestic and international reactions to words and pictures from those places the cameras and reporters can reach. In both northern Iraq and Somalia, scenes of mass misery helped draw in the United States. It is instructive that images accelerated the U.S. departure from Somalia just months after they had the opposite impact." The media urged action, raised hopes, and then criticized the mission. As Entman points out: "Even as they pushed an interventionist agenda, many top journalists tended to blame administrations for the inevitable reverses and sacrifices. They demanded immediate and coherent responses to crises, and quick if not instant evidence of success—and clear indications that no quagmire loomed."[49]

Elite Manipulation. As we have seen in many of our cases, popular views of victory tend to reflect the unity or disunity of elite opinion. The same dynamic is apparent with regard to Somalia. Initially positive about the intervention, congressmen became more skeptical in the summer of 1993 in the wake of difficulties on the ground. Elites and the public interacted in their appraisals: Congress responded to negative opinion polls about the mission while also steering the public debate.[50]

The sharply critical turn by elites came quite late and quite suddenly. Although elites had mainly concurred in the new policy of capturing Aidid in June, within a few weeks disapproval became widespread. In July the Democratic Senator Robert Byrd remarked that he did not "remember voting to grant the U.S. military the authority to chase down competing African warlords and conduct house-to-house searches in Mogadishu to confiscate weapons." In September both houses of Congress passed nonbinding resolutions urging Clinton to outline the goals of the mission and to seek congressional approval for further involvement.[51]

After the Mogadishu raid, the virulence of congressional criticism, especially by Republicans, surprised Clinton. Many members of Congress, even those who had supported a May 1993 bill to cobble together belated congressional authorization for the use of U.S. forces in Somalia, were now demanding immediate withdrawal. The public picked up on this elite dissensus: as we saw earlier, polls after October show a much greater partisan divide in approval than did earlier polls.[52]

A key part of the explanation for negative public perceptions lies with the Clinton administration. Throughout 1993 Clinton focused on domestic policy and avoided risking political capital to build a public consensus in favor of his Somalia policy. There was a lack of sustained communication with the public as the mission goals changed: the administration did not articulate its reasons for being in Somalia until the end of August, by which time public support had steadily fallen. The inherent risks of the operation were rarely discussed, neither were the stakes or what could and could not be achieved.[53]

Furthermore, the way the administration reacted to events in Mogadishu served to frame the whole intervention as a disaster. Although Clinton did send emergency troops to protect those already there (reminiscent of Johnson's decision following the Tet offensive), the overall demeanor of the Clinton administration was one of embattlement and defeat. A few days after Mogadishu, when Secretary of Defense Lee Aspin and Secretary of State Warren Christopher met with more than two hundred members of Congress, the congressmen expected them to present a plan showing that the administration was in control. The administration, however, wanted to hear congressional views, and offered little leadership on the issue. The meeting was a disaster and led to increased calls for a pullout.[54]

Clinton eventually compromised on the views of his advisors, and chose a 31 March 1994 deadline for a complete withdrawal. The search for Aidid was abandoned, and the use of force was ruled out except in self-defense. Clinton, in a speech after the Mogadishu battle, did try to justify the mission, but he offered no plan for retaliation against Aidid, and no attempt to seize the initiative or take control of the situation. In any case, only 18 percent of Americans heard Clinton's speech, far fewer than the 84 percent who saw the images of the dead American soldiers. Without the political will for renewed efforts in Somalia, the public supported the pullout. The administration's reaction to Mogadishu effectively doomed the entire Somalia mission to the category of failure.[55]

It need not have been so. The evidence suggests that, despite the waning popularity of the intervention by October 1993, Clinton did have other options available. He could have presented the Mogadishu battle as one of heroism against a brutal opponent and called for the redoubling of efforts to capture Aidid. He could also have played up the extraordinary asymmetry of the outcome even in conditions entirely unfavorable to U.S. forces.

The public may, in fact, have been amenable to a strategy of "win first, then leave." Clinton could have mobilized support for punishing Aidid, tapping into the American public's desire for retribution. In June 1993 two-thirds of Americans approved of retaliation against Aidid. Immediately after the October raid, 51 percent wanted to continue to try to capture Aidid, and later polls showed up to 71 percent supporting such action (so long as it would not significantly delay the withdrawal).[56] In one poll 46 percent considered the demands of congressmen for an immediate pullout to be an overreaction to the events in Mogadishu.[57] Three separate polls found that a majority of the public favored sending *more* troops, at least to protect the U.S. soldiers already there. Americans were also strongly supportive of any actions that safeguarded U.S. prisoners of war. Large majorities favored the use of additional force to help release American prisoners, with 75 percent supporting "a major military attack against Aidid's forces" if the prisoners could not be freed through negotiations.[58]

The public favored withdrawing as soon as practicable, and polls showed that while 35 percent wanted to capture Aidid, 56 percent preferred to pull out regardless. But Clinton could have claimed that once Aidid was captured the mission would be accomplished and America would quickly withdraw. He could have tied the deployment of additional forces to the highly salient issue of POWs by arguing that the troops would force the release of American prisoners and punish those responsible for the mistreatment of Americans. Indeed, Clinton's trouble in controlling the media framing of events was not unique to Somalia: he also had difficulty explaining the relevance to national security of interventions in Haiti, Bosnia, and Kosovo.[59]

If the mission had ended with Aidid behind bars, perceptions would have been radically different, even given the Mogadishu battle. When the United States intervened in Panama in 1989, the search for the deposed Panamanian leader Manuel Noriega became quite drawn out, as he kept escaping and then sought refuge in the Vatican embassy. After Noriega finally gave himself up, his capture framed the intervention as a success. The arrest of Saddam Hussein also increased perceptions of success in Iraq. Judged by the metric of the manhunt, the United States had failed in Somalia, and in pulling back from the search and then pulling out completely, the United States had no chance of reversing this evaluation. Instead, Aidid, still a free man, would declare in a radio address in March 1994: "Our special thanks are due to the government and the people of the United States for their courageous decision to change its policy when they fully understood the realities in Somalia."[60]

Elites encouraged a perception that the United States was not responsible for what happened in Mogadishu. For example, Bob Dole, who would later be the Republican candidate for president in 1996, argued in an article published in the spring of 1995 that the Somalia debacle had been caused by the United Nations. The Clinton administration also tried to shift the blame for the Mogadishu raid to the United Nations. Clinton was hailed as having restored command and control over the U.S. military after the battle; however, according to the Africa experts Walter Clarke and Jeffrey Herbst, this view "is simply false." In fact the Rangers were entirely under U.S. control during the whole period, the broadened UN mandate for UNOSOM II had been written in Washington, and the United States had strongly supported the strategy of capturing Aidid. The general in command of the Rangers' mission wrote to Clinton immediately following the event, accepting all blame.[61]

Conclusions

By match-fixing rather than score-keeping, Americans got the Somalia result badly wrong. The keys to negative evaluations of Somalia were mind-sets (especially high expectations and hostility toward nation-building), salient events (especially the hunt for Aidid and the images of the Mogadishu battle), and social pressures (especially media reporting and the Clinton administration's failure to build a consensus around revised goals in Somalia).

Even though by October the United States could point to several substantive successes in Somalia, the dominant view was that the United States had lost control. In September only 36 percent of Americans thought the mission was "under control," while 52 percent thought the United States was "too deeply involved in Somalia."[62] These beliefs were strongly reinforced by the battle in Mogadishu, in which Washington had apparently lost the initiative. Clinton's most effective strategy would have been to assert an image of control with a limited and focused plan to capture Aidid.

The intervention in Somalia demonstrates the causal processes by which decisiveness, ambiguity, power, and regime type can encourage match-fixing at the expense of score-keeping. First, the outcome was not the sort of decisive result that essentially forces people to score-keep. Second, Somalia was a highly ambiguous operation with few precedents and with multiple actors, objectives, and dynamics, leaving its outcome open to interpretation. Third, the great asymmetry in power between the Somali militias and the United States created expectations of rapid results that ignored the difficulties of the environment in Somalia. Fourth, the democratic nature of the United States allowed for self-critical match-fixing, including skeptical coverage by the media and a congressional outcry after Mogadishu.

Partly because of the decision to pull out, there were only modest long-term gains from the U.S. intervention in Somalia. Some limited improvements had been made in infrastructure such as schools and roads. Subsistence agriculture had recovered, and many lives had been saved from the ravages of the drought. But conflict was still rife even after Aidid died in 1996, although the situation improved somewhat in the northern part of the country in the wake of the intervention. By 1995, overall, interclan violence was less prevalent than it had been in the pre-UNITAF period.[63]

The case of Somalia illustrates the difficulties of nation-building and the problems of fielding multinational forces such as UNOSOM II. At the same time, it demonstrates the potential for dramatically successful humanitarian relief operations led by a determined country with considerable resources. According to Hirsch and Oakley, the United States "achieved an important humanitarian objective, showed that coordination of critical elements can be achieved, and produced a positive result." But these were not the lessons most people drew from the episode.[64] Perceptions of defeat in Somalia had dramatic consequences. Asked whether the Somalia experience had made them more or less willing to support the use of U.S. troops for humanitarian operations in the future, 13 percent of Americans said "more willing" and 43 percent said "less willing." After Somalia, in 1994, the U.S. government drew up new policy guidelines that limited the scope for future armed humanitarian interventions. Congress also made efforts to reduce U.S. contributions to UN peacekeeping, efforts that Clarke and Herbst call "a direct response to the perceived failures in Somalia." UN documents, too, reflected newfound pessimism about future interventions because of the Somalia experience.[65]

The most disastrous legacy of perceptions of failure in Somalia was the U.S. response to the genocide in Rwanda in 1994. Clinton refused to send troops to Rwanda, or even to support other nations' efforts to intervene, primarily because of memories of Somalia. According to the scholar of international law Simon Chesterman: "Fear of international condemnation did not prevent any state intervening in Rwanda: televised images of a downed US Ranger being dragged through the streets of Somalia did." Perceptions of Somalia reinforced the notion that civil conflicts such as the one in Rwanda were the products of ancient hatreds, impossible for the United States to solve. A *New York Times* editorial in April 1994 advised that the world should stand aside from intervening in Rwanda: "Somalia provides ample warning against plunging open-endedly into a 'humanitarian' mission." Samantha Power suggests, in her book on the U.S. response to recent genocides: "The fear, articulated mainly at the Pentagon, was that what would start as a small engagement by foreign troops [in Rwanda] would end as a large and costly one by Americans. This was the lesson of Somalia." According to Power, all the American officials she interviewed said that memories of Somalia were the main impediment to U.S. action in Rwanda.[66] Tragically, people had learned the wrong lessons—blinded to success and scarred by failure.

9 | AMERICA AT WAR

The way you keep score in this game is very simple: How many Al Qaeda people are off the street, and how many are still out there, active and plotting . . .

—EDMUND HULL

In a way, success will be if the Iraqis don't hate us.

—DREW ERDMANN

IN THE AFTERMATH of the terrorist attacks of 11 September 2001, U.S. President George W. Bush declared a global war on terror. Coalitions led by the United States subsequently invaded the Islamic states of Afghanistan and Iraq, and numerous clandestine operations were mounted around the world. To keep American hearts and minds committed to the fight, the Bush administration has strongly encouraged the belief that the United States is winning these conflicts.[1] In this chapter we examine how the U.S. public has perceived the success or failure of President Bush's wars. Our analysis focuses on the period up to the end of 2004, though we refer to later events where appropriate.

The war on terror is a very different type of conflict from the others analyzed in this book. It is not war as traditionally understood, with organized military forces and recognizable political entities fighting for control of territory. There is no enemy capital city to occupy and no precisely outlined goal or end point. Even the capture of the al-Qaeda leader Osama bin Laden would not end the conflict. The metric one should use to gauge U.S. success is particularly vague, and information about whether this metric has been achieved is often secret or unknown. Should we judge President Bush's policy by the number of terrorist attacks within the United States, or by the number of terrorist attacks worldwide? Has al-Qaeda increased its membership since September 2001? The U.S. secretary of defense, Donald Rumsfeld, commented on 16 October 2003: "Today, we lack metrics to know if we are winning or losing the global war on terror. Are we capturing, killing or deterring and dissuading more terrorists every day than the *madrassas* [Islamic schools] and the radical clerics are recruiting, training, and deploying against us?"[2]

Furthermore, one of the central questions about the war in Iraq is whether it has had a positive or negative effect on the overall war on terror. The Bush administration has argued that the invasion of Iraq had a positive impact: that by tackling terrorists in Iraq the United States avoids having to fight them in American cities, and that Saddam Hussein might have given weapons of mass destruction (WMD) to terrorists. Critics argue that the Iraq War at best is a distraction from hunting al-Qaeda, and at worst has directly undermined the struggle against terrorism. But weighing up the impact of the conflict in Iraq on the war on terror is extraordinarily difficult, partly because the counterfactual of the war on terror *without* the Iraq War can only be guessed at.

Perceptions of success in these ongoing wars have significant implications. Perceptions of U.S. victory or defeat in the war on terror and the war in Iraq were major factors influencing the outcome of the 2004 presidential election.[3] Since perceptions of success and failure exert a strong influence on public approval of foreign policies, such perceptions may determine the duration and ultimate success of the U.S. mission in Iraq.

As of the end of 2004, there was no consensus among Americans about success in the war on terror and the war in Iraq. Evaluations were deeply divided, with some Americans certain that Bush's policies were succeeding and others equally certain that they were failing. Of course, this division in opinion may simply reflect the fact that the conflict is not yet over. In fifty years' time, observers may overwhelmingly agree that the United States won or lost the war on terror or the Iraq War.

The fact that members of the public look at the same events and draw completely different conclusions is an indication that match-fixing may play an important role in many people's evaluations. This is hardly a surprise: if the U.S. secretary of defense does not have access to the relevant metrics, how is the American public to make judgments? Yet here, in contrast to our other cases, match-fixing is not the dominant explanation for evaluations. Instead, perceptions are significantly shaped both by score-keeping (for example U.S. casualty levels) and by mind-sets, salient events, and social pressures.

| History

The key historical events are well known. On 11 September 2001 the United States suffered a surprise attack by al-Qaeda suicide terrorists who hijacked four aircraft and struck the World Trade Center in New York and the Pentagon in Washington, D.C. The fourth plane crashed in the Pennsylvania countryside. Within two months, the United States and coalition allies from NATO and elsewhere attacked and deposed the Taliban government in Afghanistan, which had harbored al-Qaeda. By the end of 2004, apart from a short-lived anthrax attack, there had been no further terrorist strikes within the United States, although groups linked to al-Qaeda had carried out attacks in Bali, Spain, and the Middle East.

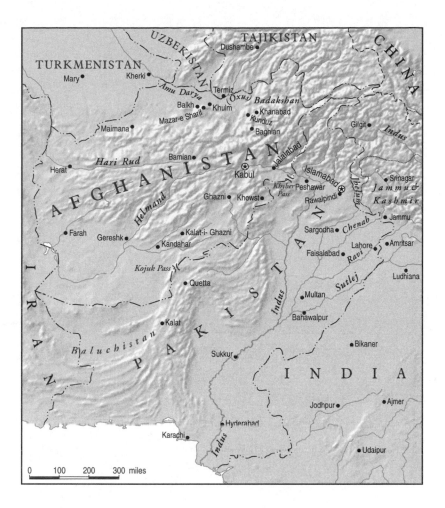

MAP 5. Afghanistan. Map by Philip Schwartzberg.

In March 2003 a U.S.-led coalition of states, without an explicit UN resolution, invaded Iraq. Although the ground campaign proceeded fairly smoothly, prompting Bush to declare the end of "major combat operations" after only six weeks, the U.S. and coalition forces soon faced an increasingly determined insurgency concentrated in the Sunni areas of central Iraq. In June 2004 the United States transferred power to an interim Iraqi government and planned for the elections of January 2005.

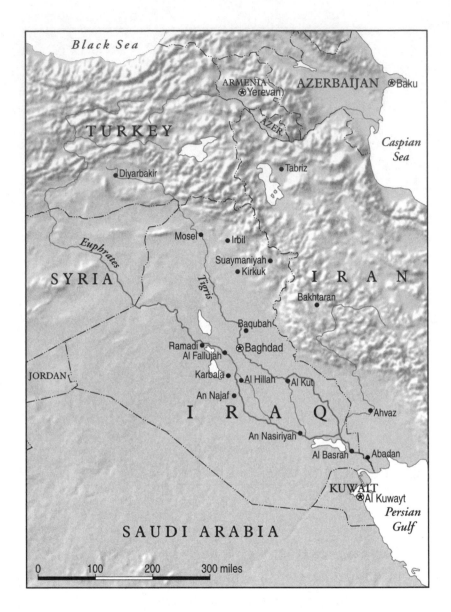

MAP 6. Iraq. Map by Philip Schwartzberg.

| Perceptions of Victory and Defeat

The Global War on Terror

How have Americans evaluated the success or failure of the war on terror? Two major indicators are available in the poll data: direct questions about who is winning, and approval ratings for presidential handling of the war. Beliefs that the United States and its allies were winning the war on terror increased sharply in the wake of the invasions of Afghanistan and Iraq, and to a lesser extent after Saddam Hussein was captured in December 2003 (see Chart 9.1). In all three of these instances, this boost in confidence quickly subsided. Over the period as a whole, the view that the terrorists were winning was quite consistently held by 10–20 percent of Americans, with the figure drifting upward slightly. These responses also indicate that the public conflated the war on terror and the war in Iraq, because the invasion of Iraq and Saddam's capture influenced views about the success of the war on terror. Approval ratings for Bush's handling of the war on terror slipped from 70 percent in December 2003 to 51 percent in May 2004, before climbing again to 59 percent in November 2004.[4]

The Iraq War

How have Americans judged success or failure in Iraq? Most polls indicate that perceptions that the United States was succeeding in Iraq peaked at over 50 percent in the first weeks of the invasion, then quickly fell once major combat ended and the focus shifted to counterinsurgency operations in the summer of 2003 (see Chart 9.2). Since that time, perceptions of U.S. success have steadily eroded, except for a positive surge when Saddam Hussein

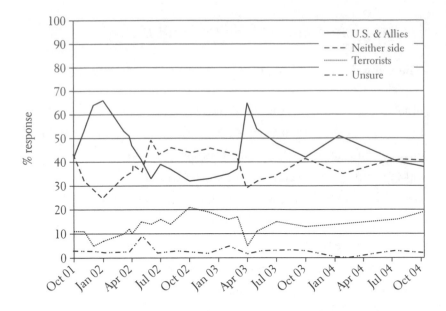

CHART 9.1. Results of poll question: "Who do you think is currently winning the war against terrorism: the U.S. and its allies, neither side, or the terrorists?" (CNN/USA *Today* poll, October 2001–October 2004.)

was captured in December 2003. Approval of Bush's policy in Iraq stood at 75 percent in April 2003 and then declined to 40 percent in May 2004 (with a spike in support when Saddam was captured), before rising slightly to 47 percent in September 2004.[5]

Beneath these broad evaluations of success, attitudes toward the Iraq War are marked by pronounced ambiguity and ambivalence. Poll questions that focus on different dimensions of success produce starkly different results, which can even appear contradictory. In August 2004, a narrow majority of the U.S. public thought the Iraq War had contributed to long-term U.S. security; at the same time, a similar majority thought the war had made the world a more dangerous place.[6] Looking to the future, Americans were quite positive. In May 2004, during a period of pronounced violence, one poll

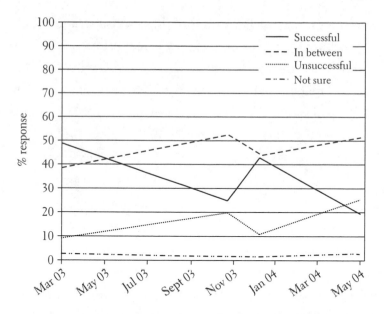

CHART 9.2. Results of poll question: "In your opinion, has the military campaign against Iraq been successful, unsuccessful, or somewhere in between?" (*Time*/CNN poll, March 2003–May 2004.)

found 55 percent "optimistic" and 43 percent "pessimistic" about the situation in Iraq in the following twelve months. This optimism was heavily qualified, however. When Americans were asked in August 2004 to rate their confidence that the United States would succeed in Iraq on a scale from zero, meaning not at all confident, to ten, meaning extremely confident, the mean response was 4.63.[7]

In 2004 a consistent majority of Americans agreed with the proposition that invading Iraq had been the "right decision" as opposed to the "wrong decision." In addition, most Americans thought the operation had improved the lives of ordinary Iraqis. However, opinions shifted when survey questions introduced the notion that the Iraq War had opportunity costs (that the resources could have been better employed elsewhere): in the fall of 2004, 52 percent thought it would have been better to use U.S. resources against al-Qaeda and to stabilize Afghanistan, while 39 percent supported the use of these resources in Iraq. In August 2004, Americans also thought by a two-to-one margin that the invasion of Iraq had made the United States "less respected" around the world, and that May, 73 percent believed the U.S. image had declined in the Arab world because of the war, while only 6 percent thought it had not declined.[8]

In summary, in 2003 and 2004 Americans were generally confident if asked about the prospects for long-term U.S. success in Iraq, the idea that the Iraq War was "right" rather than "wrong," and the benefits to the Iraqi population. However, they were more critical if asked whether the resources used in Iraq could have been better employed against al-Qaeda, whether the international image of the United States had suffered, and whether the world had become more dangerous as a result of the war.

| Framework 1: Score-keeping

Were Americans score-keeping the war on terror and the Iraq War, or were match-fixing factors influencing their evaluations? Here we test the congruence between perceptions of victory and defeat and U.S. aims, gains, and losses in Bush's wars.

The War on Terror

Material Gains and Losses. It is very difficult even to find basic agreed-upon information about the material progress of the war on terror because the relevant metrics and information are ill-defined and/or unavailable, and because political interests ensure that certain facts and not others are presented by elites.[9]

The major material change in the war on terror has been the re-

moval of the Taliban regime in Afghanistan (see Chart 9.3). Much
of the work of deposing the Taliban was carried out by Afghan
Northern Alliance troops, supplied and trained by the United States
and supported by U.S. airpower and Special Forces. Most of the
Taliban units disintegrated under determined attack, although al-
Qaeda forces did stand and fight. The CIA spent about $70 million
bribing Afghans to back Washington, an outlay that proved highly
cost effective. In the initial operation to overthrow the regime,
Taliban forces killed only two Americans, although 150 U.S. personnel had died in Afghanistan by the end of 2004.[10]

As for stabilizing Afghanistan, by the end of 2004 there had been
progress toward democratic elections. There had also been some
economic success, for example the opening in December 2003
of the Kabul-to-Kandahar highway. However, by 2004 the illegal
opium trade was worth over $2 billion. U.S. troop strength in Af-
ghanistan in 2004 was only 11,000, engaged almost solely in tracking
al-Qaeda and Taliban remnants. Much of the economic reconstruction had been slow, complicated by the continuing strength of
Afghan warlords.[11]

Has al-Qaeda membership risen or fallen since 2001? The Bush
administration claims that two-thirds of the known al-Qaeda
leadership had been captured by 2004, including Khalid Sheikh
Mohamed, the key planner for the September 2001 attacks, and
Abu Zubayda, al-Qaeda's chief recruiter. Mohamed Atef, al-
Qaeda's military chief, was also killed. However, a key unknown
is whether the number of captured or killed terrorists exceeds the
supply of new terrorists. U.S. intelligence agencies admit that they
do not know the true size of al-Qaeda or its success at recruitment.
Much of the leadership remains alive and active, including Osama
bin Laden (for whom the United States offered a $25 million
reward), and a UN report in December 2002 stated that al-Qaeda

| | | | | Importance | | Altering the credit due[a] |
Type of outcome	Event	Material gain or loss?	An aim achieved?	For leader	For observer[b]	Difficulty[c]
Positive outcomes	Regime change in Afghanistan	Gain	Achieved	Very high	Very high	Moderate/high
	Two-thirds of al Qaeda leaders captured	Gain	Partially achieved	High	High	Moderate/high
	No terrorist attacks in the U.S.	Neither	Achieved	Very high	Very high	Moderate
	Stability and democracy in Afghanistan	Gain	Partially achieved	High	Very high	Very high
Negative outcomes	150 U.S. dead in Afghanistan by end of 2004	Loss	Partially achieved	High	Moderate/high	Low (chance of avoiding)
	Cost of Afghan operations $1 billion a month	Loss	Not an aim	Low	Low	Very low (chance of avoiding)
	208 international terrorist attacks in 2003 (35 Americans killed)	Loss	Partially achieved	Moderate/high	Moderate	Moderate/low (chance of avoiding)

a. Higher values give *more* credit for positive outcomes and *less* credit for negative outcomes.
b. The importance of a gain or an aim in the minds of observers (in this case the authors) trying to fairly assess its worth.
c. The difficulty of a gain or an aim in the minds of observers (in this case the authors) trying to assess it fairly.

CHART 9.3. U.S. scorecard in the war on terror, 2001–2004.

continued to attract money and recruits.[12] In estimating gains and losses we also have to factor in al-Qaeda's ability to inspire other militant groups. Evaluating this crucial metric is, therefore, in large part guesswork.

The global war on terror is probably making it more difficult for al-Qaeda to operate. It no longer has a state-backed sanctuary in Afghanistan, for example, and multinational coordination has significantly improved worldwide antiterrorist efforts (from breaking up terrorist cells to freezing financial assets). Since 9/11 there have been no new al-Qaeda attacks in the United States. According to the Bush administration in 2005: "Overall, the United States and our partners have disrupted at least ten serious al-Qaida terrorist plots since September 11—including three al-Qaida plots to attack inside the United States. We have stopped at least five more al-Qaida efforts to case targets in the United States or infiltrate operatives into our country." The number of people killed by global terrorism in 2003 was 625, down from 725 in 2002. However, attacks classified as "significant" increased from 138 in 2002 to 175 in 2003, the highest level in twenty-one years.[13]

Material Aims. Even more difficult than determining material gains and losses is matching these gains and losses to U.S. aims, since we cannot be sure what these aims were. Bush's National Security Strategy report of 17 September 2002 set out three tasks: "We will defend the peace by fighting terrorists and tyrants. We will preserve the peace by building good relations among the great powers. We will extend the peace by encouraging free and open societies on every continent."

In its first aim, "fighting terrorists and tyrants," the Bush administration managed to overthrow the Taliban in Operation Enduring Freedom, which was for the most part, according to the foreign policy analyst Michael O'Hanlon, "a masterpiece of military creativity and finesse."[14] With relatively minor losses, U.S. forces removed the Afghan regime and captured or killed many al-Qaeda operatives (although, as noted above, the net gain or loss in al-Qaeda membership is unknown). The war on terror may also have spurred Libya to abandon its WMD program, thus removing the need to confront what many viewed as a tyrannical regime in Tripoli. The second aim, building good relations among the great powers, has not been as successful: U.S. relations with many states suffered because of Iraq. As global opinion has become more critical toward the United States, France, Germany, and Russia have pursued somewhat divergent strategies. There has not been the grand alliance against terrorism many Americans envisaged in the autumn of 2001. As for "encouraging free and open societies," Afghanistan is certainly freer than it was in 2001, having had its first even partially democratic elections. At the same time, the need for allies in the war on terror has led the United States to qualify its efforts to promote democracy in some cases, for example, in regard to Russian actions in Chechnya and the military government in Pakistan.

The Iraq War

Since the material changes in Iraq corresponded closely to the aims of U.S. decisionmakers, we will detail gains and losses in the context of espoused U.S objectives.

The core objective was to overthrow the regime in Baghdad; Bush and his top officials were determined to remove Saddam from early 2001. The attacks on September 11 of that year significantly lowered the threshold for action, as Rumsfeld explained: "The coalition did not act in Iraq because we had discovered dramatic new evidence of Iraq's pursuit of WMD; we acted because we saw the

| | | | | Altering the credit due[a] | | |
| | | | | Importance | | |
Type of outcome	Event	Material gain or loss?	An aim achieved?	For leader	For observer[b]	Difficulty[c]
Positive outcomes	Regime change in Iraq	Gain	Achieved	Very high	Very high	Moderate/high
	32,000 insurgents killed	Gain	Achieved	Very high	Very high	Moderate/high
	Nation-building	Gain	Partially achieved	Very high	Very high	Very high
	Spread democracy to the region	Gain	Partially achieved	High	Very high	Very high
	Prevent Iraq developing WMD	Neither	Achieved	Very high	High	Very low
Negative outcomes	1,300 U.S. dead in Iraq by end of 2004	Loss	Not achieved	Very high	High	Moderate (chance of avoiding)
	$150 billion cost by end of 2004	Loss	Not an aim	Low	Moderate	Very low (chance of avoiding)
	Number of insurgents increased from 5,000 to 20,000–40,000; escalation of attacks	Loss	Not achieved	Very high	Very high	Moderate/high (chance of avoiding)
	12,000–100,000 Iraqi civilian casualties	Loss	Not achieved	High	Very high	Moderate (chance of avoiding)

a. Higher values give *more* credit for positive outcomes and *less* credit for negative outcomes.

b. The importance of a gain or an aim in the minds of observers (in this case the authors) trying to fairly assess its worth.

c. The difficulty of a gain or an aim in the minds of observers (in this case the authors) trying to assess it fairly.

CHART 9.4. U.S. scorecard in the Iraq War, 2003–2004.

existing evidence in a new light—through the prism of our experience on 9/11." The United States sought to disarm Iraq's WMD and prevent an Iraqi alliance with al-Qaeda. A broader U.S. aim was to create a pro-U.S. democratic regime in Iraq that was secure and economically prosperous, with a strong civil society.[15]

Has the administration achieved these goals? As shown in Chart 9.4, the difficulty of the aims varied markedly. For example, intrinsic problems would have affected any postwar nation-building effort following the ousting of Saddam Hussein. At the same time, destroying Iraq's WMD capability and preventing the regime from allying with al-Qaeda were easily "accomplished" because there were no WMD in Iraq and Iraq's ties with al-Qaeda were minimal.

The military invasion of Iraq was successful by any standards, leading to the swift capture of Baghdad and the end of the regime, with quite light U.S. casualties (122 killed up to the fall of Baghdad on 9 April 2003). Iraqi military casualties are hard to judge, but may have been in the range of 5,000–20,000. If America won the war in Iraq, however, it failed to win the peace. At the end of 2003, with most of the top Ba'ath party leaders having been captured, Michael O'Hanlon and his co-worker Adriana Lins de Albuquerque concluded: "Things are gradually getting better even as we progress toward an exit strategy that should further defuse extremist sentiment."[16] But by the summer of 2004 the same writers saw a worsening security situation and escalating violence. A multidimensional rebellion developed, encompassing disaffected Sunnis, Shia groups including Moqtada al-Sadr's militia, and foreign terrorists. The Brookings Institution estimated that 32,000 insurgents had been killed or captured since April 2003, but insurgent strength had actually increased from about 5,000 in January 2004 to around 20,000 after July 2004. The head of Iraq's intelligence service claimed that by January 2005 there were 40,000 hard-core rebels and 160,000 sympathizers providing support. In the last four months of 2004, about 1,300 Iraqi police officers were killed. The number of attacks on U.S. soldiers rose throughout 2004, peaking in November. A broad consensus has arisen among commentators that the Bush administration did not commit enough troops to secure the country, and that significant errors were made in planning for postwar security.[17]

Economically, there was some progress in Iraq. Most of the courts, schools, and hospitals were soon in operation, and the electricity supply improved. During 2004 oil production reached 2.5 million barrels a day (close to prewar levels), although it did not increase as much as expected. Many problems evidently remained; for example, in 2004 unemployment in some areas was 30 percent or higher, and the United States was slow to spend the $18 billion available for Iraqi reconstruction. Politically, the United States had some success in promoting democratic pluralism: although a broadly based democratic regime had not yet been established, civil organizations flourished and there was a vigorous free press. At the same time, however, Iraqi public opinion turned against the United States. Polls found that most Iraqis were fairly optimistic about the future, but that majorities thought the invasion had done more harm than good and saw the coalition troops as occupiers, not liberators. Estimates of civilian casualties vary widely, with one of the highest being 100,000 (cited in *The Lancet*). O'Hanlon and Lins de Albuquerque estimated that by the end of 2004 12,000–13,000 civilians had been killed in "acts of war."[18]

The ousting of Saddam Hussein probably did not have a significant direct effect on international terrorism, since Iraqi sponsorship of international terrorism had been limited anyway.[19] U.S. actions may have played a role in encouraging Libya to renounce its WMD programs. North Korea and possibly Iran, however, responded to the Iraq War by stepping up their nuclear programs on the grounds that they feared being attacked by the United States. As for the aim of encouraging wider democratization, some signs of democratic reform could be detected in Saudi Arabia, Egypt, Lebanon, and elsewhere, but establishing a causal link with the Iraq War is problematic.

In summary, at the end of 2004 the U.S. record in Iraq in terms of material gains and losses and the achievement of material aims was decidedly mixed. The moderately difficult task of overthrowing the regime was achieved with skill and speed; the even easier task of disarming Iraq of nonexistent WMD and breaking the Iraqi government's tenuous, if not imaginary, links with al-Qaeda were both quickly "accomplished." There was progress in economic development, and especially in the growth of civil society. However, security was a major issue, as were mounting Iraqi and U.S. casualties. The effect on rogue states was complex: arguably pushing Libya to abandon its WMD program, but having the opposite effect on North Korea, and strengthening the position of Iran by removing its chief adversary, Saddam Hussein.

Do perceptions of victory and defeat in America's ongoing wars match the scorecard outcome? This is hard to judge compared with our other case studies because neither evaluations nor the outcomes on the ground are clear-cut. Score-keeping does appear to play a significant but not overriding role in American evaluations. Events on the ground are one important source of judgments about success. The peaks and troughs in confidence about the progress of the Iraq War are closely linked to periods of heightened U.S. casualties. For example, in April 2004, a month when 137 U.S. soldiers were killed, there was a considerable increase in those who thought the war was going badly. Survey questions that mention

U.S. casualties find significantly lower popular support for the war than similar questions that do not mention casualties. Controlling for the rally effect, the political scientists Richard Eichenberg and Richard Stoll found that for every 100 additional American casualties, approval of Bush's handling of Iraq fell 3 percent, and his overall approval rating fell 1 percent.[20]

| Framework 2: Match-Fixing

Although aggregate perceptions of success and failure in America's ongoing wars are loosely related to material aims, gains, and losses, many observers' perceptions are partially or wholly shaped by match-fixing factors. As summarized in Chart 9.5, the key match-fixing factors influencing perceptions were mind-set (demographics, partisanship, cognitive dissonance, beliefs, and analogies), salient events (symbolic events and the rally phenomenon), and social pressures (media spin and elite manipulation).

Mind-sets

It is sometimes apparent that a variable shapes overall evaluations of success but hard to tell whether this variable influences metric selection or information selection (or both). Basic data on demographic characteristics and political party affiliation reveal that Americans' perceptions of issues such as whether the Iraq war has helped the war on terror depend on factors other than score-keeping (see Chart 9.6). For example, while 48 percent of men believed, in June 2004, that the Iraq War had helped the war on terror, only 39 percent of women held this belief. [21] Also, the higher people's income, the more likely they were to say the Iraq War had helped the war on terror. Racial differences were more substantial: whites be-

Match-fixing factors	Affected aspect of judgment	
	Metrics	Information
Mind-sets		
Demographics	X	X
Partisanship	X	X
Cognitive dissonance	X	X
American beliefs	X	X
Historical analogies		X
Salient events		
Symbolic events		X
Rally phenomenon		X
Social pressures		
Media and elite manipulation	X	X

CHART 9.5. Key match-fixing factors influencing perceptions of victory and defeat in the war on terror and the Iraq War.

lieved the Iraq War had helped the war on terror by a margin of 47 percent to 39 percent, while blacks believed it had *not* helped by 71 percent to 20 percent. Race tends to covary with political preferences, so it is unclear how much of this is independent of partisan differences.

Of all the variables included in Chart 9.6, the clearest factor shaping American perceptions of the Iraq War is political partisanship. When questioned in June 2004, Republicans believed the war had helped rather than hurt the war on terror by a margin of 69 percent to 20 percent, while Democrats believed it had *hurt* the war on terror by a similar margin, 63 percent to 23 percent. In a poll in October 2004, when asked who was winning the war on terror, the "United States and its allies" or the terrorists, Republicans thought the United States was winning by 81 percent to 8 percent; Democrats thought the terrorists were winning by 46 percent to 25 percent. When asked in November 2005 why the U.S. and U.K. governments had claimed that Iraq had WMD, 69 percent of Re-

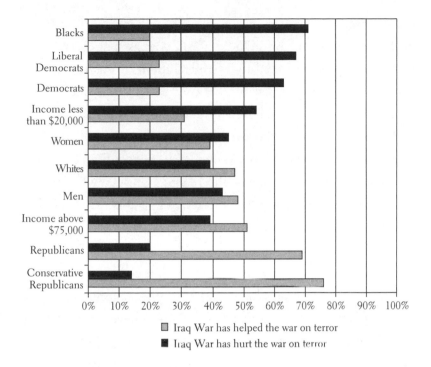

Iraq War has helped the war on terror
Iraq War has hurt the war on terror

CHART 9.6. Variation among groups in opinions on whether the Iraq War has helped or hurt the war on terror. (Pew Research Center for the People and the Press, "Public Support for War Resilient· Bush's Standing Improves," 17 June 2004.)

publicans but only 20 percent of Democrats said "they were misinformed," while 67 percent of Democrats but only 12 percent of Republicans said "they lied."[22]

Partisanship had a much greater impact on evaluations of Iraq and the war on terror than it did in our other case studies. In the Cuban missile crisis, for example, a single dominant image of who had won emerged and was broadly accepted across party lines. There are several reasons why partisanship has become more important to American perceptions of victory in today's conflicts. First, there is a long-term process evident, since the 1960s, whereby views about foreign policy are increasingly predictable from one's choice of party. Republicans were more likely than Democrats to see President George H. W. Bush's 1991 Gulf War as a success. In the Kosovo campaign in 1999 under Bill Clinton, it was Republicans who were more skeptical about the war.[23] Second, the Iraq War was divisive from the start, and the president failed to build a consensus for the invasion. Third, the war on terror and the Iraq conflict were ongoing as of the end of 2004. When (or if) the conflicts end, Democrats and Republicans may come to agree on who won and who lost (because match-fixing or score-keeping factors may become so dominant as to create a consensus across party lines).

Mind-sets and Metrics of Success. Cultural, social, and political beliefs in the United States have tended to produce metrics for success in Iraq that are increasingly difficult to achieve. As we saw with the U.S. intervention in Somalia, Americans tend to judge "nation-building" efforts in a very unforgiving fashion. In Iraq, any situation that falls short of U.S. democratic standards is typically viewed as a failure. This is partly the Bush administration's own fault: grandiose rhetoric about transforming Iraqi society, designed to mobilize Americans, has come back to haunt its proponents. "Victory" in Iraq is no longer about regime change: "victory" is now being equated with making Iraq into a full-fledged and secure democracy.

In a series of surveys from February to June 2004, when Americans were asked what success in Iraq would mean and had to choose one criterion for success from a list, 28–33 percent said when Iraq had a stable and democratic government, 22–27 percent said when Iraqis led normal lives, and 21–25 percent said when Iraqis were able to provide for their own security. When Americans were asked to specify the best measure of success in Iraq from a list, the most popular response (29–39 percent) was whether Iraqis were cooperating with the United States and not with the insurgents.

Using these criteria, it is hard to see how success for the United States will be achievable in the short to medium term. It is even harder to see how the Bush administration will be able to maintain public support given that to do so it must satisfy several different metrics. After all, the best way to create short-term security in Iraq might be to slow down or abandon democratic reforms. In contrast, few Americans selected criteria for success based on the original core premises for the war, premises that were relatively easy to achieve. Only 9–12 percent said that the key criterion for success was the Iraqi government having no links to terror, and only 3–5 percent said it was the Iraqi government having no WMD.[24] This suggests that Americans' selection of metrics predisposes them to view the Iraq mission in a negative light. If success in Iraq requires the creation of a full-fledged and stable democracy, in which Iraqis lead normal lives, provide for their own security, and cooperate with U.S. forces, then the United States may never be able to declare victory.

Metrics for victory also depend upon whether U.S. observers' thresholds for "democracy," "normal lives," and "providing for their own security" are based on Iraqi or American standards. The political scientist Samuel Huntington has argued that Americans expect national interests to be upheld abroad, but in addition, they have "distinctive political principles and values" which provide "a second set of standards" by which they judge the success of U.S. foreign policy. A regime supported by the United States that fails to live up to American standards of liberty and equality is deemed illegitimate. In evaluating actions abroad, Americans "hold the United States to standards that they do not generally apply to other countries," a tendency that encourages the perception that Washington has failed.[25]

We decided to test whether partisanship influences people's

Criterion	Favorable for Bush?	Predicted importance for Democrats
1. Whether the U.S. captures, or does not capture, key Al-Qaeda commanders	Yes	Low
2. Whether the U.S. captures, or does not capture, Osama bin Laden	No	High
3. Whether the U.S. has international support for its war on terror, especially in Islamic countries	No	High
4. Whether there are, or there are not, terrorist attacks inside the USA	Yes	Low
5. Whether the U.S. has accurate intelligence in the war on terror	No	High
6. Whether Bush retains the support of a majority of Americans for the war on terror	Yes	Low

CHART 9.7. Criteria for success offered to experimental subjects judging President Bush's performance in the war on terror.

choice of metrics of success. In the fall of 2004 we gave one group of Harvard University undergraduates (19 of whom identified themselves as Democrats, 12 as Republicans) a list of six possible metrics for evaluating Bush's success in the war on terror, which they were asked to rank in importance from 1 to 6 (see Chart 9.7). We chose three metrics by which Bush had performed favorably (criteria 1, 4, and 6 in the chart), and three by which he had performed poorly (criteria 2, 3, and 5). We predicted that, because of cognitive dissonance, Democrats would scan the list and, partly subconsciously, rank the metrics by which Bush failed as being most important. Republicans were predicted to do the opposite.[26]

One objection might be that some third factor drives both partisan beliefs and the selection of metrics. For example, a passionate belief in the importance of multilateralism might produce both party preference and metric selection. To control for this possibility, we asked a second group of undergraduates (15 Democrats, 7 Republicans) to rank the same criteria for judging success, but in reference to the following (fictional) scenario about Uzbekistan:

> In 1999 the country of Uzbekistan suffered a series of devastating terrorist attacks in which hundreds of people died. An Islamic terrorist group, led by Mohammed al-Badr, claimed responsibility. Since 1999, the leaders of Uzbekistan have launched a campaign against terrorism, including military intervention in nearby Kazakhstan.

In the list of criteria for this group, "al-Qaeda" was changed to "Islamic terrorist," "bin Laden" to "Mohammed al-Badr," and "the U.S." to "Uzbekistan," but otherwise the wording was identical. If a third factor were responsible for driving both partisanship and criteria selection, then we would expect little or no difference between the rankings chosen by Republicans in the two groups, or in those chosen by Democrats in the two groups.

Our findings are summarized in Chart 9.8. First, let's look at Republicans—the bar graphs on the right in the chart (note that we are dealing with ranks, so small numbers correspond to high importance for those particular metrics). As predicted, Republicans ranked the three criteria favorable to Bush (marked by bars with plus signs) among the most important. However, Republicans' criteria rankings were hardly influenced by whether they were judging the United States or Uzbekistan. Perhaps the Ivy League Republicans in our sample were either less strongly partisan or more moderate than average Republicans.

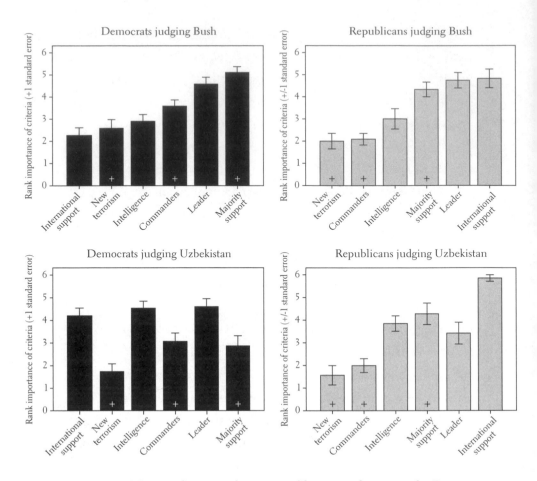

CHART 9.8. Mean ranks assigned to six possible criteria for success by Democrats and Republicans when judging Bush's performance in the war on terror and when judging a fictional situation in Uzbekistan. Because they are ranks, low numbers signify criteria that are judged as are *more* important. Bars with plus signs denote criteria favorable to Bush.

Democrats, however, were quite another story (as shown in the bar graphs on the left side of the chart). They ranked the three criteria favorable to Bush as being among the *least* important. Moreover, their criteria rankings were heavily influenced by whether they were judging Bush or Uzbekistan. Mean rankings were completely different between the two groups. When Democrats judged

Bush they ranked all three criteria that were favorable to him as being less important than other Democrats did when picking criteria for Uzbekistan. Democrats judging Bush also ranked all three criteria that were *not* favorable to Bush as more important than other Democrats did when picking criteria for judging Uzbekistan (although the difference in the leader category was very small). In other words, among Democrats all the criteria rankings fell in the predicted direction: Democrats were punishing Bush by selecting metrics by which he would fail, metrics that Democrats did not rank as highly when judging another country.[27]

Mind-sets and Information on Success. Mind-sets also influence American evaluations of incoming information about the war on terror and the war in Iraq. Low U.S. casualties are a component of many people's metric for success, but the amount of information people receive on this issue varies widely, for example, according to political awareness. Research by William Boettcher and Michael Cobb suggests that observers' estimates of total casualties in Iraq are extremely poor (often far exceeding the actual numbers), and that people are much better at recognizing *changes* in the number of casualties from month to month, as measured by the intensity of negative reports in the media, than at counting cumulative casualties. Strong Republicans are much more likely than Democrats to underestimate casualties. In a survey in September 2004, 54 percent of Democrats but only 36 percent of Republicans correctly said that U.S. casualties in the previous month had been higher than in recent months.[28]

There is additional evidence that the reception of incoming information about Iraq is shaped by cognitive dissonance, and that this in turn influences perceptions of success and failure. Americans who support the Iraq War tend to hold a number of associated beliefs: that the wider war on terror is going well; that Saddam Hussein had WMD; that Iraq provided substantial support to al-Qaeda; and that world opinion supports the U.S. invasion of Iraq or is evenly divided on the issue. In one poll in April 2004, 68 percent of those who felt it was right to intervene in Iraq, but only 18 percent of those who said the intervention was wrong, thought the United States was winning the war on terror. As negative feelings about the Iraq War grew, associated beliefs also shifted in parallel. In August 2003, 57 percent of respondents considered the Iraq War to be part of the war on terror, and 41 percent considered it a separate action. By March 2004, when approval of Bush's Iraq policy was declining, only 50 percent considered Iraq part of the war on terror, while 48 percent saw it as a separate action. Americans were perhaps more comfortable being skeptical about a conflict that they no longer thought of as part of the wider fight against terror.[29]

This cognitive dissonance is often related to partisanship. Supporters of Bush appear to receive information that bolsters his foreign policy positions less critically than information that undermines his positions. Researchers who analyzed three popular misperceptions about the Iraq War (that WMD were found in Iraq; that Iraq was closely linked to al-Qaeda; and that the war was popular around the world during 2003) found that the key factor correlated with holding these misperceptions was support for the president. Respondents who said they would vote for Bush were far more likely to hold such misperceptions than those who backed the Democrats. These misperceptions are, in turn, highly correlated with support for the decision to go to war in Iraq. Among those who held none of the three misperceptions, only 23 percent supported the Iraq War; among those who held one of these misperceptions the figure rose to 53 percent; two misperceptions and the figure was 78 percent; all three misperceptions and 86 percent supported the war.[30]

Notions of causality can also hinge on cognitive dissonance. Supporters of the Iraq War sometimes argue that the war caused greater democratization of the region, pointing to elections, for example, in Lebanon. Opponents of the war depict it as having caused bombings elsewhere in the world, such as in Spain or Britain. But there is a striking gap between the *confidence* with which these claims are made and the *evidence* — which is unclear to say the least — that the war in Iraq caused either democratization in the region or bombings elsewhere.

In addition, American perceptions are shaped by an aversion to counterinsurgency and nation-building missions. As we saw with Somalia, Americans tend to be skeptical about success when they fight against insurgents rather than against a state. The number of Americans who thought the Iraq War was going "very well" (as opposed to "fairly well," "not too well," or "not at all well") fell from 61 percent in April 2003 to just 23 percent two months later. This collapse in optimism followed the switch from a war between states to a counterinsurgency war. Even though the United States had deposed Saddam and captured Baghdad, in mid-July only 39 percent of Americans considered the U.S. effort to be a success, and by November only 25 percent viewed the war as a success.[31]

Memories of Vietnam reside in the American mind-set and may subtly influence evaluations of information about how well the United States is doing in conflicts that are perceived as analogous. A poll in April 2004 asked. "How concerned are you that Iraq will become another Vietnam in which the United States does not accomplish its goals despite many years of military involvement?" In response, 40 percent said they were "very concerned," 24 percent were "somewhat concerned," 14 percent were "not too concerned" and only 20 percent were "not at all concerned." It is possible to elicit additional negative responses about the Iraq War by using phrases such as "bogged down" that evoke memories of the defeat in Vietnam. During 2003–2004 a Harris poll asked: "How likely do you think it is that the U.S. will get bogged down for a long time in Iraq and not be able to create a stable government there?" From October 2003 to June 2004, only 5–8 percent of Americans stated that it was "not at all likely"; 37–45 percent thought it "very likely"; and an additional 28–34 percent thought it "somewhat likely." We can contrast these results with responses to similar questions about U.S. progress in Iraq that did not invoke Vietnam. One poll which asked how the U.S. effort was going in Iraq during the same period in 2003–2004 found that 10–28 percent of Americans (rather than 5–8 percent) chose the most optimistic option: that the U.S. military effort was going "very well."[32]

Salient Events

Salient Events and Information on Success. A number of symbolic events also had a substantial effect on perceptions of victory and defeat in America's ongoing wars. These events appeared to most potently shape the information, rather than the metrics, observers employed in their judgments. The capture of Saddam Hussein on 15 December 2003, for example, was partly a genuine battlefield success, partly a symbolic event, and it had a major effect on perceptions of success in Iraq. A few weeks earlier, in November, 25 percent of Americans thought the Iraq campaign had been a success, and 20 percent considered it unsuccessful. Shortly after the capture of Saddam, at the end of December, 43 percent considered the mission a success and 11 percent thought it was unsuccessful.[33] Confidence in success soon fell, however, and by early January 2004 a majority of Americans thought that the United States was not safer after the capture of Saddam.[34]

Graphic accounts of certain events may also have affected perceptions of success and failure. In March 2004 the U.S. media provided vivid coverage of cheering Iraqis in Fallujah celebrating the murder of four American security contractors; the bodies were burned, mutilated, and strung up for public view. According to the communications researcher Cara Finnegan: "The media is linking the Fallujah incident to Mogadishu [in Somalia in 1993] and those images are already imprinted on our collective visual memory. Images are always processed through the previous knowledge that we have."[35] Although the causal link is hard to prove, support for the Iraq war fell sharply in the early spring and summer of 2004.

Another example of a symbolic event unrelated to the material gains and losses of the war is the death of former President Ronald Reagan on 5 June 2004, which favorably shaped perceptions of President Bush. The Pew Research Center carried out a poll from 3 June to 13 June 2004. Prior to Reagan's death, Bush's approval rating was the same as in May (44 percent approve/48 percent disapprove). After Reagan's death (June 6–13), Bush's approval rating increased to 50 percent.[36] The praise for Reagan in the press partly rebounded onto the president.

The unfolding of dramatic events can also shape perceptions over and above material gains and losses by invoking a rally phenomenon. When people rally around their leader, they look at the same information about success in a very different way. Roosevelt received an enormous approval jump after Pearl Harbor, which was hardly a triumph for the United States (if anything, it exposed grave errors in foreign policy and intelligence). The terrorist attacks of 9/11 and the U.S. invasion of Iraq both had a major positive effect on evaluations of presidential performance (but in the second case, the effect was quite short-lived). After the invasion was announced on 17 March 2003, presidential approval ratings rose 13 percentage points (from 58 to 71 percent), but they fell back within a few months.[37]

Social Pressures

Manipulation by the media and by elites also shaped perceptions of success in Bush's wars. These pressures tended to shape metrics and information in parallel.

Media Manipulation. Although the two sides in the Iraq War have an asymmetry of capabilities, with the United States being far more powerful, this is partly balanced by what we call an *asymmetry of spectacle.* U.S. failures are spectacular and U.S. successes are unspectacular: therefore the U.S. media tend to focus on negative rather than positive news from Iraq. U.S. casualties are clear-cut, striking, and reported, while improvements in Iraqi services (such as the establishment of a free press, or clean water in a desert town) are vague, hard to judge, and usually unreported—and when they are reported, they rarely grab attention. During setbacks in Iraq, many have suggested that the press were unduly pessimistic. The scholar of legal and international affairs Robert Alt compared al-Sadr's uprising of April 2004 to the Tet offensive of 1968 and asserted: "By objective criteria, the past week has witnessed victories for Coalition forces, and stunning losses for the extreme anti-Coalition factions. But for all the cries of despair, the only real crisis in Iraq is in the subjective eyes of a media unwittingly being used by extremists." "The media got Tet wrong and they're getting Iraq wrong," lamented one U.S. officer serving in Iraq. "We are winning but people won't know that if all they are hearing about is death and violence." Americans tend to agree: according to one poll conducted in October 2003, 60 percent thought the media focused on negative stories over positive stories, with only 19 percent thinking that the media concentrated mainly on positive stories.[38]

Particular news organizations appear to shape the information observers receive about Iraq. An analysis by three scholars of public opinion—Steven Kull, Clay Ramsay, and Evan Lewis—found that misperceptions about the Iraq War during 2003 were especially likely to be held by those Americans who relied on Fox News as their major news source. Some 80 percent of those who named Fox as their primary source of news held one or more of the three common misperceptions (that WMD had been found in Iraq; that Iraq had strong ties with al-Qaeda; and that the Iraq War was popular in the rest of the world). At the other extreme, only 23 percent of those who named NPR/PBS as their primary source of news held one or more of these misperceptions. This was not simply because Fox viewers are Republicans. The study found that Republicans who got their news from Fox were much more likely to misperceive than Republicans who got their news mainly from NPR/PBS. Of course, it may be that a certain *type* of Republican watches Fox: one predisposed to hold these misperceptions. However, other effects suggest that the different news sources have a genuine influence. Among those who mainly watched Fox, the more attention they paid to the news, the more likely they were to hold misperceptions. In contrast, for those who watched other news channels, the effect of closely following the news on the tendency to hold misperceptions was minimal, and for those who got their news from the print media, the more attention they paid, the less likely they were to hold misperceptions.[39]

Experimental subjects at Princeton University in the fall of 2004 appeared to acknowledge media bias by discounting reports of victory from certain sources.[40] One group was told that the following (fictional) story came from the *New York Times*; a second group was told it came from Fox News:

> U.S. forces engaged in a firefight Monday in Afghanistan with suspected Taliban or al-Qaeda members. Ten of the U.S. soldiers were killed. Fifty suspected Taliban were killed and injured, and one hundred escaped into the mountains.

Asked to judge whether the battle was a "victory" or "not a victory" for the United States, 17 percent of those who thought the report was from Fox News called it a victory, but 27 percent of those who thought the report was from the *New York Times* did so.[41] The implication is that when our subjects heard that a battle report was from Fox, a number of them assumed that the battle was being favorably reported, and might have gone worse for the United States than the story indicated. This can be considered a defense mechanism against media manipulation. Alternatively, it may represent another form of bias if people overcompensate by discounting media reports more than the media actually distort events.

There is also evidence of media manipulation in shaping the wording of opinion poll questions. As noted earlier, Americans hold ambivalent attitudes about the Iraq War, being positive about some aspects of the war and negative about others. This ambivalence gives pollsters substantial power to manipulate the wording to get a desired result. Such bias may not be evident when a particular question and its results are viewed in isolation, but it is demonstrable when we compare the results of different questions asked at the same time. Certain news organizations appear to consistently select questions to promote a political agenda. Fox News, for example, tends to encourage answers favoring the Iraq War, and CBS/*New York Times* tends to encourage answers opposing the war. Both of these organizations sometimes ask neutral questions, but when the wording of their questions about the Iraq War is biased, it is usually in the predicted direction. From the results of Fox polls, one might think that the American public was solidly behind the Iraq War, confident about its successful outcome, unilateralist, and positive about how Iraqis view the United States. The results of CBS/*New York Times* polls, in contrast, would suggest that Americans were multilateralist, thought the Iraq War was going badly, and believed it was not worth the costs. These news organizations are not directly shaping people's evaluations of success, in the sense of influencing their beliefs about the war. What they are doing is using question wording to shape what public evaluations *appear* to be. This is important because considerable attention is paid to poll results: leaders often refer to the polls to see how much room for maneuver they have, and the public may be influenced by reports from polling organizations about what other Americans are thinking. Here are two questions asked in June 2004:

> Fox News/Opinion Dynamics poll:
> "Do you support or oppose the United States having taken military action to disarm Iraq and remove Iraqi President Saddam Hussein?"
> *Responses:* 60 percent support, 34 percent oppose.
> ABC News/*Washington Post* poll:
> "All in all, considering the costs to the United States versus the benefits to the United States, do you think the war with Iraq was worth fighting, or not?"
> *Responses:* 47 percent it was worth fighting, 52 percent it was not.[42]

Fox News cued a "pro-war" response in its question by focusing attention on Saddam Hussein and by assuming that Iraq was, in fact, "disarmed" (an ambiguous notion given Iraq's lack of WMD before the war). In contrast to the apparently impressive majority support of 60 percent attained by Fox, the second poll, carried out just over a week later, which did not include cues about Saddam and disarmament, found that only 47 percent of Americans thought the Iraq War was worth fighting and a small majority thought it was not worth fighting.

Similarly, consider two questions from April 2004 on the issue of how Americans perceive the reaction of ordinary Iraqis to the war:

> Fox News/Opinion Dynamics poll:
> "In general, do you think most Iraqi people are glad that the United States removed Saddam Hussein from power or do they wish the United States troops had stayed home?"
> *Responses:* 69 percent glad, 18 percent wish U.S. troops had stayed home.
> Pew Research Center poll:
> "Based on what you've seen and read, do *most* people in Iraq support or do most oppose America's current policies in Iraq?"
> *Responses:* 37 percent support, 48 percent oppose.[43]

Fox News phrased its question to promote an optimistic view by focusing only on the removal of Saddam. Yet, contrary to what the Fox poll suggests, the second poll indicated that Americans tended to think U.S. policies were unpopular among Iraqis.

CBS/*New York Times* polls often appear to include questions that promote negative evaluations of the Iraq War. Here are two questions from April 2004:

> CBS News/*New York Times* poll:
> "How would you say things are going for the U.S. in its ef-

forts to bring stability and order to Iraq?"

Responses: 4 percent "very well."

Fox News/Opinion Dynamics poll:

"How well do you think the war with Iraq is going for the United States and coalition allies?"

Responses: 11 percent "very well."[44]

In response to a question that specified a particular metric for success ("stability and order"), only 4 percent said the war was going "very well" (as opposed to "somewhat well," "somewhat badly," or "very badly"). The Fox News question does not promote a particular metric. With this wording Fox found that almost three times as many Americans thought the war was going "very well."

To illustrate that such effects are stable over time, Chart 9.9 tracks responses to two questions that were asked repeatedly:

CBS/*New York Times* poll:

"Do you think the result of the war with Iraq was worth the loss of American life and other costs of attacking Iraq, or not?"

ABC News/*Washington Post* poll:

"All in all, considering the costs to the United States versus the benefits to the United States, do you think the war with Iraq was worth fighting, or not?"[45]

Americans were consistently between 7 and 20 percent less likely to say the war was "worth it" in response to the question that referred only to the costs of the war (and specified loss of life as a cost) than in response to the question that mentioned both costs and benefits and left both unspecified.

For a final example, consider the effect of question wording on attitudes toward unilateralism.

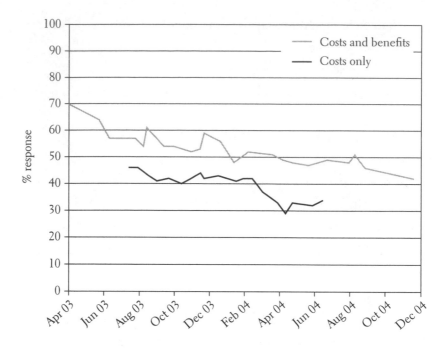

CHART 9.9. Effect of question wording on support for the Iraq War. *Black Line:* percentage of Americans who said the war was worth it when asked: "Do you think the result of the war with Iraq was worth the loss of American life and other costs of attacking Iraq, or not?" (CBS/*New York Times* poll, August 2003–July 2004.) *Gray Line:* percentage who said the war was worth it when asked: "All in all, considering the costs to the United States versus the benefits to the United States, do you think the war with Iraq was worth fighting, or not?" (ABC News/*Washington Post* poll, April 2003–December 2004.)

CBS/*New York Times* poll:

"When it comes to Iraq, do you think the United States should do what it thinks is right no matter what its allies think, or should the U.S. take into account the views of its allies before taking action?"

Responses: 60 percent multilateral, 36 percent unilateral.

Fox News/Opinion Dynamics poll:

"If other countries in the international alliance oppose mili-

> tary action against Iraq, do you think it is more important for the U.S. to go along with its allies, or is it more important for the U.S. to maintain its ability to act alone if necessary to protect U.S. citizens?"
>
> *Responses:* 40 percent multilateral, 51 percent unilateral.[46]

A majority supports taking into account the views of allies, but also a majority supports overriding the opinions of allies to protect U.S. citizens. In fact, it is surprising that anyone rejected taking the views of allies "into account," since this implies only a minimal commitment. At the same time, the idea of protecting U.S. citizens when "necessary" is highly attractive to respondents since the wording implies that the United States *ought* to act alone.

The obvious conclusion to draw from these examples is that the results of opinion polls on Iraq need to be read carefully and compared with those of other polls asked at the same time. This analysis also raises troubling questions about how news organizations (Fox News and CBS/*New York Times* are not the only culprits) can alter the wording of questions, apparently to encourage a particular result.

Elite Manipulation. There is also evidence that deliberate manipulation by elites shapes American perceptions of victory. The Bush administration has, unsurprisingly, made efforts to keep the war news positive. In his 2003 State of the Union address, Bush declared: "We have the terrorists on the run. We're keeping them on the run." On 6 October 2005 he addressed the National Endowment for Democracy, stating: "In Iraq, there is no peace without victory. We will keep our nerve and we will win that victory." In November 2005 he issued the "National Strategy for Victory in Iraq." The Republican Convention, 30 August to 2 September 2004, provided a public platform for promoting the idea that the United States was winning in Iraq. This event co-occurred with a 10 percent fall in the number of Americans who thought that the Iraq War was a mistake, from 48 percent to 38 percent.[47]

As we have seen in other case studies, positive spin can backfire when it creates high expectations of future success. Public support rises and then crashes down as inflated expectations are not met. The Bush administration built support for the invasion of Iraq, for example, by promising that U.S. troops would be greeted as liberators and would quickly return home. When Bush declared the end of major combat operations on 1 May 2003, he made the announcement from the deck of an aircraft carrier, standing in front of a banner that read "Mission Accomplished." While perhaps convincing some doubters to back the war, such messages ultimately produced disappointment at the slow rate of progress. Furthermore, in response to the failure to find WMD in Iraq, the administration shifted its rationale for the war toward the creation of a stable and democratic Iraq. If WMD had been found, that discovery would have provided a firm basis for positive evaluations of success; societal stability is a much harder metric to achieve.[48]

At the same time, the Bush administration's talk of Iraq becoming a beacon of freedom and democracy for the region actually makes it more likely that the Iraq War will be viewed as a success.[49] Since there is little historical precedent for democracy in the region, *any* evidence of democratization in the Arab world is likely to be seen by American observers as having been caused by the Iraq mission, even if there is no direct evidence of cause and effect. If no democratization occurs, this is unlikely to encourage perceptions of failure; if some democratization occurs, it will be lauded as a huge success. Therefore the administration's rhetoric of democratization makes the mission more likely to be viewed as having failed in Iraq itself, but also more likely to be viewed as having succeeded in regional terms.

The state department's report *Patterns of Global Terrorism*, released in 2003, claimed that worldwide terrorism had dropped 45 percent between 2001 and 2003. "You will find in these pages," Deputy Secretary of State Richard Armitage told reporters, "clear evidence that we are prevailing in the fight." Closer examination revealed that the report contained many errors, and actually included data indicating that "significant" attacks in 2003 stood at their highest level in twenty years. Although Secretary of State Colin Powell suggested that the errors had been due to imprecise data collection rather than political scheming, the social scientists Alan Kruger and David Laitin astutely conclude: "If the errors had gone in the opposite direction—making the rise in terrorism on George W. Bush's watch look even greater than it has been—it is a safe bet that the administration would have caught them before releasing the report. And such asymmetric vetting is a form of political manipulation."[50]

Kruger and Laitin suggest that government reports on terrorism should follow rules similar to those on the production and dissemination of economic data: "Only accurate information, presented without political spin, can help the public and decisionmakers know where the United States stands in the war on terrorism and how best to fight it." The state department ceased publication of the annual *Patterns of Global Terrorism* report in 2004 after its methodology was challenged, and perhaps more pertinently, because the data suggested that terrorist attacks had risen sharply since 2003. "Significant" attacks increased from 175 in 2003 to 625 in 2004. The replacement publication, *Country Reports on Terrorism*, offered no similar statistics.[51]

| Conclusions

In each of our other case studies, evaluations of success and failure coalesced around a coherent dominant impression of who the winners and losers were. We were then able to investigate which factors explained the emergence of this dominant perception. However, with America's ongoing wars, judgments are marked by diversity and ambiguity.

In the aggregate, Americans are partially responsive to actual battlefield gains and losses—that is, they base their judgments partly on score-keeping. However, despite the influence of material realities, a large number of Americans view the war on terror and the war in Iraq through heavily biased lenses. Observer's mind-sets, notably political partisanship, appear to be a primary explanation for the diversity of perceptions. As John Mueller notes: "The partisan divide over the war in Iraq is considerably greater than for any military action over the last half-century."[52] Mind-sets tend to shape all stages of the evaluation process. Our experimental results suggest that people often select their metrics after the event to ensure that they reach the "right" judgment. Evidence also indicates that information by which to assess metrics is viewed selectively. In addition, several symbolic but irrelevant events such as the death of Reagan have had a noticeable effect on evaluations. Meanwhile, manipulation by media and elites influences the information that Americans receive about the conflict, and the ways in which Americans interpret this information.

Clearly, match-fixing in the war on terror and the Iraq War cuts both ways. Partisanship makes some Americans hostile to any hint of success by President Bush, and others unwilling to acknowledge any significant failures by his administration. Symbolic events such as the capture of Saddam Hussein favored Bush, while the mutilation of American corpses in Fallujah may have favored negative evaluations of the war. The media influence is also complex: the effects of the pro-Bush slant of Fox News must be contrasted with an arguably wider media tendency toward negative coverage of events in Iraq.

Perceptions of America's ongoing wars illustrate the causal processes by which our four independent variables—decisiveness, ambiguity, power, and regime type—can encourage match-fixing. Certainly, U.S. success in Iraq or the war on terror has not reached the threshold of *decisive* victory, where a triumph is sufficiently undeniable that people score-keep the outcome. It is even unclear what events, if any, would constitute such a decisive victory. The war on terror is also one of the most inherently *ambiguous* conflicts in American history, with no precedent, and with much of the conduct of the war on both sides kept secret. This ambiguity has allowed people to choose their own criteria for success, thus encouraging the selection of arbitrary or self-serving metrics. The great disparity in *power* between the United States and its terrorist and insurgent opponents promoted expectations of rapid American victory, and people may not have sufficiently considered the difficulties involved in stabilizing Iraq. And U.S. *democracy* provided an outlet for self-critical match-fixing by those with an interest in promoting negative perceptions of the Bush administration. Together, these factors have primed both the war in Iraq and the war on terror for high levels of match-fixing.

Ironically, however, while any one person's perceptions may be quite contrary to the realities on the ground, the evident diversity in perceptions about America's ongoing wars may mean that the *average* perception is surprisingly similar to the scorecard result. Members of the biased majority may, by fixing the match in different directions across party, ideological, or social lines, serve to cancel one another out. As the journalist and author James Surowiecki points out in *The Wisdom of Crowds*, collective judgments can approximate reality even if many individuals get it wrong.[53] Public opinion *shifts* could, in theory, be driven by a relatively small group of scorekeepers who follow the news from Iraq and elsewhere and revise their judgments about U.S. success and failure on the basis of new data.

10 | CONCLUSION

The fight is won or lost far away from witnesses—behind the lines, in the gym and out there on the road, long before I dance under those lights.

— MUHAMMAD ALI

You know how to win victory, Hannibal, you do not know how to use it.

— MAHARBAL

NIKITA KHRUSHCHEV, LYNDON JOHNSON, and Golda Meir form an unlikely triumvirate, but they share at least one characteristic: they were all victims of match-fixing. This was not match-fixing in the sense familiar from the 1919 World Series, where some of the players conspired to arrange the result. Rather, it was psychological match-fixing, with actual successes on the ground perceived as failures, as if the Boston Red Sox won a four-game sweep of the World Series in 2004, but across America the St. Louis Cardinals received the laurels of victory. In such a case, the Red Sox might think they really were cursed.

Perhaps Khrushchev, Johnson, and Meir wondered why their achievements seemed to go unrecognized; why people viewed them as having lost in spite of their gains. Or perhaps they themselves were subject to match-fixing factors and concurred with the dominant perception of failure, unknowingly accepting an illusory view of the outcome. In the end, all three paid with their careers and their reputations for the psychological biases of observers. How and why did this happen?

In this book we have compared two potential frameworks or explanations for the way observers perceive victory and defeat in international disputes. Framework 1, score-keeping, focuses on material gains and aims achieved as criteria for determining success and failure. Framework 2, match-fixing, focuses on mind-sets, salient events, and social pressures to explain perceptions of victory and defeat. Both frameworks contribute to people's overall perceptions of victory and defeat, but their relative importance depends upon key characteristics of the dispute and the participating states.

The case studies illustrated how the decisiveness of the outcome, the ambiguity of the dispute, the relative power of the countries involved, and regime type all shaped the likelihood of match-fixing. In none of the cases was the outcome sufficiently decisive that observers were essentially forced to score-keep. The ambiguous nature of the disputes encouraged the use of arbitrary metrics and information. In most of the cases the more powerful side was the victim of match-fixing. In addition, people in democracies appear to be more likely to match-fix against their own side: free societies produce maximum latitude for opposition politicians and the media to downplay their own government's successes and exaggerate its failures.

Of course, individuals vary. Better-educated and more politically attentive people are likely to show greater awareness about an outcome, and may seek and receive information from a wider range of sources. But the story of the case studies is how match-fixing can engulf individual variation. In most of our examples, a majority of people, despite their differences in education and political attentiveness, ended up subscribing to the same dominant evaluation of the outcome.

	Cuban missile crisis	Tet offensive	Yom Kippur War	Somalia	War on terror and Iraq
Mind-sets					
Expectations	X	XX	XX	XX	X
Cognitive dissonance (shaping metrics)	—	—	X	—	XX
Cognitive dissonance (shaping information)	X	X	X	X	XX
Salient events					
Symbolic events	XX	XX	XX	XX	X
Rally phenomenon	X	X	—	—	XX
Social pressures					
Enemy state manipulation	—	X	X	—	—
Media manipulation	—	XX	X	XX	XX
Elite manipulation	XX	XX	XX	XX	XX

CHART 10.1. The importance of match-fixing factors in shaping perceptions of victory and defeat in the case studies. XX indicates primary importance, X indicates secondary importance, and a dash indicates minor or no importance.

Chart 10.1 indicates the relative importance of mind-sets, salient events, and social pressures across the case studies. In the cases we examined, the most important element within observers' mind-sets was expectations, especially in biasing metric selection. In the Tet offensive and the Yom Kippur War, expectations were probably the single greatest factor pushing judgments away from the material scorecard. The most crucial salient events were those with symbolic power, which operated to a significant degree in every case, although somewhat less so in the war on terror and the war in Iraq, where partisanship tended to dominate evaluations. As for social pressures, manipulation by elites and by the media was important in shaping evaluations in all the cases.

Complex interactions can occur between mind-sets, salient events, and social pressures. For example, mind-sets can increase or decrease observers' sensitivity toward certain salient events or social pressures. In the Cuban missile crisis, prior beliefs made Chinese leaders especially sensitive to evidence that the Soviets were appeasing the capitalist states by turning their ships around and pulling out the missiles. Similarly, salient events can affect the extent to which elites can manipulate opinion, as well as the nature of that manipulation. President Kennedy could frame the Cuban missile crisis solely in terms of the missiles, in part because of the timing of the discovery of the missiles. Social pressures can also interact with observers' mind-sets, shaping the information available in the public domain. For example, leaders can compound or utilize preexisting prejudices. Hitler was able to exploit the German mind-set of victimization in order to encourage the belief that Germany had been betrayed rather than defeated in World War I.

Match-fixing factors do not always push in the same direction. Partisanship may encourage observers to perceive their favored leader as winning while symbolic events suggest defeat. These factors may cancel each other out, or one match-fixing factor may dominate another. For example, individuals with extremely deep-rooted ideological mind-sets may resist the conclusions suggested by symbolic events or elite manipulation if those conclusions challenge their core beliefs.

| A Guide for Observers

The best way to evaluate success and failure is score-keeping, carefully weighing up aims and gains while factoring in importance and difficulty. Score-keeping is not perfectly objective because people may give different weights to the importance and difficulty of gains and the difficulty of aims according to their personal preferences. But score-keeping is a reasonably fair and balanced process of judgment. A population of people who are properly score-keeping will tend to produce evaluations that are clustered together, even if they are not identical.

The best way to avoid match-fixing biases is by being self-aware and open to contrary information. But this advice is by no means easy to follow. People usually prefer sources of information that confirm or support their cherished beliefs. Critical and lateral thinking are required on precisely the occasions—wars and crises—in which the media and the public tend to rally around their leaders, and to become decisively unified, anchored to core beliefs, and especially subject to self-serving illusions.

People should score-keep if one very important assumption holds true: everyone else is score-keeping. But if others are *not* score-keeping, then match-fixing judgments may rebound onto the international stage and create secondary gains and losses, which must be factored into evaluations. If, for example, match-fixing alters everyone else's judgment of which side was the victor in a particular conflict, then it may be incorrect to disagree with them even if the scorecard indicates that they are wrong. Suppose Side A loses a battle on the ground, but 99 percent of Side B's population consider Side A the winner, and as a result, Side B withdraws its troops: in this situation, Side A will emerge as the winner after all.

Perceptions of victory can therefore become self-fulfilling prophecies, altering international relations in such a way that the perceived outcome becomes the reality. When perceptions that the Soviets had been defeated in the Cuban missile crisis exacerbated the Sino-Soviet split, the defeat became very real for Moscow. Perceptions of American defeat in the Tet offensive led President Johnson to stop the bombing of Vietnam, offer negotiations, and begin scaling back U.S. efforts in the Vietnam war, handing a victory to the North Vietnamese. Perceptions that Israel had lost the Yom Kippur War meant that after 1973 Israel and Egypt acted as if Israel really had lost, with both sides showing a greater willingness to work toward peace. Similarly, perceptions of the 1993 battle in Mogadishu

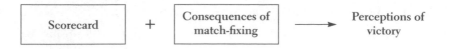

CHART 10.2. "Total score-keeping": how people *should* evaluate victory in situations where others are match-fixing.

as a failure for the United States prompted President Clinton to announce the withdrawal of U.S. forces and to give up trying to capture Aidid, undermining the long-term benefits of the intervention.

Therefore, in cases where at least some people are match-fixing, there are two parallel pathways by which gains are accrued: via the outcome on the ground (the scorecard), and via perceptions of that outcome. Both need to be taken into account in what we term "total score-keeping" (see Chart 10.2). In such a scenario, perceptions of victory and defeat can matter more than the reality on the ground in determining who *really* won.

The potential repercussions of match-fixing mean that evaluations in the immediate aftermath of a crisis or a war are almost always inaccurate or incomplete. It is very hard to predict in advance the full material ramifications that may arise from other people's match-fixing.

| A Guide for Leaders

It is essential for leaders to understand the processes by which people perceive victory and defeat. Machiavelli's advice in *The Prince* rings true for leaders today. A prince, he maintained, must "appear to him who sees and hears him altogether merciful, faithful, humane, upright, and religious . . . Every one sees what you appear to be, few really know what you are, and those few dare not oppose themselves to the opinion of the many."[1] Leaders can manipulate opinion to ameliorate defeats and exaggerate victories. At the extreme, they may be able to draw a political victory from the jaws of a military defeat by highlighting illusory achievements. Here we make seven suggestions for policymakers—in both democracies and dictatorships—if they are to manage perceptions of victory and defeat.

Be seen to control events. Leaders will benefit from investing their energy, not just in the details of the settlement terms, but in shaping the process by which the settlement comes about. It is enormously important to generate the perception that one is in control. In our case studies, the side that was perceived as being in control (for example, the communists in the Tet offensive) was also usually perceived as the victor—even when it lost in material terms.

How can the perception of control be established? One way is through decisive military victory, but this is not the only way. Leaders can try to publicly establish ground rules for the dispute, and then coerce or trick the opposing side into conforming to these rules (or at least appearing to). In the Cuban missile crisis, President Kennedy publicly announced the discovery of the Soviet missiles in Cuba and the "rule" that the crisis would end when the missiles were removed. When the missiles were withdrawn it created a sense that Kennedy was in control. Leaders can also create standoffs in which the other side is forced to symbolically retreat, as Kennedy did with his quarantine of Cuba. In a battle, leaders can target the enemy's symbolically strongest point, such as the U.S. embassy in the Tet offensive. Observers may base their evaluations mainly on implications drawn from such actions: an enemy who can strike at the safest point on one's own side appears to be in control of the fighting.

Focus on metrics. Leaders should single out one clear and achievable metric for success, relentlessly highlight it, and then accomplish it at all costs. As the political scientist Robert Mandel notes in his book *The Meaning of Military Victory*: "Powerful states engaged in warfare may lose focus on what precisely they are trying to achieve. Having sharply delineated outcomes in warfare seems like a no-brainer but has frequently been missing in many post–Cold War international conflicts."[2]

Shape perceptions of one's aims. After a dispute, leaders can suggest that the outcome (whatever it was) satisfied their initial core objectives, while claiming that an opponent's gains were largely unwanted and accidental by-products of the settlement. Sadat made the result of the Yom Kippur War look like the accomplishment of his objectives by deceiving the Egyptian public, after the fighting was over, about what his prewar aims had been.

Beware of expectations. Leaders need to be very careful about managing expectations. It is tempting to build support by focusing on positive news and rosy prospects, but this tends to heighten expectations, producing more difficult metrics for success and thereby increasing the probability and severity of later negative evaluations.

States need to be wary even when matches are fixed in their own favor, because after a perceived victory observers will expect the country to perform at a new higher level. If a boxer becomes expert at tricking the judges into thinking he won on points, and keeps getting moved up the rankings, he may be in for a mighty fall.

If a leader avoids predicting victory, reverses will be less shocking. This may make it harder to garner support for particular policies in the first place, but it will make successes look far more impressive. As Europe crumbled before Hitler's advancing legions, Churchill promised the British people just four things: "blood, sweat, toil and tears."

Exaggerate past failure. Leaders can encourage perceptions of success in the current dispute by focusing on the negative aspects of previous disputes. Playing up yesterday's failure highlights today's relative progress. The Arab states depicted their own defeat in the 1967 Six-Day War as far more terrible *after* the 1973 Yom Kippur War than they had done in the previous six years, because the worse the 1967 outcome looked, the better the 1973 outcome looked in contrast. Of course, playing up past disasters is easier for a leader who was not responsible for them. For example, Sadat came to power in 1970 and could thus safely paint the 1967 Six-Day War in negative hues.

Steer negative perceptions. Even when perceptions of defeat are inescapable, leaders can propagate a desired account of why the defeat occurred, and who was to blame, as a form of damage limitation. After the American Civil War, Southern leaders claimed that the South had lost only to the North's overwhelmingly greater numbers, not to any superior heroism, tactics, or man-for-man fighting ability. After World War I, many German leaders propagated the view that the German army had been stabbed in the back by domestic forces in 1918 as a means of reconciling the reality of defeat with the belief that Germany had not lost on the battlefield. Such rationalizations often find attentive audiences in defeated nations.

Feign defeat to obtain indirect gains. Leaders usually want to convince their people that they won—but not always. Occasionally a leader may accept or even encourage an image of defeat as a means of mobilizing additional resources. General Wheeler, the chairman of the U.S. joint chiefs of staff, deliberately wrote a report portraying the Tet offensive as a near-disaster for the United States to try to force the Johnson administration to send more troops to Vietnam and also to absolve the U.S. army from responsibility if Johnson said no and the United States ultimately lost (in fact the report had the effect of further pressuring Johnson to de-escalate). Another example may be Israel's historic withdrawal from Gaza in 2005. By demonstrating the domestic unpopularity and political costs of withdrawal, Prime Minister Ariel Sharon sent a strong signal that a complete withdrawal from the (more important) West Bank would be impossible.

| Advice for U.S. Policymakers

There are three specific lessons for U.S. policymakers that emerge from this book.

The United States is likely to be a victim of match-fixing. The chances of being the victim of match-fixing are greatest for a democratic superpower. Expectations of U.S. performance in all disputes are sky-high. Starting with the 1991 Gulf War, "smart" weapons led people to believe that the United States should be able to win wars quickly, cleanly, and with little loss of life. "In one sense," notes the journalist and author Stephen Budiansky, "the victory against Saddam [in 1991] had vanquished the Vietnam syndrome; in another sense it had arguably only made it worse by creating an illusory, impossible standard of perfection. No one of course regretted the miraculously low American losses, but some Air Force officers worried they had made it look too easy."[3]

Our cases indicate that observers do not always recognize the extent to which fighting in a difficult environment (such as that of Vietnam, Somalia, or Iraq) can equalize the odds between the United States and an opponent. Furthermore, the democratic U.S. system allows for criticism of the government's performance. Indeed, match-fixing could be America's Achilles' heel. As the United

States achieves tactical and strategic gains in a war, the U.S. public may nevertheless perceive the events as a failure for their side and force concessions or withdrawal.

Match-fixing by U.S. governments should be a subtle weapon—not a blunt instrument. America's experience in the Cuban missile crisis, the Tet offensive, and the intervention in Somalia was a tale of three presidents. Kennedy successfully created the illusion of personal and national triumph; Johnson was swept out of office in part by perceptions of failure; and Clinton stumbled toward withdrawal from Somalia. To a large extent, perceptions of success and failure in each of these cases were products of factors beyond the president's control, such as the different mind-sets of Americans in 1962, 1968, and 1993. Manipulating perceptions is not easy for leaders because they compete with media and other influences, and because their claims may fall on deaf ears, at least among political opponents. But U.S. presidents can make a difference.

As a general rule, leaders in democracies have to be subtler about their match-fixing than leaders in autocracies. Types of manipulation that leaders may find attractive—as simple as hiding information—tend to backfire in democracies, where the public has access to a range of alternative news sources, and may in the end only serve to undermine the leaders' credibility. The Israeli government's half-hearted efforts to control the media in the Yom Kippur War probably contributed to perceptions of defeat more than either a free press or a completely restricted press would have done. Partial control of information, tempting as it is, inevitably leads to leaks, exposures, and skeptical citizens. U.S. leaders would be wise to avoid trying to restrict bad news from Iraq, for example, that is likely to reach American audiences from other sources.

The key for U.S. policymakers is to exploit opportunities in the political environment to shape and structure public perceptions of victory. It is easier to encourage people to select from a range of frames that already coexist in their minds than it is to force them to adopt a wholly new frame. Policymakers can highlight the aspects of an outcome toward which the public is already favorably disposed. The trick is to figure out what these are. In the Iraq War, one of the most favorable aspects for many Americans is the capture of Saddam Hussein, and policymakers would be well served by frequently reminding the public of this result. Policymakers should also be on the lookout for powerful symbolic images to exploit, such as the medical student kissing American soil on the return from Grenada. That image ended the debate over Grenada, particularly when Reagan reinforced its positive message in a speech about the mission.

The public is defeatist toward nation-building. The United States may be especially likely to match-fix against itself in missions that feature nation-building or counterinsurgency. In two of our case studies (the Tet offensive and Somalia), the U.S. public evaluated American performance in such interventions more negatively than the battlefield outcome warranted. In the case of the Iraq War, confidence in U.S. success also nose-dived the moment the war shifted from being an inter-state war to being a counterinsurgency and nation-building mission.

This follows a broader pattern in which recent U.S. interventions in other countries' civil wars have been perceived negatively at home. The intervention in Haiti in 1994–1996 was a partial success, reinstalling an elected government, mitigating suffering, rebuilding health and police services in a desperately poor country—all at a low cost in American lives. But notably, within a few months of U.S. troops arriving in Haiti, a plurality of Americans judged the mission as a failure.[4] Similarly, once 20,000 U.S. troops arrived in Bosnia after the 1995 peace deal, reasonable stability ensued, the economy grew, elections were held, and U.S. casualties were zero. But by 1998, 69 percent of Americans were "not satisfied" with the intervention in Bosnia, and only 26 percent were willing to say that the mission had gone even "fairly well."[5] In 1999, following the deployment of U.S. forces in Kosovo, nation-building efforts were generally more successful than in Bosnia because lessons had been learned, for example about the need for more effective coordination with international organizations.[6] Kosovo became fairly stable, and U.S. casualties were again zero. But again Americans were skeptical: in 2000, only 37 percent said that the United States had made progress toward its aims in Kosovo.[7]

Why do Americans tend to perceive nation-building missions as failures? Memories of Vietnam play a role in making Americans especially concerned about fighting against insurgents, promoting expectations that such operations will be protracted, inconclusive, and costly—that the United States will be trapped in a quagmire. Furthermore, rather than judging nation-building efforts on the basis of how much progress has been made since U.S. forces arrived, Americans often judge them on the basis of the gap between U.S. levels of social stability and democracy and those in the target state. Observers would arrive at more accurate judgments if they recognized the difficulties involved in nation-building and lowered the threshold for a successful outcome. Another reason for negative judgments has to do with media presentation. In nation-building missions, the fact that electricity production is up or unemployment is down is rarely reported, but dramatic events like bombings are front-page news.

U.S. leaders will not have an easy time countering this quagmire mentality, but they can at least try to encourage more reasonable standards of judgment. Often U.S. presidents actually reinforce the quagmire mentality by using grandiose rhetoric to mobilize support for a nation-building mission, promising to transform the target society and construct a democracy. When the outcome inevitably falls short of the president's words, the public turns against the effort. Instead, to take one example, President Clinton would have been well advised to focus on other aspects of the intervention in Somalia: the dismal situation in that country when U.S. troops arrived, the impressive progress made as a result of the intervention, the important stakes involved in staying the course for the future of Somalia, the fact that the United States could not solve all Somalia's problems but could do an enormous amount of good, and the likelihood of some U.S. casualties.

Leaders since time immemorial have expended vast resources to defeat their enemies on the field of battle. As we have shown, success on the battlefield does not guarantee victory. Human nature commonly elevates the influence of mind-sets, salient events, and social pressures over and above the outcome on the ground. Without more attention to the way victory is determined by perception as well as by reality, nations may sacrifice copious amounts of blood and treasure, only to find themselves failing to win.

NOTES

Chapter 1. Introduction

1 Harris Survey poll, 23–27 May 1975; J. F. Guilmartin, *A Very Short War: The Mayaguez and the Battle of Koh Tang* (College Station: Texas A & M University Press, 1995); R. Wetterhahn, *The Last Battle: The Mayaguez Incident and the End of the Vietnam War* (New York: Carroll and Graf, 2001).

2 Gallup/CNN/*USA Today* poll, 5 Oct. 1993.

3 R. C. DiPrizio, *Armed Humanitarians: U.S. Interventions from Northern Iraq to Kosovo* (Baltimore: Johns Hopkins University Press, 2002), 71, 148–149. In September 1999 UN Secretary General Kofi Annan attributed the failure to intervene in Rwanda to "the reluctance of Member States to place their forces in harm's way where no perceived vital interests are at stake, a concern over costs, and doubts — in the wake of Somalia — that intervention could succeed." See J. F. Miskel, "Some Lessons about Humanitarian Intervention," *Journal of Humanitarian Assistance* (2000), *www.jha.ac/greatlakes/b006.htm*.

4 J. S. Nye, *Soft Power: The Means to Success in World Politics* (New York: Public Affairs, 2004), ix.

5 R. Mandel, *The Meaning of Military Victory* (Boulder: Lynne Rienner, 2006); J. E. Mueller, *Retreat from Doomsday: The Obsolescence of Major War* (New York: Basic Books, 1989). R. E. Wagner-Pacifici, *The Art of Surrender: War and Politics at Conflict's End* (Chicago: University of Chicago Press, 2005); V. P. Fortna, "Where Have All the Victories Gone? War Outcomes in Historical Perspective," paper delivered at the annual International Studies Association Convention, Honolulu, Mar. 2005; M. Toft, "End of Victory? Civil War Termination in Historical Perspective," paper delivered at the annual International Studies Association Convention, Honolulu, Mar. 2005.

6 D. R. Hickey, *The War of 1812: A Forgotten Conflict* (Urbana: University of Illinois Press, 1989), 309. J. W. Loewen, *Lies My Teacher Told Me: Everything Your American History Textbook Got Wrong* (New York: Simon and Schuster, 1995), 124.

7 P. Corner and G. Procacci, "The Italian Experience of 'Total' Mobilization, 1915–1920," in J. Horne, ed., *State, Society, and Mobilization in Europe during the First World War* (Cambridge: Cambridge University Press, 1997), 223.

8 H. Strachan, *The First World War* (New York: Viking, 2003), 58, 330–331. W. Schivelbusch, *The Culture of Defeat: On National Trauma, Mourning, and Recovery* (London: Granta Books, 2003), 60.

9 D. Dutton, *Neville Chamberlain* (London: Arnold, 2001). R. J. Beck, "Munich's Lessons Reconsidered," *International Security* 14 (1989): 161–191.

10 R. B. A. Dimuccio, "The Study of Appeasement in International Relations: Polemics, Paradigms and Problems," *Journal of Peace Research* 35 (1988): 245–259; B. Farnham, *Roosevelt and the Munich Crisis: A Study of Political Decision-Making* (Princeton: Princeton University Press, 1997), ch. 5; E. R. May, *Lessons of the Past: The Use and Misuse of History in American Foreign Policy* (Oxford: Oxford University Press, 1973). A. J. P. Taylor, *The Origins of the Second World War* (London: Penguin, 1964), 9.

11 R. Jenkins, *Churchill* (London: Pan Books, 2002), 597.

12 J. Garofano, "Tragedy or Choice in Vietnam? Learning to Think Outside the Archival Box," *International Security* 26 (2002): 143–168.

13 Y. F. Khong, *Analogies at War: Korea, Munich, Dien Bien Phu, and the Vietnam Decisions of 1965* (Princeton: Princeton University Press, 1992), 114–115.

14 D. D. P. Johnson and D. Tierney, "Essence of Victory: Winning and Losing International Crises," *Security Studies* 13 (2004): 350–381.

15 Baskin's views summarized in Dan Ephron, "Sharon Said to Modify Withdrawal Plan from Gaza Strip," *Boston Globe*, 23 May 2004.

16 B. B. de Mesquita, A. Smith, R. M. Siverson, and J. D. Morrow, *The Logic of Political Survival* (Cambridge, Mass.: MIT Press, 2003).

17 Schivelbusch, *Culture of Defeat.*

18 P. Feaver and C. Gelpi, *Choosing Your Battles: American Civil-Military Relations and the Use of Force* (Princeton: Princeton University Press, 2004). See also S. Kull and R. Clark, "The Myth of the Reactive Public: American Public Attitudes on Military Fatalities in the Post-Cold War Period," in P. Everts and P. Isneria, eds., *Public Opinion and the International Use of Force* (London: Routledge, 2001); R. C. Eichenberg, "Victory Has Many Friends: The American Public and the Use of Military Force, 1981–2005," *International Security* 30 (2005): 140–177; R. C. Eichenberg, "Gender Differences in Public Attitudes towards the Use of Force by the United States, 1990–2003," *International Security* 28 (2003): 135.

19 George Patton, speech to U.S. forces in England, 31 May 1944, available at *webpages.charter.net/wjpbr/patton.html.* Perceptions of success shape presidential approval ratings, which may in turn affect policy decisions through a process of "dynamic representation"; see J. A. Stimson, M. Mackuen, and R. S. Erikson, "Dynamic Representation," *American Political Science Review* 89 (1995): 543–565.

20 R. K. White, *Nobody Wanted War: Misperception in Vietnam and Other Wars* (Garden City, N.Y.: Doubleday, 1968), 207.

21 Khong, *Analogies at War;* May, *Lessons of the Past.* D. Reiter, *Crucibles of Belief: Learning, Alliances, and World Wars* (Ithaca: Cornell University Press, 1996).

22 R. Jervis, *Perception and Misperception in International Politics* (Princeton: Princeton University Press, 1976), 232–233, 275–279.

23 R. N. Lebow, "Domestic Politics and the Cuban Missile Crisis," *Diplomatic History* 14 (1990): 488. Moyers quoted in I. L. Janis, *Victims of Groupthink: Psychological Studies of Policy Decisions and Fiascoes* (Boston: Houghton Mifflin, 1972), 120. Plato quoted in R. Hobbs, *The Myth of Victory: What Is Victory in War?* (Boulder: Westview, 1979), 1.

24 B. Woodward, *Bush at War* (New York: Simon and Schuster, 2002), 38–39, 79.

25 *Wars* are defined as large-scale institutionally organized lethal violence, usu-

ally fought for the control of territory. B. Russett, "The Fact of Democratic Peace," in M. E. Brown, S. M. Lynn-Jones, and S. E. Miller, eds., *Debating the Democratic Peace* (Cambridge, Mass.: MIT Press, 2001), 69. *Crises* are characterized by the perception of an increased probability of war, the existence of a threat to basic values, and an awareness that finite time exists to resolve matters. M. Brecher and J. Wilkenfeld, *A Study of Crisis* (Ann Arbor: University of Michigan Press, 1997), 3–4.

Chapter 2. Score-keeping

1 W. R. Neuman, "The Paradox of Mass Politics: Knowledge and Opinion in the American Electorate," in N. J. Kressel, ed., *Political Psychology: Classic and Contemporary Readings* (New York: Paragon, 1993); see also P. E. Converse, "The Nature of Belief Systems in Mass Publics," in D. E. Apter, ed., *Ideology and Discontent* (New York: Free Press, 1964). J. Mueller, "American Foreign Policy and Public Opinion in a New Era: Eleven Propositions," in B. Norrander and C. Wilcox, eds., *Understanding Public Opinion* (Washington: CQ Press, 2002). 2002 Roper survey commissioned by the National Geographic Society; see *www.nationalgeographic.com/geosurvey/*.

2 CBS News Poll, 15–18 Aug. and 6–8 Sept. 2004. Neuman, "Paradox of Mass Politics," 268.

3 This, as it happens, closely resembles some previous analyses of war outcomes: T. H. Dupuy's logic in his analysis of battle data, in which he wanted to reveal only the performance of the leaders and the soldiers once all other factors had been stripped away; and Scott Gartner's definition of strategy: "Strategy is a plan for pursuing specific aims against an adversary, such as the physical possession of an adversary's city, the destruction of an enemy's port, or the capture of an individual or group. By specific, I mean tangible, measurable objectives . . . strategy does not include notions of military approach, such as aggressiveness, or efforts to destroy nonspecific intangibles, like enemy morale." T. N. Dupuy, *Numbers, Prediction, and War: Using History to Evaluate Combat Factors and Predict the Outcome of Battles* (New York: Bobbs-Merrill, 1985); S. S. Gartner, *Strategic Assessment in War* (New Haven: Yale University Press, 1997), 19.

4 See R. Powell, "Absolute and Relative Gains in International Relations Theory," *American Political Science Review* 85 (1991): 1303–20; M. Nicholson, "Interdependent Utility Functions: Implications for Co-Operation and Conflict," in P. Allan and C. Schmidt, eds., *Game Theory and International Relations: Preferences, Information and Empirical Evidence* (Aldershot, UK: Edward Elgar, 1994); A. Stein, *Why Nations Cooperate: Circumstance and Choice in International Relations* (Ithaca: Cornell University Press, 1990).

5 D. A. Baldwin, "The Sanctions Debate and the Logic of Choice," *International Security* 24 (1999): 80–107; D. A. Baldwin, *Economic Statecraft* (Princeton: Princeton University Press, 1985), ch. 7.

Chapter 3. Match-fixing

1 John Hughes, *Ferris Bueller's Day Off*, *www.hundland.com/scripts/ FerrisBuellersDayOff.txt*.

2 See, e.g., R. Jervis, *Perception and Misperception in International Politics* (Princeton: Princeton University Press, 1976); T. Gilovich, D. Griffin, and D. Kahneman, eds., *Heuristics and Biases: The Psychology of Intuitive Judgment* (New York: Cambridge University Press, 2002); P. E. Tetlock, "Social Psychology and World Politics," in D. Gilbert, S. Fiske, and G. Lindzey, eds., *Handbook of Social Psychology* (New York: McGraw Hill, 1998); D. O. Sears, L. Huddy, and R. Jervis, eds., *Oxford Handbook of Political Psychology* (Oxford; New York: Oxford University Press, 2003); Y. Y. I. Vertzberger, *The World in Their Minds: Information Processing, Cognition, and Perception in Foreign Policy Decisionmaking* (Stanford: Stanford University Press, 1990); S. T. Fiske, "What We Know Now about Bias and Intergroup Conflict, the Problem of the Century," *Current Directions in Psychological Science* 11 (2002): 123–128; for a popular account, see M. Gladwell, *Blink: The Power of Thinking without Thinking* (Boston: Little, Brown, 2005).

3 D. Kahneman, P. Slovic, and A. Tversky, eds., *Judgment under Uncertainty: Heuristics and Biases* (Cambridge: Cambridge University Press, 1982); D. Kahneman and A. Tversky, "Prospect Theory: An Analysis of Decisions under Risk," *Econometrica* 47 (1979): 263–291; D. Kahneman, "A Perspective on Judgment and Choice: Mapping Bounded Rationality," *American Psychologist* 58 (2003): 697–720.

4 A. G. Greenwald, "The Totalitarian Ego: Fabrication and Revision of Personal History," *American Psychologist* 35 (1980): 603–618.

5 There are several related concepts and their exact definitions are often debated. According to Rose McDermott, "Emotion . . . encompasses thoughts, motivations, bodily sensations, and an internal sense of experience. However, this definition requires further refinement in order to differentiate emotion from *affect, mood,* and *feeling,* which, though often used synonymously, refer to different phenomena. Affect refers to the way people represent the value of things as good or bad; it can include preferences as well as emotions and moods. Moods are amorphous states—like emotions, but without specific objects or referents. Finally, feelings are the actual experience of value." R. McDermott, "The Feeling of Rationality: The Meaning of Neuroscientific Advances for Political Science," *Perspectives on Politics* 2 (2004): 692.

6 R. J. Davidson, "Cognitive Neuroscience Needs Affective Neuroscience (and Vice Versa)," *Brain and Cognition* 42 (2000): 89–92. A. R. Damasio, *Descartes' Error: Emotion, Reason, and the Human Brain* (New York: Avon, 1994). D. L. Schacter, "Memory Distortion: History and Current Status," in D. L. Schacter, ed., *Memory Distortion: How Minds, Brains, and Societies Reconstruct the Past* (Cambridge, Mass.: Harvard University Press, 1995); S. P. Rosen, *War and Human Nature* (Princeton: Princeton University Press, 2004).

7 E. R. May, *Lessons of the Past: The Use and Misuse of History in American Foreign Policy* (Oxford: Oxford University Press, 1973); Y. F. Khong, *Analogies at War: Korea, Munich, Dien Bien Phu, and the Vietnam Decisions of 1965* (Princeton: Princeton University Press, 1992).

8 See, e.g., R. E. Nisbett, *The Geography of Thought: How Asians and Westerners Think Differently—and Why* (Yarmouth, Me.: Nicholas Brealey, 2003).

9 Schacter, "Memory Distortion," 3; M. Schudson, "Dynamics of Distortion

in Collective Memory," in Schacter, ed., *Memory Distortion.* L. LeShan, *The Psychology of War: Comprehending Its Mystique and Its Madness* (New York: Helios, 2002); see also R. K. White, *Nobody Wanted War: Misperception in Vietnam and Other Wars* (Garden City, N.Y.: Doubleday, 1968); A. F. Eldridge, *Images of Conflict* (New York: St. Martin's, 1979).

10 Jervis, *Perception and Misperception in International Politics.*

11 See, e.g., D. Dunning and G. L. Cohen, "Egocentric Definitions of Traits and Abilities in Social Judgement," *Journal of Personality and Social Psychology* 63 (1992): 341–355.

12 Vertzberger, *World in Their Minds,* 262.

13 See, e.g., R. McDermott, *Political Psychology in International Relations* (Ann Arbor: University of Michigan Press, 2004); Sears, Huddy, and Jervis, *Oxford Handbook of Political Psychology.*

14 E. Kam, *Surprise Attack: The Victim's Perspective* (Cambridge, Mass.: Harvard University Press, 2004), 54.

15 Schacter, ed., *Memory Distortion.*

16 H. A. Simon, "Rationality as Process and as Product of Thought," *American Economic Review* 68 (1978): 1–16; J. A. Rosati, "The Power of Human Cognition in the Study of World Politics," *International Studies Review* 2 (2001): 45–75.

17 R. Jervis, "The Confrontation between Iraq and the U.S.: Implications for the Theory and Practice of Deterrence," *European Journal of International Relations* 9 (2003): 315–337. Jervis, *Perception and Misperception,* 117–202, 232–233. T. J. Lomperis, *The War Everyone Lost — and Won: America's Intervention in Viet Nam's Twin Struggles* (Washington: CQ Press, 1993). White, *Nobody Wanted War,* ch. 10. A black-and-white image of a messy world may be encouraged by Western culture; see Nisbett, *Geography of Thought.*

18 Kahneman and Tversky, "Prospect Theory"; J. S. Levy, "Loss Aversion, Framing Effects, and International Conflict," in M. I. Midlarsky, ed., *Handbook of War Studies* 2 (Ann Arbor: University of Michigan Press, 2000).

19 S. M. Walt, "Beyond Bin Laden: Reshaping U.S. Foreign Policy," *International Security* 26 (2001): 71n37.

20 Schudson, "Dynamics of Distortion," 355.

21 Vertzberger, *World in Their Minds,* 111–112; K. M. McGraw, "Political Impressions: Formation and Management," in Sears, Huddy, and Jervis, eds., *Oxford Handbook of Political Psychology,* 394; A. George, "The 'Operational Code': A Neglected Approach to the Study of Political Leaders and Decision Making," *International Studies Quarterly* 13 (1969): 190–222.

22 D. D. P. Johnson, *Overconfidence and War: The Havoc and Glory of Positive Illusions* (Cambridge, Mass.: Harvard University Press, 2004); C. A. Blainey, *The Causes of War* (New York: Free Press, 1973); S. Van Evera, *Causes of War* (Ithaca: Cornell University Press, 1999).

23 McDermott, "Feeling of Rationality," 693, 699.

24 F. I. Greenstein, *The Presidential Difference: Leadership Style from F.D.R. To Bill Clinton* (New York: Free Press, 2000), 112. Harris Survey poll, 23–27 May 1975.

25 See Johnson, *Overconfidence and War,* ch. 2 and appendix, and references therein.

26 May, *Lessons of the Past;* Khong, *Analogies at War;* D. P. Houghton, "The

Role of Analogical Reasoning in Novel Foreign-Policy Situations," *British Journal of Political Science* 26 (1996): 523–552; D. P. Houghton, "Analogical Reasoning and Policymaking: Where and When Is It Used?" *Policy Sciences* 31 (1998): 151–176.

27 Jervis, *Perception and Misperception*, 275.

28 L. Festinger, *A Theory of Cognitive Dissonance* (Stanford: Stanford University Press, 1957); Vertzberger, *World in Their Minds*, 137. Dunning and Cohen, "Egocentric Definitions of Traits and Abilities."

29 E. Katz and J. J. Feldman, "The Debates in the Light of Research: A Survey of Surveys," in S. Kraus, ed., *The Great Debates: Background, Perspective, Effects* (Bloomington: Indiana University Press, 1962). ABC News poll, 8 Oct. 2004.

30 "Reaction Shots May Tell Tale of Debate: Bush's Scowls Compared to Gore's Sighs," *Washington Post*, 2 Oct. 2004, A10.

31 O. R. Holsti, *Public Opinion and American Foreign Policy* (Ann Arbor: University of Michigan Press, 2004), ch. 5.

32 By one estimate, around 30 percent of the population are solid hawks, supporting almost all uses of force abroad, while about 10–30 percent are solid doves, opposing virtually all uses of force abroad. P. Feaver and C. Gelpi, *Choosing Your Battles: American Civil-Military Relations and the Use of Force* (Princeton: Princeton University Press, 2004), 145.

33 Holsti, *Public Opinion and American Foreign Policy*; E. Wittkopf, *Faces of Internationalism: Public Opinion and American Foreign Policy* (Durham, N.C.: Duke University Press, 1990). Bruce Jentleson and Rebecca Britton have argued that the U.S. public is ready to use force to restrain the foreign policy actions of other states, and for humanitarian purposes, but is reluctant to use force for internal political change; B. W. Jentleson and R. L. Britton, "Still Pretty Prudent: Post-Cold War American Public Opinion on the Use of Military Force," *Journal of Conflict Resolution* 42 (1998): 395–417.

34 D. Kearns, *Lyndon Johnson and the American Dream* (New York: Harper and Row, 1976), 327.

35 J. E. Mueller, *War, Presidents and Public Opinion* (New York: Wiley, 1973), 168–169.

36 Festinger, *Theory of Cognitive Dissonance*; A. L. George, *Presidential Decisionmaking in Foreign Policy: The Effective Use of Information and Advice* (Boulder: Westview, 1980).

37 J. Fallows, "Blind into Baghdad," *Atlantic Monthly* 293 (2004): 53–74.

38 Mueller, *War, Presidents and Public Opinion*, 116–118.

39 R. E. Wagner-Pacifici, *The Art of Surrender: Decomposing Sovereignty at Conflict's End* (Chicago: University of Chicago Press, 2005), 21–22; K. Inoue, *MacArthur's Japanese Constitution: A Linguistic and Cultural Study of Its Making* (Chicago: University of Chicago Press, 1991), 7; N. Ferguson, "Prisoner Taking and Prisoner Killing in the Age of Total War," *War in History* 11 (2004): 148–192.

40 Wagner-Pacifici, *Art of Surrender*, 85. W. Schivelbusch, *The Culture of Defeat: On National Trauma, Mourning, and Recovery* (London: Granta Books, 2003); G. W. Gallagher and A. T. Nolan, eds., *The Myth of the Lost Cause and Civil War History* (Bloomington: Indiana University Press, 2000).

41 J. Assmann, "Ancient Egyptian Antijudaism: A Case of Distorted Memory," in Schacter, ed., *Memory Distortion*, 374–375.

42 McDermott, "Feeling of Rationality," 695.

43 H. H. Kelley, "The Warm-Cold Variable in First Impressions of Persons," *Journal of Personality* 18 (1950): 431–439. R. D. Ashmore, D. Bird, F. K. D. Boca, and R. C. Vanderet, "An Experimental Investigation of the Double Standard in the Perception of International Affairs," *Political Behavior* 1 (1979): 123–135. R. N. Lebow and J. G. Stein, *We All Lost the Cold War* (Princeton: Princeton University Press, 1994), ch. 8; M. G. Bonham, M. J. Shapiro, and T. L. Trumble, "The October War: Changes in Cognitive Orientation toward the Middle East Conflict," *International Studies Quarterly* 23 (1979): 3–44; Eldridge, *Images of Conflict*.

44 LeShan, *Psychology of War*, 110. Rosen, *War and Human Nature*.

45 S. Kernell, *Going Public: New Strategies for Presidential Leadership* (Washington: CQ Press, 1998), 163. G. C. Edwards, *On Deaf Ears: The Limits of the Bully Pulpit* (New Haven: Yale University Press, 2003), 60.

46 M. D. Toft, *The Geography of Ethnic Conflict: Identity, Interests, and the Indivisibility of Territory* (Princeton: Princeton University Press, 2003).

47 B. L. Fredrickson, "Extracting Meaning from Past Affective Experiences: The Importance of Peaks, Ends, and Specific Emotions," *Cognition and Emotion* 14 (2000): 577; D. Redelmeier and D. Kahneman, "Patients' Memories of Painful Medical Treatments: Real-Time and Retrospective Evaluations of Two Minimally Invasive Procedures," *Pain* 116 (1996): 3–8; D. Thomas and E. Diener, "Memory Accuracy in the Recall of Emotions," *Journal of Personality and Social Psychology* 59 (1990): 291–297.

48 Edwards, *On Deaf Ears*, 108–123.

49 *Washington Post* polls, 9 Sept. 2001, 6 Nov. 2001, 27 Jan. 2002; Mueller, *War, Presidents and Public Opinion*; B. Russett, *Controlling the Sword: The Democratic Governance of National Security* (Cambridge, Mass.: Harvard University Press, 1990); P. James and J. Oneal, "The Influence of Domestic and International Politics on the President's Use of Force," *Journal of Conflict Resolution* 35 (1991): 307–332; R. A. Brody, *Assessing the President: The Media, Elite Opinion, and Public Support* (Stanford: Stanford University Press, 1991), ch. 3.

50 Kernell, *Going Public*, 160–168. *Washington Post* polls, 9 Sept. 2001, 6 Nov. 2001, 27 Jan. 2002.

51 T. E. Patterson and R. D. McClure, *The Unseeing Eye: The Myth of Television Power in National Elections* (New York: Putnam, 1976); J. Mueller, "American Foreign Policy and Public Opinion in a New Era," in B. Norrander and C. Wilcox, eds., *Understanding Public Opinion* (Washington: CQ Press, 2002), 153–155. D. R. Kinder, "Communication and Politics in the Age of Information," in Sears, Huddy, and Jervis, eds., *Oxford Handbook of Political Psychology*.

52 M. Schudson, *The Power of News* (Cambridge, Mass.: Harvard University Press, 1995), 114. M. E. McCombs and D. L. Shaw, "The Agenda-Setting Function of the Media," *Public Opinion Quarterly* 36 (1972): 176–187.

53 S. Iyengar, M. D. Peters, and D. R. Kinder, "Experimental Demonstrations of the 'Not-So-Minimal' Consequences of Television News Programs," in

N. J. Kressel, ed., *Political Psychology: Classic and Contemporary Readings* (New York: Paragon House, 1993), 297. Kinder, "Communication and Politics in the Age of Information," 376–377. See also S. Iyengar and A. Simon, "News Coverage of the Gulf Crisis and Public Opinion: A Study of Agenda-Setting, Priming and Framing," in W. L. Bennett and D. L. Paletz, eds., *Taken by Storm: The Media, Public Opinion, and U.S. Foreign Policy in the Gulf War* (Chicago: University of Chicago Press, 1994), ch. 8.

54 S. Iyengar and D. R. Kinder, *News That Matters: Television and American Opinion* (Chicago: University of Chicago Press, 1987). J. A. Krosnick and D. R. Kinder, "Altering the Foundations of Popular Support for the President through Priming: Reagan and the Iran-Contra Affair," *American Political Science Review* 84 (1990): 495–512.

55 T. E. Patterson, *The Mass Media Election: How Americans Choose Their President* (New York: Praeger, 1980), ch. 11.

56 S. Aday, J. Cluverius, and S. Livingston, "As Goes the Statue, So Goes the War: The Evolution and Effects of the Victory Frame in Television Coverage of the Iraq War," *Broadcasting and Electronic Media* 49 (2005): 326.

57 J. Western, *Selling Intervention and War: The Presidency, the Media, and the American Public* (Baltimore: Johns Hopkins University Press, 2005), 19. Edwards, *On Deaf Ears*, 179. J. Zaller, *The Nature and Origins of Mass Opinion* (New York: Cambridge University Press, 1992), 16–22; R. M. Entman, *Projections of Power: Framing News, Public Opinion, and U.S. Foreign Policy* (Chicago: University of Chicago Press, 2004).

58 N. Machiavelli and P. E. Bondanella, *The Prince* (Oxford: Oxford University Press, 2005), ch. 15.

59 G. Orwell, *1984: A Novel* (New York: Plume, 1983), part 1, ch. 2.

60 V. D. Hanson, *Carnage and Culture: Landmark Battles in the Rise of Western Power* (New York: Anchor, 2001), 436.

61 Speech by President G. W. Bush, United States Naval Academy, Annapolis, Md., 30 Nov. 2005.

62 Edwards, *On Deaf Ears*. R. Glaros and B. Miroff, "Watching Ronald Reagan: Viewers' Reaction to the President on Television," *Congress and the Presidency* 10 (1983): 25–46.

63 Mueller, *War, Presidents and Public Opinion*; Edwards, *On Deaf Ears*, 27–28. C. Kaufmann, "Threat Inflation and the Failure of the Marketplace of Ideas: The Selling of the Iraq War," *International Security* 29 (2004): 37–41.

64 L. R. Jacobs and R. Y. Shapiro, *Politicians Don't Pander: Political Manipulation and the Loss of Democratic Responsiveness* (Chicago: University of Chicago Press, 2000). Edwards, *On Deaf Ears*, 110–112.

65 C. S. Taber, "Information Processing and Public Opinion," in Sears, Huddy, and Jervis, eds., *Oxford Handbook of Political Psychology*, 454–455. D. A. Baldwin, "The Sanctions Debate and the Logic of Choice," *International Security* 24 (1999): 89. Edwards, *On Deaf Ears*, 159. K. H. Jamieson, *Eloquence in an Electronic Age* (New York: Oxford University Press, 1988), 127–133.

66 W. K. Clark, *Winning Modern Wars: Iraq, Terrorism, and the American Empire* (New York: Public Affairs, 2003); Entman, *Projections of Power*.

67 R. Jenkins, *Churchill* (London: Macmillan, 2001), 660, 675, 702.

68 Brody, *Assessing the President*; E. V. Larson, "Casualties and Consensus: The Historical Role of Casualties in Domestic Support for U.S. Military Operations," RAND Corporation report M.R.-726, 1996; Jentleson and Britton, "Still Pretty Prudent," 412.

69 Zaller, *Nature and Origins of Mass Opinion*, 8–9, 100–113.

70 White, *Nobody Wanted War*, ch. 9. M. Gladwell, *The Tipping Point: How Little Things Can Make a Big Difference* (Boston: Little, Brown, 2000).

Chapter 4. Sources of Variation

1 W. Schivelbusch, *The Culture of Defeat: On National Trauma, Mourning, and Recovery* (London: Granta Books, 2003), 220.

2 M. Toft, "End of Victory? Civil War Termination in Historical Perspective" (paper delivered at the International Studies Association Conference, Honolulu, Mar. 2005); V. Fortna, "Where Have All the Victories Gone? War Outcomes in Historical Perspective" (paper delivered at the International Studies Association Conference, Honolulu, Mar. 2005).

3 Thucydides, *History of the Peloponnesian War* (London: Penguin, 1954), bk. 7, 499.

4 J. A. Rosati, "The Power of Human Cognition in the Study of World Politics," *International Studies Review* 2 (2001): 57, 58.

5 See Z. Maoz, *Paradoxes of War* (Boston: Unwin Hyman, 1990); A. Arreguín-Toft, "How the Weak Win Wars: A Theory of Asymmetric Conflict," *International Security* 26 (2001): 93–128; T. V. Paul, *Asymmetric Conflicts: War Initiation by Weaker Powers* (Cambridge: Cambridge University Press, 1994).

6 L. Jensen, *Explaining Foreign Policy* (Englewood Cliffs, N.J.: Prentice Hall, 1982). S. Van Evera, "Hypotheses on Nationalism and War," *International Security* 18 (1998): 5–39. B. Silverstein, "Enemy Images: The Psychology of U.S. Attitudes and Cognitions Regarding the Soviet Union," *American Psychologist* 44 (1989): 903–913.

7 J. Zaller, *The Nature and Origins of Mass Opinion* (New York: Cambridge University Press, 1992), 19.

8 The four predictions in this chapter emerged partly from deductive logic and partly from inductive thinking about historical cases of score-keeping and match-fixing. Therefore, the five detailed case studies we present in the following chapters are not meant to be a scientific test of our predictions (such a test would require a set of cases that did not contribute to the creation of the theory). Instead, the case studies provide more detailed explorations of the processes by which cause becomes effect—for example, how greater power tends to make a state the victim of match-fixing.

Our five case studies are not selected on the dependent variable: that is, we did not choose them because they are examples of particular judgments of victory. Instead we chose recent cases in which the most obvious independent variable (score-keeping) is insufficient to explain perceptions of victory and defeat, and we then examine whether match-fixing provides a better explanation. Throughout the book we also make frequent reference to more clear-cut disputes in which score-keeping explains evaluations very well (such as World War II). To aid the development of our theory, ideally we would have many more cases than variables; thus we complement our five main case studies with counterfactuals, comparisons with historically analogous disputes, and references to other examples of match-fixing. As well as being methodologically appropriate, the cases we study in depth are some of the most important events in international relations in the past half-century, events in which perceptions of victory had dramatic consequences. J. Gerring, "What Is a Case Study and What Is It Good For?" *American Political Science Review* 98 (2004): 348; G. King, R. O. Keohane, and S. Verba, *Designing Social Inquiry: Scientific Inference in Qualitative Research* (Princeton: Princeton University Press, 1994).

9 See A. L. George, "Case Studies and Theory Development: The Method of Structured Focused Comparison," in G. Lauren, ed., *Diplomatic History: New Approaches* (New York: Free Press, 1979). It is difficult to prove the direct or indirect causal links between these factors and subsequent evaluations of victory. However, this difficulty does not invalidate the causal link, it just introduces substantial caution into our claims. We aim to show that our causes are independent of their effects (that is, that Framework 2 factors are not merely phenomena driven by perceptions of victory). However, it should be noted that Framework 2 factors are not independent of one another; indeed, they often reinforce and shape one another (a further twist which we explore in the Conclusion). See J. Gerring, *Social Science Methodology: A Criterial Framework* (Cambridge: Cambridge University Press, 2001), 138–151.

Chapter 5. The Cuban Missile Crisis

1 G. Allison and P. Zelikow, *Essence of Decision: Explaining the Cuban Missile Crisis* (New York: Longman, 1999), 79. L. Freedman, *Kennedy's Wars: Berlin, Cuba, Laos, Vietnam* (Oxford: Oxford University Press, 2000), 216; P. Nash, *The Other Missiles of October: Eisenhower, Kennedy, and the Jupiters, 1957–1963* (Chapel Hill: University of North Carolina Press, 1997).

2 Interview with Robert McNamara in the film *Fog of War* (2003). W. Taubman, *Khrushchev: The Man and His Era* (New York: Norton, 2003), 581. T. C. Reeves, *A Question of Character: A Life of John F. Kennedy* (London: Bloomsbury, 1991), 388. *Economist*, 2 Feb. 2002, 41.

3 Gallup poll, 26–31 July, 16–21 Nov. 1962, 13–18 Dec. 1962 (see similar polls asked from 1959–1979); T. W. Smith, *The Impact of the Cuban Missile Crisis on American Public Opinion* (Chicago: National Opinion Research Center, University of Chicago, 2002). E. Alterman, *When Presidents Lie: A History of Official Deception and Its Consequences* (New York: Viking, 2004), 159. Z. Brzezinski, "The Implications of Change for United States Foreign Policy," *U.S. Department of State Bulletin* 52 (1967): 19–21.

4 J. G. Blight and P. Brenner, *Sad and Luminous Days: Cuba's Struggle with the Superpowers after the Missile Crisis* (Lanham, Md.: Rowman and Littlefield, 2002), 15. Anatoly Dobrynin, the USSR's ambassador to the United States, said the Soviet leadership saw the outcome as "a blow to its prestige bordering on humiliation." Taubman, *Khrushchev*, 579.

5 Reeves, *Question of Character*, 391; D. A. Brugioni, *Eyeball to Eyeball: The*

inside Story of the Cuban Missile Crisis (New York: Random House, 1991), 558; R. N. Lebow and J. G. Stein, *We All Lost the Cold War* (Princeton: Princeton University Press, 1994), 144. Polyansky quoted in A. Fursenko and T. Naftali, *One Hell of a Gamble: Khrushchev, Castro, and Kennedy, 1958–1964* (New York: Norton, 1997), 354.

6   E. Abel, *The Missiles of October: The Story of the Cuban Missile Crisis of 1962* (London: Cox and Wyman, 1966), 193–194. Taubman, *Khrushchev*, 579. Blight and Brenner, *Sad and Luminous Days*, xv–xvi. Reeves, *Question of Character*, 391.

7   A. L. George, *Awaiting Armageddon: How Americans Faced the Cuban Missile Crisis* (Chapel Hill: University of North Carolina Press, 2003), 139. Louis Harris poll, 6–14 Dec. 1974. Market Opinion Research poll, 7–18 Sept. 1988; Smith, *Impact of the Crisis on American Public Opinion*, 26.

8   Reeves, *Question of Character*, 392; A. M. Schlesinger, *A Thousand Days: John F. Kennedy in the White House* (London: Andre Deutsch, 1965), 715; see also T. C. Sorenson, *Kennedy* (New York: Harper and Row, 1965); R. Hilsman, *To Move a Nation: The Politics of Foreign Policy in the Administration of John F. Kennedy* (Garden City, N.Y.: Doubleday, 1967); R. Kennedy, *Thirteen Days* (New York: Norton, 1969); A. Stein, *Why Nations Cooperate: Circumstance and Choice in International Relations* (Ithaca: Cornell University Press, 1990), 141.

9   V. Zubok and C. Pleshakov, *Inside the Kremlin's Cold War: From Stalin to Khrushchev* (Cambridge, Mass.: Harvard University Press, 1996), 259. R. Service, *A History of Twentieth-Century Russia* (Cambridge, Mass.: Harvard University Press, 1997), 374. W. Poundstone, *Prisoner's Dilemma: John Von Neumann, Game Theory, and the Puzzle of the Bomb* (Oxford: Oxford University Press, 1992), 211. M. Brecher and J. Wilkenfeld, *A Study of Crisis* (Ann Arbor: University of Michigan Press, 1997), 703.

10 Lebow and Stein, *We All Lost the Cold War*, 140–145. "The Reprieve and What Needs to Be Done with It," *I. F. Stone's Weekly*, 5 Nov. 1962, 1; R. Hagan, "Cuba: Triumph or Tragedy," *Dissent* 10 (1963): 13–26. R. Nixon, "Castro, Cuba, and John F. Kennedy," *Reader's Digest* (1964): 297. Interview with McNamara in the film *Fog of War* (2003).

11 Khrushchev quoted in Reeves, *Question of Character*, 390, and Abel, *Missiles of October*, 197. N. S. Khrushchev, *Khrushchev Remembers* (Boston: Little, Brown, 1970), 500.

12 R. N. Lebow, "Domestic Politics and the Cuban Missile Crisis," *Diplomatic History* 14 (1990): 488. Taubman, *Khrushchev*, 579.

13 D. C. Copeland, *The Origins of Major War* (Ithaca: Cornell University Press, 2000), 195.

14 Allison and Zelikow, *Essence of Decision*; Lebow, "Domestic Politics and the Cuban Missile Crisis"; W. I. Cohen, *America in the Age of Soviet Power, 1945–1991* (Cambridge: Cambridge University Press, 1999), 144–145; R. N. Lebow, *Between Peace and War: The Nature of International Crisis* (Baltimore: John Hopkins University Press, 1981), 64–65.

15 Allison and Zelikow, *Essence of Decision*, 79. Reeves, *Question of Character*, 364; R. S. Thompson, *The Missiles of October: The Declassified Story of John F. Kennedy and the Cuban Missile Crisis* (New York: Simon and Schuster,

1992), 121. R. L. Garthoff, "Documenting the Cuban Missile Crisis," *Diplomatic History* 24 (2000): 297–303.

16 Fursenko and Naftali, *One Hell of a Gamble*, 327. For the argument that Kennedy might have attempted an invasion of Cuba without the missile crisis, but never seriously considered this option after the crisis, see J. L. Gaddis, *We Now Know: Rethinking Cold War History* (Oxford: Oxford University Press, 1997), 279.

17 Allison and Zelikow, *Essence of Decision*, 242. Alterman, *When Presidents Lie*, 115. D. P. Houghton, "Essence of Excision: A Critique of the New Version of Essence of Decision," *Security Studies* 10 (2000): 151–178; Freedman, *Kennedy's Wars*, 206. Nash, *The Other Missiles of October.*

18 *Khrushchev Remembers*, 182.

19 M. J. White, "New Scholarship on the Cuban Missile Crisis," *Diplomatic History* 26 (2002): 147–153; Lebow and Stein, *We All Lost the Cold War*, chs. 2–3.

20 Lebow, *Between Peace and War*, 82, 64. Taubman, *Khrushchev*, ch. 19. Freedman, *Kennedy's Wars*, 171–173, 223. Allison and Zelikow, *Essence of Decision*, 99–109.

21 B. Kuklick, "Reconsidering the Missile Crisis and Its Interpretations," *Diplomatic History* 25 (2001): 520.

22 In a letter sent privately to Kennedy on 26 October 1962, Khrushchev said: "Give us a pledge not to invade Cuba, and we will remove the missiles." Fursenko and Naftali, *One Hell of a Gamble*, 257–258; Allison and Zelikow, *Essence of Decision*, 349. Khrushchev publicly proposed the removal of missiles from Turkey the next day, without having received a response to the letter.

23 M. R. Beschloss, *The Crisis Years: Kennedy and Khrushchev, 1960–1963* (New York: Edward Burlingame, 1991); T. G. Paterson, "Fixation with Cuba: The Bay of Pigs, Missile Crisis, and Covert War against Fidel Castro," in Paterson, ed., *Kennedy's Quest for Victory: American Foreign Policy, 1961–1963* (New York: Oxford University Press, 1989); Lebow and Stein, *We All Lost the Cold War*, 28–50; Blight and Brenner, *Sad and Luminous Days*, 9; Reeves, *Question of Character*, 365; Gaddis, *We Now Know*, 262–263, 274–275.

24 Fursenko and Naftali, *One Hell of a Gamble*, 355; Taubman, *Khrushchev*, 533–535; S. M. Stern, *Averting "the Final Failure": John F. Kennedy and the Secret Cuban Missile Crisis Meetings* (Stanford: Stanford University Press, 2003), 20.

25 Letter available in R. Kennedy, *Thirteen Days*, 162. When vacationing on the Black Sea, Khrushchev would gaze out over the waters toward Turkey, telling guests that what he saw were "U.S. missiles in Turkey aimed at *my dacha.*" Gaddis, *We Now Know*, 264.

26 Fursenko and Naftali, *One Hell of a Gamble*, 272, 284–285; Gaddis, *We Now Know*, 106; Lebow and Stein, *We All Lost the Cold War*, 123–140.

27 Lebow, "Domestic Politics and the Cuban Missile Crisis"; Hilsman, *To Move a Nation.* Freedman, *Kennedy's Wars*, 225, 175. Fursenko and Naftali, *One Hell of a Gamble*, 355. P. Zelikow, "American Policy and Cuba, 1961–63," *Diplomatic History* 24 (2000): 321. Blight and Brenner, *Sad and Lumi-*

nous Days, 2. M. J. White, *The Cuban Missile Crisis* (London: Macmillan, 1996), 225.

28 J. G. Hershberg, "Before the 'Missiles of October': Did Kennedy Plan a Military Strike against Cuba?" in J. A. Nathan, ed., *The Cuban Missile Crisis Revisited* (New York: St. Martin's, 1992), 237; Alterman, *When Presidents Lie*, 112–113, 133. Fursenko and Naftali, *One Hell of a Gamble*, 335–336, 320.

29 The U.S. air force favored keeping the missiles in Turkey. Lebow and Stein, *We All Lost the Cold War*, 123.

30 Reeves, *Question of Character*, 387–388. Freedman, *Kennedy's Wars*, 215.

31 Gaddis, *We Now Know*, 278. D. D. P. Johnson and D. Tierney, "Essence of Victory: Winning and Losing International Crises," *Security Studies* 13 (2004): 350–381.

32 Alterman, *When Presidents Lie*, 123.

33 Q. Zhai, *Beijing and the Vietnam Conflict, 1964–1965, New Chinese Evidence* (Washington: Cold War International History Project, 1995); M. Y. Prozumenschikov, "The Sino-Indian Conflict, the Cuban Missile Crisis, and the Sino-Soviet Split, October 1962: New Evidence from the Russian Archives," *Cold War International History Project Bulletin* 8–9 (1996/97): 251–257; Taubman, *Khrushchev*, 534.

34 Blight and Brenner, *Sad and Luminous Days*, 1, 20–22, 75. "Literally overnight, the Cuban perception of the Soviets shifted from that of savior to traitor . . . stunned at what they saw in the crisis as Soviet ineptitude, spinelessness, and callous disregard for the fate of the Cubans and their revolution . . . the Cubans would never fully trust the Soviets again for the security of their island. This was the first psychological scar left in Cuban memory by the missile crisis. The second was that the outcome of the crisis crushed their idealistic hopes for the success of an immediate world revolution, along the lines of the Cuban revolution." Castro said that it was "as if we were deprived of not only the missiles, but of the very symbol of solidarity." Ibid., 74–78.

35 Brugioni, *Eyeball to Eyeball*, 557, 492–493. Freedman, *Kennedy's Wars*, 194.

36 Zubok and Pleshakov, *Inside the Kremlin's Cold War*, 262–268; Lebow and Stein, *We All Lost the Cold War*, 58–59.

37 J. Weldes, *Constructing National Interests: The United States and the Cuban Missile Crisis* (Minneapolis: University of Minnesota Press, 1999); R. Weisbrot, *Maximum Danger: Kennedy, the Missiles, and the Crisis of American Confidence* (Chicago: Ivan R. Dee, 2002). Smith, *Impact of the Crisis on American Public Opinion*.

38 Poundstone, *Prisoner's Dilemma*; Stein, *Why Nations Cooperate*. Allison and Zelikow, *Essence of Decision*, 232–235. Rusk quoted in Freedman, *Kennedy's Wars*, 197.

39 Walter Trohan, *Chicago Tribune*, 27 Oct. 1962. *Time*, 2 Nov. 1962. Lebow and Stein, *We All Lost the Cold War*, 144. For historians, see, e.g., Reeves, *Question of Character*, ch. 16; K. O'Donnell, D. F. Powers, and J. McCarthy, *Johnny We Hardly Knew Ye: Memories of John Fitzgerald Kennedy* (New York: Pocket Books, 1973); Brugioni, *Eyeball to Eyeball*.

40 Harold Macmillan was aware of the dangers of a negotiated settlement. "If Khrushchev comes to a conference hall he will of course try to trade his

Cuban position against his ambitions in Berlin and elsewhere. This we must avoid at all costs, as it will endanger the unity of the Alliance." The Americans similarly saw a summit meeting as a potential trap. Despite this, a UN-sponsored agreement remained a very real possibility given the involvement of Secretary-General U Thant in the crisis. Freedman, *Kennedy's Wars*, 194, 203.

41 *Washington Post*, 5 Feb. 2003.

42 M. Kern, P. W. Levering, and R. B. Levering, *The Kennedy Crises: The Press, the Presidency, and Foreign Policy* (London: University of North Carolina Press, 1983), pt. 4. On muted criticism of the administration's deception, see C. Wyatt, *Paper Soldiers: The American Press and the Vietnam War* (New York: Norton, 1993), 45.

43 J. S. Levy, "Loss Aversion, Framing Effects, and International Conflict," in M. I. Midlarsky, ed., *Handbook of War Studies* 2 (Ann Arbor: University of Michigan Press, 2000). Blight and Brenner, *Sad and Luminous Days*.

44 E. R. May and P. Zelikow, *The Kennedy Tapes: Inside the White House during the Cuban Missile Crisis* (Cambridge, Mass.: Belknap Press, 1997).

45 Alterman, *When Presidents Lie*, 118–119; George, *Awaiting Armageddon*, 109–112; Freedman, *Kennedy's Wars*, 220. G. T. Allison, *Essence of Decision: Explaining the Cuban Missile Crisis* (Boston: Little, Brown, 1971), 209. Ironically, Stevenson did much to generate worldwide support for the United States with his theatrical performance in the UN Security Council on 25 October 1962. White, *Cuban Missile Crisis*, 206.

46 May and Zelikow, *The Kennedy Tapes*, 29; Freedman, *Kennedy's Wars*, 221.

47 Lebow, *Between Peace and War*, 302–303; I. N. Gallhofer and W. E. Saris, *Foreign Policy Decision-Making: A Qualitative and Quantitative Analysis of Political Argumentation* (Westport, Conn.: Praeger, 1996). B. J. Bernstein, "Reconsidering the Missile Crisis: Dealing with the Problems of the American Jupiters in Turkey," in J. A. Nathan, ed., *The Cuban Missile Crisis Revisited* (New York: St. Martin's, 1992), 104, 125–126.

48 M. Bundy, *Danger and Survival: Choices about the Bomb in the First Fifty Years* (New York: Random House, 1988), 432–433, 434. *New York Times*, 29 Oct. 1962. Fursenko and Naftali, *One Hell of a Gamble*, 321. Bundy quoted in Lebow and Stein, *We All Lost the Cold War*, 123.

49 Fursenko and Naftali, *One Hell of a Gamble*, 324, 328; Alterman, *When Presidents Lie*, 106.

50 White, "New Scholarship on the Cuban Missile Crisis." Cohen, *America in the Age of Soviet Power*, 145. George, *Awaiting Armageddon*, 137.

51 Alterman, *When Presidents Lie*, 132; Dobrynin in CNN, *The Cold War*, episode 10, "Cuba," 29 Nov. 1998.

52 Copeland, *Origins of Major War*, 202. In one plan Kennedy considered, the United States would have agreed to a public trade of missiles following a request by the UN secretary general. Fursenko and Naftali, *One Hell of a Gamble*, 284; Freedman, *Kennedy's Wars*, 215; Lebow and Stein, *We All Lost the Cold War*, 127–129; May and Zelikow, *The Kennedy Tapes*, 207; Alterman, *When Presidents Lie*, 105–107.

53 Alterman, *When Presidents Lie*, 123. Polyansky quoted in Fursenko and Naftali, *One Hell of a Gamble*, 354.

54 Blight and Brenner, *Sad and Luminous Days*, 73, 106.

55 Bernstein, "Reconsidering the Missile Crisis," 106.

Chapter 6. The Tet Offensive

1 M. J. Gilbert and W. Head, eds., *The Tet Offensive* (Westport, Conn.: Praeger, 1996). Our colloquial "North Vietnam" refers to the Democratic Republic of Vietnam (DRV), and "South Vietnam" refers to the Republic of Vietnam (RVN).

2 B. Brodie, "The Tet Offensive," in N. Frankland and C. Dowling, eds., *Decisive Battles of the Twentieth Century: Land, Sea, Air* (New York: McKay, 1976).

3 By referring to the insurgents as communists, we do not mean to imply that communism was the primary motivation for all the fighters. The major motivation was often nationalism rather than communism, but such insurgents were still communist led.

4 R. E. Ford, *Tet 1968: Understanding the Surprise* (London: Frank Cass, 1995); J. J. Wirtz, *The Tet Offensive: Intelligence Failure in War* (Ithaca: Cornell University Press, 1991).

5 R. H. Spector, *After Tet: The Bloodiest Year in Vietnam* (New York: Free Press, 1993).

6 S. F. Hayward, *The Age of Reagan: The Fall of the Old Liberal Order* (Roseville, Calif.: Prima, 2001), 191.

7 W. S. Turley, "Tactical Defeat, Strategic Victory for Hanoi," in R. J. McMahon, ed., *Major Problems in the History of the Vietnam War* (Boston: Houghton Mifflin, 2003), 371–372; M. J. Gilbert, "The Cost of Losing the 'Other War' in Vietnam," in Gilbert, ed., *Why the North Won the Vietnam War* (New York: Palgrave, 2002); Military History Institute of Vietnam, *Victory in Vietnam: The Official History of the People's Army of Vietnam, 1954–1975*, trans. M. L. Pribbenow (Lawrence: University Press of Kansas, 2002)

8 N. V. Long, "The Tet Offensive and Its Aftermath," in Gilbert and Head, *Tet Offensive*, 93. Ford, *Tet 1968*, 139; D. Oberdorfer, *Tet! The Turning Point in the Vietnam War* (Baltimore: Johns Hopkins University Press, 2001), 252–253.

9 B. Diem, "My Recollections of the Tet Offensive," in Gilbert and Head, *Tet Offensive*, 131.

10 L. B. Johnson and D. K. Goodwin, *The Johnson Presidential Press Conferences* (New York: E. M. Coleman, 1978), 897. L. B. Johnson, *The Vantage Point: Perspectives of the Presidency, 1963–1969* (New York: Holt, Rinehart and Winston, 1971), 383; S. S. Gartner, *Strategic Assessment in War* (New Haven: Yale University Press, 1997), 139–140. W. C. Westmoreland, *A Soldier Reports* (Garden City, N.Y.: Doubleday, 1976), 332; Spector, *After Tet*, 5–6.

11 Gilbert and Head, eds., *The Tet Offensive*.

12 Spector, *After Tet*, 23, 5. B. Tuchman, *The March of Folly: From Troy to Vietnam* (New York: Knopf, 1984), 348. R. Buzzanco, "The Myth of Tet: American Failure and the Politics of War," in Gilbert and Head, *Tet Offensive*, 231. H. A. Kissinger, *Ending the Vietnam War: A History of America's Involvement in and Extrication from the Vietnam War* (New York: Simon and Schuster, 2003), 47; *Wall Street Journal*, 23 Feb. 1968. D. C. Hallin, *The*

"Uncensored War": The Media and Vietnam (New York: Oxford University Press, 1986), 161–162.

13 J. E. Mueller, *War, Presidents, and Public Opinion* (New York: Wiley, 1973), 54–55; Hallin, *Uncensored War*, 168; R. Sobel, *The Impact of Public Opinion on U.S. Foreign Policy since Vietnam: Constraining the Colossus* (New York: Oxford University Press, 2001), 36.

14 Gallup polls, 1967–1968. Hallin, *Uncensored War*, 169, 173; W. M. Hammond, *Reporting Vietnam: Media and Military at War* (Lawrence: University Press of Kansas, 1998), 121–122. G. C. Herring, *America's Longest War: The United States and Vietnam, 1950–1975* (Boston: McGraw-Hill, 2002), 199. D. C. Foyle, "Public Opinion and Bosnia: Anticipating Disaster," in R. G. Carter, ed., *Contemporary Cases in U.S. Foreign Policy: From Terrorism to Trade* (Washington: C.Q. Inc., 2005), 28, and Mueller, *War, Presidents, and Public Opinion*, 106–107.

15 Herring, *America's Longest War*, 189, 197. Gilbert, "Cost of Losing the 'Other War,'" 183. Gartner, *Strategic Assessment*, 127. Clifford quoted in Tuchman, *March of Folly*, 354.

16 Long, "Tet Offensive and Its Aftermath," 93.

17 Herring, *America's Longest War*, 188.

18 Estimates of numbers killed in Tet offensive: S. C. Tucker, *Encyclopedia of the Vietnam War: A Political, Social, and Military History* (Oxford: Oxford University Press, 1998), 396: over 58,000 VC and North Vietnamese, 3,895 U.S., 4,954 ARVN, and 214 non-U.S. allies; See also Gartner, *Strategic Assessment in War*; Long, "Tet Offensive and Its Aftermath"; *www.vietnamwall.org*.

19 Turley, "Tactical Defeat, Strategic Victory," 369. Hayward, *Age of Reagan*, 184. See also M. W. Woodruff, *Unheralded Victory: Who Won the Vietnam War?* (London: HarperCollins, 1999).

20 P. Feaver and C. Gelpi, *Choosing Your Battles: American Civil-Military Relations and the Use of Force* (Princeton: Princeton University Press, 2004), 138–139; C. Gelpi, P. D. Feaver, and J. Reifler, "Success Matters: Casualty Sensitivity and the War in Iraq," *International Security* 30 (2005): 7–46. Hallin, *Uncensored War*, 174–175.

21 G. H. Hess, *Vietnam and the United States: Origins and Legacy of War* (Boston: Twayne, 1990), 108.

22 R. Brigham, "The N.L.F. and the Tet Offensive," in Gilbert and Head, *Tet Offensive*. Gilbert, "Cost of Losing the 'Other War,'" 180–181. A. C. Guan, "Decision-Making Leading to the Tet Offensive (1968)—The Vietnamese Communist Perspective," *Journal of Contemporary History* 33 (1998): 341–353. W. J. Duiker, "Victory by Other Means: The Foreign Policy of the Democratic Republic of Vietnam," in M. J. Gilbert, ed., *Why the North Won the Vietnam War* (New York: Palgrave, 2002), 67.

23 Peter Brush, "The Battle of Khe Sanh, 1968," in Gilbert and Head, *Tet Offensive*.

24 Guan, "Decision-Making Leading to the Tet Offensive." Turley, "Tactical Defeat, Strategic Victory"; Anonymous, "A Communist Party Evaluation, 1968," in McMahon, *Major Problems in the History of the Vietnam War*. Tucker, *Encyclopedia of the Vietnam War*, 397. V. Pohle, *The Viet Cong in*

Saigon: Tactics and Objectives during the Tet Offensive (Santa Monica, Calif.: RAND, 1969).

25 Woodruff, *Unheralded Victory*, 33; T. L. Cubbage, "Westmoreland vs. C.B.S.: Was Intelligence Corrupted by Policy Demands?" in Handel, ed., *Leaders and Intelligence*, 119. S. Karnow, *Vietnam: A History* (New York: Penguin, 1984), 544. M. Handel, "Leaders and Intelligence," in Handel, ed., *Leaders and Intelligence*, 27. Ford, *Tet 1968*, 116, 121.

26 Woodruff, *Unheralded Victory*, 46. Hess, *Vietnam and the United States*, 117.

27 Although the U.S. had won most previous wars, Korea is somewhat ambiguous. The U.S. initially saw the war as a defeat, then later as more of a success. This "we always win" mind-set was based on previously perceiving unclear or drawn outcomes as U.S. victories (e.g. the War of 1812 or the Cuban missile crisis).

28 Brogan quoted in D. Halberstam, *The Best and the Brightest* (New York: Penguin, 1972), 123. D. A. Armor and S. E. Taylor, "Situated Optimism: Specific Outcome Expectancies and Self-Regulation," *Advances in Experimental Social Psychology* 30 (1998): 361. D. Kaiser, *American Tragedy: Kennedy, Johnson, and the Origins of the Vietnam War* (Cambridge, Mass.: Harvard University Press, 2000). Tuchman, *March of Folly*, 321.

29 C. Wyatt, *Paper Soldiers: The American Press and the Vietnam War* (New York: Norton, 1993), 178, 179. Hallin, *Uncensored War*, 165. Johnson's speech, WGBH, transcripts of *Vietnam: A Television History*, "Tet (1968)" (1983), www.pbs.org. Gartner, *Strategic Assessment*, 131; Herring, *America's Longest War*, 182–187. Halberstam, *Best and Brightest*; Diem, "Recollections of the Tet Offensive," 130; Buzzanco, "Myth of Tet," 233. C. Pach, "The War on Television," in Young and Buzzanco, *Companion to the Vietnam War*, 460.

30 L. Gelb and R. K. Betts, *The Irony of Vietnam: The System Worked* (Washington: Brookings Institution, 1980); D. D. P. Johnson, *Overconfidence and War: The Havoc and Glory of Positive Illusions* (Cambridge, Mass.: Harvard University Press, 2004); I. L. Janis, *Victims of Groupthink: Psychological Studies of Policy Decisions and Fiascoes* (Boston: Houghton Mifflin, 1972). Johnson, *Vantage Point*, 380.

31 Diem, "Recollections of the Tet Offensive," 130. "Bloody Path to Peace," *New York Times*, 1 Feb. 1968, quoted in Hammond, *Reporting Vietnam*, 112. P. Braestrup, *Big Story: How the American Press and Television Reported and Interpreted the Crisis of Tet 1968 in Vietnam and Washington* (New Haven: Yale University Press, 1977), 133. Rusk quoted in Spector, *After Tet*, 19.

32 Cronkite quoted in Herring, *America's Longest War*, 198. R. Komer, "Robert Komer Recalls Tet's Impact," in McMahon, *Major Problems in the History of the Vietnam War*, 352–354.

33 Herring, *America's Longest War*, 198; Oberdorfer, *Tet*, 174.

34 Mueller, *War, Presidents, and Public Opinion*, 116–118.

35 Tucker, *Encyclopedia of the Vietnam War*, 396.

36 N. C. Ky, *How We Lost the Vietnam War* (New York: First Cooper Square, 2002), 158. Komer, "Komer Recalls Tet's Impact," 352–354. Clifford quoted in Buzzanco, "Myth of Tet," 232.

37 Woodruff, *Unheralded Victory*, 37. K. W. Nolan, *The Battle for Saigon* (New York: Pocket Books, 1996); Hammond, *Reporting Vietnam*, 111.

38 Braestrup, *Big Story*, 120–121.

39 Wyatt, *Paper Soldiers*, 165. E. Durschmied, *How Chance and Stupidity Have Changed History: The Hinge Factor* (New York: MJF Books, 1999), 330.

40 V. D. Hanson, *Carnage and Culture: Landmark Battles in the Rise of Western Power* (New York: Anchor, 2001), 418. Hess, *Vietnam and the United States*, 111.

41 Hammond, *Reporting Vietnam*, 115.

42 J. S. Olson and R. Roberts, *Where the Domino Fell: America and Vietnam 1945–1995* (New York: St. Martin's, 1996), 187.

43 Hess, *Vietnam and the United States*, 103–104; Turley, "Tactical Defeat, Strategic Victory," 363; WGBH, transcripts of "Tet (1968)"; Herring, *America's Longest War*, 185; J. Hughes-Wilson, *Military Intelligence Blunders* (New York: Carroll and Graf, 1999), 177.

44 Wyatt, *Paper Soldiers*; W. M. Hammond, *Public Affairs: The Military and the Media, 1968–1973* (Washington: Center of Military History, U.S. Army, 1995). Hallin, *Uncensored War*, 174–175.

45 Durschmied, *Chance and Stupidity*, 326. Hammond, *Reporting Vietnam*, 110. K. Willenson, *The Bad War: An Oral History of the Vietnam War* (New York: New American Library, 1987).

46 Herring, *America's Longest War*, 197. Braestrup, *Big Story*, 467. A. J. Joes, *America and Guerrilla Warfare* (Lexington: University Press of Kentucky, 2000), 232.

47 Braestrup, *Big Story*, 138, 219. Hallin, *Uncensored War*, 171. Ky, *How We Lost the Vietnam War*, 152–153. Joes, *America and Guerrilla Warfare*, 234; R. Elegant, "Viet Nam: How to Lose a War," *Encounter* 57 (1981): 73–90.

48 Braestrup, *Big Story*, 508.

49 Oberdorfer, *Tet*, 176.

50 Gartner, *Strategic Assessment*, 131.

51 Ibid., 121.

52 WGBH, transcripts of "Tet (1968)." R. K. White, *Nobody Wanted War: Misperception in Vietnam and Other Wars* (Garden City, N.Y.: Doubleday, 1968), 222. Braestrup, *Big Story*, 127.

53 Herring, *America's Longest War*, 192; E. G. Wheeler, "Earle G. Wheeler's Report on Military Prospects after Tet, 1968," in McMahon, *Major Problems in the History of the Vietnam War*, 344–347. L. Berman, "The Tet Offensive," in Gilbert and Head, *Tet Offensive*, 24–25. Tucker, *Encyclopedia of the Vietnam War*, 397. Komer, "Komer Recalls Tet's Impact," 352–354.

54 A. F. Krepinevich, *The Army and Vietnam* (Baltimore: Johns Hopkins University Press, 1986), 248. G. Warner, "Lyndon Johnson's War? Part 2: From Escalation to Negotiation," *International Affairs* 81 (2005). Buzzanco, "Myth of Tet," 247.

55 Braestrup, *Big Story*, 509.

56 Long, "Tet Offensive and Its Aftermath," 93.

57 Hallin, *Uncensored War*, 162–163; Braestrup, *Big Story*, 472.

58 Diem, "Recollections of the Tet Offensive," 133.

Chapter 7. The Yom Kippur War

1 C. S. Liebman, "The Myth of Defeat: The Memory of the Yom Kippur War in Israeli Society," *Middle Eastern Studies* 29 (1993): 413. M. Gilbert, *Israel:*

A History (New York: William Morrow, 1998), 452–453. Hisdai quoted in Herb Keinon, "A Victory Remembered as a Defeat," *Jerusalem Post*, online ed., 25 Sept. 1998.

2 M. Tamir, *Yom Kippur War Children's and Youth Art: Story and Drawing, Poem and Painting* (Jerusalem: Ministry of Education and Culture, 1973/4), 125. C. S. Liebman, "Paradigms Sometimes Fit: The Haredi Response to the Yom Kippur War," *Israeli Affairs* 1 (1995): 177. K. Nakhleh, "The Political Effects of the October War on Israeli Society," in N. H. Aruri, ed., *Middle East Crucible: Studies on the Arab-Israeli War of October 1973* (Wilmette, Ill: Medina University Press International, 1975), 157; Liebman, "Myth of Defeat."

3 G. Meir, *My Life* (New York: Putnam, 1975), 420, 452–453. *Jerusalem Post*, 26 Nov. 1973. H. Blum, *The Eve of Destruction: The Untold Story of the Yom Kippur War* (New York: HarperCollins, 2003), 228–229.

4 L. Guttman and S. Levy, "Dynamics of Three Varieties of Morale: The Case of Israel," in S. Breznitz, ed., *Stress in Israel* (New York: Van Nostrand Reinhold, 1983), 102–113; E. Etzioni-Halevy and R. Shapiro, *Political Culture in Israel: Cleavage and Integration among Israeli Jews* (New York: Praeger, 1977), 183–204; Liebman, "Myth of Defeat," 401.

5 Etzioni-Halevy and Shapiro, *Political Culture in Israel*, 116–117; B. Morris, *Righteous Victims: A History of the Zionist-Arab Conflict, 1881–1999* (New York: Knopf, 1999), 442. Nakhleh, "Political Effects of the October War," 159, 170.

6 Etzioni-Halevy and Shapiro, *Political Culture in Israel*, 212.

7 Y. Meital, "Drums of War and Bells of Peace: Egypt's Perspective on the 1973 War," in B. Rubin, J. Ginat, and M. Ma'oz, eds., *From War to Peace: Arab-Israeli Relations 1973–1993* (New York: New York University Press, 1994), 55; E. O'Ballance, *No Victor, No Vanquished* (San Rafael, Calif.: Presidio, 1978), 349.

8 Sadat, Isma'il, and Faisal quoted in J. W. Amos, *Arab-Israeli Military/Political Relations: Arab Perceptions and the Politics of Escalation* (New York: Pergamon, 1979), 208. M. A. G. El-Gamasy, *The October War: Memoirs of Field Marshal El-Gamasy of Egypt* (Cairo: American University Press, 1993), 4. D. Hirst and I. Beeson, *Sadat* (London: Faber and Faber, 1981).

9 D. Starr, "The October War and Arab Students' Self-Conceptions," *Middle East Journal* 32 (1978): 444–456. Associated Press, "Egypt Marks Anniversary of Yom Kippur War," *Jerusalem Post*, online ed., 7 Oct. 1998. K. J. Beattie, *Egypt during the Sadat Years* (New York: Palgrave, 2000), 134. *Al-Ahram*, weekly online ed., 9–15 Oct. 2003, *weekly.ahram.org.eg/2003/659/pr1.htm*.

10 G. Ben-Dor, "Confidence-Building and the Peace Process," in Rubin, Ginat, and Ma'oz, *From War to Peace*, 73. R. Patai, *The Arab Mind* (Long Island City, N.Y.: Hatherleigh, 2002), 363–364, 375. Associated Press, "Egypt Marks Anniversary of Yom Kippur War," *Jerusalem Post*, online ed., 7 Oct. 1998.

11 C. Herzog, *The War of Atonement* (London: Weidenfeld and Nicolson, 1975), 284–285.

12 A. Shlaim, "Failure in National Intelligence Estimates: The Case of the Yom Kippur War," *World Politics* 28 (1976): 348–380.

13 I. S. Minerbi, "Western Europe: Overview," in M. Davis, ed., *The Yom Kippur War: Israel and the Jewish People* (New York: Arno, 1974), 183–184.

14 Rabinovich, *Yom Kippur War*, 54–55; Morris, *Righteous Victims*, 394–396.

15 K. M. Pollack, *Arabs at War: Military Effectiveness, 1948–1991* (Lincoln: University of Nebraska Press, 2002), 512–513. R. B. Parker, ed., *The October War: A Retrospective* (Gainesville: University Press of Florida, 2001), 247.

16 Rabinovich, *Yom Kippur War*, 495, 488. El-Gamasy, *October War*, 336. Morris, *Righteous Victims*, 438.

17 *Jerusalem Post*, 15 Oct. 1973; O'Ballance, *No Victor*, 349. Liebman, "Myth of Defeat," 400–402.

18 J. Slater, "Lost Opportunities for Peace in the Arab-Israeli Conflict: Israel and Syria, 1948–2001," *International Security* 27 (2002): 94.

19 Rabinovich, *Yom Kippur War*, 41; Meital, "Drums of War," 57.

20 A. Sella, "Policy and Back Channels, 1970–1973," in Rubin, Ginat, and Ma'oz, *From War to Peace*, 42; Morris, *Righteous Victims*, 388–399; Gilbert, *Israel*, 406, 414, 423. Rabinovich, *Yom Kippur War*, 220, 340.

21 *Jerusalem Post*, 27 Nov. 1973.

22 R. N. Lebow and J. G. Stein, *We All Lost the Cold War* (Princeton: Princeton University Press, 1994). M. Gazit, "Egypt and Israel: Was There a Peace Opportunity Missed in 1971?" *Journal of Contemporary History* 32 (1997): 97–115; S. Dinitz, "The Yom Kippur War: Diplomacy of War and Peace," in R. Kumaraswamy, ed., *Revisiting the Yom Kippur War* (London: Frank Cass, 2000), 105; Rabinovich, *Yom Kippur War*, 11–15; S. Shamir, "The Yom Kippur War as a Factor in the Peace Process," in Rubin, Ginat, and Ma'oz, *From War to Peace*, 32.

23 Sella, "Policy and Back Channels," 42; Z. Ma'oz, "Decision-Making and Bargaining in the Arab-Israeli Conflict," in Rubin, Ginat, and Ma'oz, *From War to Peace*, 50–51; Parker, *October War*, 39.

24 Rabinovich, *Yom Kippur War*, 320. J. G. Stein, "Calculation, Miscalculation, and Conventional Deterrence 1: The View from Cairo," in R. Jervis, R. N. Lebow, and J. G. Stein, eds., *Psychology and Deterrence* (Baltimore: Johns Hopkins University Press, 1985), 37.

25 El-Gamasy, *October War*, 136; Rabinovich, *Yom Kippur War*, 320–321, 414–415; Gilbert, *Israel*, 462. J. Waterbury, *Egypt: Burdens of the Past, Options for the Future* (Bloomington: Indiana University Press, 1978), 32.

26 Rabinovich, *Yom Kippur War*, 432–433.

27 Morris, *Righteous Victims*, 387; Rabinovich, *Yom Kippur War*, 144; El-Gamasy, *October War*, 138; A. Drysdale and R. A. Hinnebusch, *Syria and the Middle East Peace Process* (New York: Council on Foreign Relations, 1991), 108.

28 Morris, *Righteous Victims*, 427.

29 Liebman, "Myth of Defeat," 400–401; O. Grosbard, *Israel on the Couch: The Psychology of the Peace Process* (Albany: State University of New York Press, 2003).

30 Blum, *Eve of Destruction*, 14. Gilbert, *Israel*, 423.

31 Rabinovich, *Yom Kippur War*, 7–8, 34; R. Jervis, "Perceiving and Coping with Threat," in Jervis, Lebow, and Stein, *Psychology and Deterrence*, 19. I. L. Janis, *Victims of Groupthink: Psychological Studies of Policy Decisions and Fiascoes* (Boston: Houghton Mifflin, 1972).

32 Elazar quoted in Rabinovich, *Yom Kippur War*, 52. Blum, *Eve of Destruction*, 92. Dayan quoted in Gilbert, *Israel*, 423. Yossi Klein Halevi, "War and

Atonement," *Jerusalem Post*, online ed., 2003 feature on the Yom Kippur War.

33 Rabinovich, *Yom Kippur War*, 498. A. Sharon and D. Chanoff, *Warrior* (New York: Simon and Schuster, 1989), 295. Herzog, *War of Atonement*, 281. Blum, *Eve of Destruction*, 149.

34 Pollack, *Arabs at War*; T. H. Dupuy, *Elusive Victory: The Arab-Israeli Wars, 1947–74* (New York: Harper and Row, 1978).

35 Amos, *Arab-Israeli Military/Political Relations*, 71, 64, 3, 164. Waterbury, *Egypt*, 17.

36 Patai, *The Arab Mind*, 95–100. Amos, *Arab-Israeli Military/Political Relations*, 26, xiii (Sa'ad al-Din Shadhili), 14, 18, 208. El-Gamasy, *October War*, 167. Shamir, "Yom Kippur War as a Factor in the Peace Process," 35–36. Meital, "Drums of War," 56. Herzog, *Arab-Israeli Wars*, 315.

37 Liebman, "Myth of Defeat," 409–410. D. J. Elazar, "United States of America: Overview," in M. Davis, ed., *The Yom Kippur War: Israel and the Jewish People* (New York: Arno, 1974), 34. *Jerusalem Post*, 2 Nov. 1973. Liebman, "Paradigms Sometimes Fit."

38 *Jerusalem Post*, 19 Oct. 1973. Meir, *My Life*, 433. Etzioni-Halevy and Shapiro, *Political Culture in Israel*, 188. Liebman, "Myth of Defeat," 417n38. Wiesel's address in H. H. Hart, *Yom Kippur Plus 100 Days: The Human Side of the War and Its Aftermath, as Shown through the Columns of the Jerusalem Post* (New York: Hart Publishing, 1974), 441–446.

39 Liebman, "Myth of Defeat," 410. C. S. Liebman and E. Don-Yehiya, *Civil Religion in Israel: Traditional Judaism and Political Culture in the Jewish State* (Berkeley: University of California Press, 1983), 149–150. Gottschalk, "United States of America," 38. Rabinovich, *Yom Kippur War*, 175, 218–219; Morris, *Righteous Victims*, 406, 416. For a critical view of this episode see Arieh O'Sullivan, "Debunking a Myth: Dayan Never Feared Israel's Destruction in '73," *Jerusalem Post*, online ed., 28 Sept. 2001. Blum, *Eve of Destruction*.

40 Rabinovich, *Yom Kippur War*, 440.

41 B. Thomas, *How Israel Was Won: A Concise History of the Arab-Israeli Conflict* (Oxford: Lexington, 1999), 198. Morris, *Righteous Victims*, 395. El-Gamasy, *October War*, 129–131. Stein, "Calculation, Miscalculation, and Conventional Deterrence," 48, 55; Gilbert, *Israel*, 432. Lebow and Stein, *We All Lost the Cold War*, 183.

42 Amos, *Arab-Israeli Military/Political Relations*, 198. Waterbury, *Egypt*, 30, 14. Beattie, *Egypt during the Sadat Years*, 135. Blum, *Eve of Destruction*, 313.

43 Rabinovich, *Yom Kippur War*, 22–23, 50, 56. Blum, *Eve of Destruction*, 38, 100. Stein, "Calculation, Miscalculation, and Conventional Deterrence," 66, 73–74; Gilbert, *Israel*, 423; Morris, *Righteous Victims*, 398–399.

44 Minerbi, "Western Europe," 190.

45 Shoufani, "The October War and the Israeli Press," 192. Liebman, "Myth of Defeat," 401.

46 Pollack, *Arabs at War*, 131. Rabinovich, *Yom Kippur War*, 454.

47 Lebow and Stein, *We All Lost the Cold War*, 185. Benny Morris has a lower figure of 63,000 tons of Soviet equipment reaching Syria and Egypt by sea by 30 October. Morris, *Righteous Victims*, 434; Gilbert, *Israel*, 448.

48 Lebow and Stein, *We All Lost the Cold War,* 193, 224. Rabinovich, *Yom Kippur War,* 491, 484.

49 Amos, *Arab-Israeli Military/Political Relations,* 7, 69–70. Patai, *The Arab Mind,* 110–111. El-Gamasy, *October War,* 217–218.

50 O'Ballance, *No Victor,* 349. K. W. Stein, *Heroic Diplomacy: Sadat, Kissinger, Carter, Begin, and the Quest for Arab-Israeli Peace* (New York: Routledge, 1999), 82, 97.

51 Rabinovich, *Yom Kippur War,* 12, 320. A. el-Sadat, *Sadat, in Search of Identity* (New York: Harper and Row, 1977); Amos, *Arab-Israeli Military/Political Relations,* 203.

52 H. El Badri, T. El Magdoub, and M. D. El Din Zohdy, *The Ramadan War, 1973* (Dunn Loring, Va.: T. N. Dupuy, 1978), 201–204. el-Sadat, *Sadat,* 263; Gazit, "Egypt and Israel," 99–100.

53 Amos, *Arab-Israeli Military/Political Relations,* 180, 203.

54 Rabinovich, *Yom Kippur War,* 486. Lebow and Stein, *We All Lost the Cold War,* 189; Parker, *October War,* 263; W. Isaacson, *Kissinger: A Biography* (New York: Simon and Schuster, 1992), 514–515.

55 Shoufani, "The October War and the Israeli Press," 175.

56 Pollack, *Arabs at War,* 130.

57 Stein, "Calculation, Miscalculation, and Conventional Deterrence," 63.

58 Ibid., 54.

Chapter 8. The U.S. Intervention in Somalia

1 R. C. DiPrizio, *Armed Humanitarians: U.S. Interventions from Northern Iraq to Kosovo* (Baltimore: Johns Hopkins University Press, 2002), 189.

2 D. Byman and M. Waxman, *The Dynamics of Coercion: American Foreign Policy and the Limits of Military Might* (Cambridge: Cambridge University Press, 2002), 181n7.

3 J. Western, "Sources of Humanitarian Intervention: Beliefs, Information, and Advocacy in the U.S. Decisions on Somalia and Bosnia," *International Security* 26 (2002): 115. J. Hillen, *Blue Helmets: The Strategy of U.N. Military Operations* (Washington: Brassey's, 2000), 186; T. G. Weiss and C. Collins, *Humanitarian Challenges and Intervention: World Politics and the Dilemmas of Help* (Boulder: Westview, 1996), 77–78, 80; J. Stevenson, *Losing Mogadishu: Testing U.S. Policy in Somalia* (Annapolis: Naval Institute Press, 1995); N. Wheeler, *Saving Strangers: Humanitarian Intervention in International Society* (New York: Oxford University Press, 2000), 174.

4 R. Cornwell, "Somalia: 14th Time Lucky?" *Institute for Security Studies Paper* no. 87 (2004): 1–10.

5 R. M. Entman, *Projections of Power: Framing News, Public Opinion, and U.S. Foreign Policy* (Chicago: University of Chicago Press, 2004), 20. DiPrizio, *Armed Humanitarians,* 44. M. Bowden, *Black Hawk Down: A Story of Modern War* (New York: Penguin, 1999), 332. J. L. Hirsch and R. B. Oakley, *Somalia and Operation Restore Hope: Reflections on Peacemaking and Peacekeeping* (Washington: U.S. Institute of Peace Press, 1995), 161. C. A. Crocker, "The Lessons of Somalia: Not Everything Went Wrong," *Foreign Affairs* 74 (1995): 2–8.

6 J. L. Woods, "U.S. Government Decisionmaking Processes during Humani-

tarian Operations in Somalia," in W. S. Clarke and J. I. Herbst, eds., *Learning from Somalia: The Lessons of Armed Humanitarian Intervention* (Boulder: Westview, 1997), 158. Western, "Sources of Humanitarian Intervention," 138. Americans Talk Issues Foundation and the W. Alton Jones Foundation poll, 23 Mar.–4 Apr. 1993.

7 R. C. Eichenberg, "Victory Has Many Friends: U.S. Public Opinion and the Use of Military Force, 1981–2005," *International Security* 30 (2005): 140–177; CBS News/*New York Times* poll, 21–24 June 1993; Times Mirror poll, 9–15 Sept. 1993.

8 CBS News poll, 6 Oct. 1993; NBC News poll, 6 Oct. 1993; D. C. Foyle, *Counting the Public In: Presidents, Public Opinion, and Foreign Policy* (New York: Columbia University Press, 1999), 220.

9 CBS News poll, 6–7 Oct., 18–19 Oct., 5–7 Dec. 1993. C. J. Logan, "U.S. Public Opinion and the Intervention in Somalia: Lessons for the Future of Military-Humanitarian Interventions," *Fletcher Forum of World Affairs* 20 (1996): 161–162. Gallup/CNN/*USA Today* poll, 5 Oct. 1993.

10 Bowden, *Black Hawk Down*, 337. M. J. Gray, E. E. Bolton, and B. T. Litz, "A Longitudinal Analysis of P.T.S.D. Symptom Course: Delayed-Onset P.T.S.D. in Somalia Peacekeepers," *Journal of Consulting and Clinical Psychology* 72 (2004): 912.

11 Some 25 percent thought an intervention in Haiti would be like Somalia; 21 percent thought it would be like Vietnam; and 46 percent thought it would be quick and successful like the first Gulf War. *Time*/CNN poll, 16 Sept. 1994.

12 Hirsch and Oakley, *Somalia and Operation Restore Hope*, 149.

13 Woods, "U.S. Government Decisionmaking Processes," 157.

14 Stevenson, *Losing Mogadishu*, 56. T. G. Weiss, *Military-Civilian Interactions: Humanitarian Crises and the Responsibility to Protect* (New York: Rowman and Littlefield, 2005), 66–67; DiPrizio, *Armed Humanitarians*, 47, 190. For a skeptical view see A. De Waal, "Dangerous Precedents? Famine Relief in Somalia 1991–93," in J. Macrae and A. Zwi, eds., *War and Hunger* (London: Zed Books, 1994), 152.

15 S. Baynham, *Somalia: U.N. at the Crossroads*, African Defence Review, A Working Paper Series, no. 15 (Halfway House, South Africa: Institute for Defence Policy, 1994).

16 Weiss, *Military-Civilian Interactions*, 69, 66. Woods, "U.S. Government Decisionmaking Processes," 159; DiPrizio, *Armed Humanitarians*, 47. W. J. Durch, "Introduction to Anarchy: Humanitarian Intervention and 'State Building' in Somalia," in Durch, ed., *U.N. Peacekeeping, American Politics, and the Uncivil Wars of the 1990s* (New York: St. Martin's, 1996), 325, 321. Wheeler, *Saving Strangers*, 192. Clarke and Herbst, *Learning from Somalia*, 220. J. Mueller, *The Remnants of War* (Ithaca: Cornell University Press, 2004), 127.

17 Weiss, *Military-Civilian Interactions*; D. D. Laitin, "Somalia: Civil War and International Intervention," in B. F. Walter and J. L. Snyder, eds., *Civil Wars, Insecurity, and Intervention* (New York: Columbia University Press, 1999); A. Roberts, "From San Francisco to Sarajevo: The U.N. and the Use of Force," *Survival* 37 (1996): 7–28.

18 Crocker, "Lessons of Somalia," 3. Hirsch and Oakley, *Somalia and Operation Restore Hope*.

19 Bowden, *Black Hawk Down*, 333.

20 DiPrizio, *Armed Humanitarians*, 52–54. Craig Hines, "Pity, Not U.S. Security, Motivated Use of GIs in Somalia, Bush Says," *Houston Chronicle*, 24 Oct. 1999, A11; Woods, "U.S. Government Decisionmaking Processes," 155– 158. S. Power, *A Problem from Hell: America and the Age of Genocide* (New York: Perennial, 2003), 293.

21 Mueller, *Remnants of War*, 126–127; Durch, "Introduction to Anarchy," 319; Western, "Sources of Humanitarian Intervention," 137. W. P. Strobel, *Late Breaking Foreign Policy: The News Media's Influence on Peace Operations* (Washington: U.S. Institute of Peace, 1997), 131–137; E. V. Larson, "Casualties and Consensus: The Historical Role of Casualties in Domestic Support for U.S. Military Operations," RAND Corporation report M.R.-726, 1996, 45; Wheeler, *Saving Strangers*, 179–180.

22 Woods, "U.S. Government Decisionmaking Processes," 159. Durch, "Introduction to Anarchy," 320.

23 Durch, "Introduction to Anarchy," 322–325.

24 Albright quoted in Laitin, "Somalia," 164. UN resolutions available at *www.un.org*.

25 Weiss, *Military-Civilian Interactions*, 67; K. Allard, *Somalia Operations: Lessons Learned* (Washington: National Defense University Press, 1995), available at *www.au.af.mil/au/awc/awcgate/ndu/allard_somalia/allardcont.html*.

26 UN Security Council Resolution 814, 4, 5, *www.un.org*.

27 Hillen, *Blue Helmets*, 212.

28 Byman and Waxman, *Dynamics of Coercion*, 229.

29 P. Feaver and C. Gelpi, *Choosing Your Battles: American Civil-Military Relations and the Use of Force* (Princeton: Princeton University Press, 2004), 136.

30 *Los Angeles Times* poll, 14–17 Jan. 1993. CBS/*New York Times* poll, 21–24 June 1993. ABC News/*Washington Post* poll, 11–14 Nov. 1993. *Newsweek* poll, 30 June–1 July 1993.

31 Gallup/CNN/*USA Today* poll, 5 Oct. 1993.

32 CBS News/*New York Times* poll, 21–24 June 1993. R. C. Eichenberg, "Gender Differences in Public Attitudes towards the Use of Force by the United States, 1990–2003," *International Security* 28 (2003): 135.

33 Stevenson, *Losing Mogadishu*, xiv.

34 Mueller, *Remnants of War*, 128, 146–148; R. Mandel, *Security, Strategy, and the Quest for Bloodless War* (Boulder: Lynne Rienner, 2004), 177.

35 S. Kull, I. M. Destler, and C. Ramsay, "The Foreign Policy Gap: How Policymakers Misread the Public," Program on International Policy Attitudes, Center for International and Security Studies at the University of Maryland, report, 1997. Eichenberg, "Victory Has Many Friends."

36 Bush, Speech to Congress, 6 Mar. 1991. Logan, "U.S. Public Opinion," 162; A. Kohut and R. C. Toth, "Arms and the People," *Foreign Affairs* 73 (1994): 51; Gallup/*Newsweek* poll, 3–4 Dec. 1992; *Time*/CNN poll, 13–14 Jan. 1993; Gallup/*Newsweek* poll, 14–15 Jan. 1993. NBC News/*Wall Street Journal* poll, 12–15 Dec. 1992.

37 Crocker, "Lessons of Somalia," 4. Stevenson, *Losing Mogadishu*, 58. Hirsch and Oakley, *Somalia and Operation Restore Hope*, 159.

38 B. W. Jentleson and R. L. Britton, "Still Pretty Prudent: Post-Cold War American Public Opinion on the Use of Military Force," *Journal of Conflict Resolution* 42 (1998): 395–417. Logan, "U.S. Public Opinion," 163. For the unpopularity of intervention in civil wars, see B. Russett and M. Nincic, "American Public Opinion on the Use of Military Force Abroad," *Political Science Quarterly* 91 (1976): 411–423; Chicago Council on Foreign Relations, *Worldviews 2002: American Public Opinion and Foreign Policy*, available at www.worldviews.org.

39 B. W. Jentleson, "The Pretty Prudent Public: Post-Post Vietnam American Opinion on the Use of Military Force," *International Studies Quarterly* 36 (1992): 49–74; Jentleson and Britton, "Still Pretty Prudent." Stevenson, *Losing Mogadishu*, xiii. Hirsch and Oakley, *Somalia and Operation Restore Hope*, 155. ABC News/*Washington Post* poll, 11–14 Dec. 1992; NBC News/*Wall Street Journal* poll, 12–15 Dec. 1992; Harris poll, 4–8 Dec. 1992.

40 *Washington Post* poll, 7–10 Oct. 1993. NBC News/*Washington Post* poll, 22–26 Oct. 1993.

41 Jentleson and Britton, "Still Pretty Prudent," 401.

42 Woods, "U.S. Government Decisionmaking Processes," 162. Weiss and Collins, *Humanitarian Challenges and Intervention*, 128.

43 C. Dauber, "Image as Argument: The Impact of Mogadishu on U.S. Military Intervention," *Armed Forces and Society* 27 (2001): 213. M. Bowden, "The Lesson of Mogadishu," Wall Street Journal, 5 Apr. 2004.

44 CNN/*USA Today* poll, 5 Oct. 1993; National Research Inc. poll, 15–18 Oct. 1993. Entman, *Projections of Power*, 104, 100. Larson, "Casualties and Consensus," 71. J. E. Sharkey, "When Pictures Drive Foreign Policy," *American Journalism Review* 15 (1993): 14–19.

45 *Time*/CNN poll, 7 Oct. 1993; Times Mirror poll, 21–24 Oct. 1993; Logan, "U.S. Public Opinion," 161, 160.

46 M. Maren, *The Road to Hell: The Ravaging Effects of Foreign Aid and International Charity* (New York: Free Press, 1997), 213. *Economist*, 9 Oct. 1993, 22.

47 Dauber, "Image as Argument."

48 Logan, "U.S. Public Opinion," 167, 175. National Research Inc. poll, 15–18 Oct. 1993. S. Kull and I. M. Destler, *Misreading the Public: The Myth of a New Isolationism* (Washington: Brookings Institution, 1999), 107–108. Gephardt quoted in Sharkey, "When Pictures Drive Foreign Policy."

49 Dauber, "Image as Argument," 211. Kohut and Toth, "Arms and the People," 53. R. Haass, *Intervention: The Use of American Military Force in the Post-Cold War World* (Washington: Carnegie Endowment for International Peace, 1994), 86. Entman, *Projections of Power*, 100.

50 Logan, "U.S. Public Opinion," 159.

51 J. Burk, "Public Support for Peacekeeping in Lebanon and Somalia: Assessing the Casualties Hypothesis," *Political Science Quarterly* 114 (1999): 75. Byrd quoted in H. Johnston and T. Dagne, "Congress and the Somalia Crisis," in Clarke and Herbst, *Learning from Somalia*, 198.

52 Foyle, *Counting the Public In*, 221. Johnston and Dagne, "Congress and the Somalia Crisis," 200. CBS News/*New York Times* poll, 21–24 June 1993; ABC News/*Washington Post* poll, 11–14 Nov. 1993.

53 Foyle, *Counting the Public In*, 219. Durch, "Introduction to Anarchy," 327.

Woods, "U.S. Government Decisionmaking Processes," 165, 167. Crocker, "Lessons of Somalia," 7.

54 Foyle, *Counting the Public In*, 221.

55 Logan, "U.S. Public Opinion," 161. Kull, Destler, and Ramsay, "Foreign Policy Gap."

56 CBS News/*New York Times* poll, 21–24 June 1993; ABC News poll, 5 Oct. 1993; Feaver and Gelpi, *Choosing Your Battles*, 134; Burk, "Public Support for Peacekeeping"; Kull and Destler, *Misreading the Public*; Larson, "Casualties and Consensus," 70.

57 The figures included 27 percent who thought certain congressmen "overreacted a lot" and 19 percent who thought certain congressmen "overreacted a little." National Research Inc. poll, 15–18 Oct. 1993.

58 Kull, Destler, and Ramsay, "Foreign Policy Gap," 92. *Time*/CNN poll, 7 Oct. 1993. ABC News poll, 5 Oct. 1993; NBC News poll, 6 Oct. 1993; Gallup poll, 8–10 Oct. 1993.

59 CBS News poll, 6 Oct. 1993. Entman, *Projections of Power*.

60 Radio address, 10 Mar. 1994, in Hirsch and Oakley, *Somalia and Operation Restore Hope*, appendix G.

61 B. Dole, "Shaping America's Global Future," *Foreign Policy* 98 (1995): 29–43. Foyle, *Counting the Public In*, 223; Michael R. Gordon and John H. Cushman Jr., "After Supporting Hunt for Aidid, U.S. is Blaming U.N. for Losses," *New York Times*, 18 Oct. 1993, A1, A8. W. S. Clarke and J. I. Herbst, "Somalia and the Future of Humanitarian Intervention," in Clarke and Herbst, *Learning from Somalia*, 241. B. Clinton, *My Life* (New York: Knopf, 2004).

62 NBC News/*Wall Street Journal* poll, 10–13 Sept. 1993.

63 Mueller, *Remnants of War*, 128. Weiss and Collins, *Humanitarian Challenges and Intervention*, 80.

64 Hirsch and Oakley, *Somalia and Operation Restore Hope*, 161. Haass, *Intervention*, 78.

65 Gallup/CNN/*USA Today* poll, 5 Oct. 1993. Logan, "U.S. Public Opinion," 164; *Time*/CNN poll, 4 Aug. 1994. Clarke and Herbst, "Somalia and Humanitarian Intervention," 239.

66 S. Chesterman, *Just War or Just Peace: Humanitarian Intervention and International Law* (Oxford: Oxford University Press, 2001), 231. Bowden, *Black Hawk Down*, 334–335. *New York Times*, 23 Apr. 1994. Power, *Problem from Hell*, 366. Romeo Dallaire, the Canadian general in command of the hopelessly understrength UN operation in Rwanda, argued that the Rwandan militias had learned their own lesson from Somalia: if enough westerners are killed, they will withdraw. R. Dallaire and B. Beardsley, *Shake Hands with the Devil: The Failure of Humanity in Rwanda* (Toronto: Random House, 2003), 240.

Chapter 9. America at War

1 See, e.g., "National Strategy for Victory in Iraq," 30 Nov. 2005, at *www.whitehouse.gov*.

2 M. Mandelbaum, "Diplomacy in Wartime: New Priorities and Alignments,"

in J. F. Hoge and G. Rose, eds., *How Did This Happen? Terrorism and the New War* (New York: Public Affairs, 2001), 255. Rumsfeld's memorandum available at *www.usatoday.com/news/washington/executive/rumsfeld-memo.htm.*

3   *Washington Post* poll, 12 Oct. 2004. All poll data from *www.pollingreport.com* unless otherwise stated. PIPA, "U.S. Public Beliefs and Attitudes about Iraq," 20 Aug. 2004; C. Gelpi, P. D. Feaver, and J. Reifler, "Success Matters: Casualty Sensitivity and the War in Iraq," *International Security* 30, no. 3 (Winter 2005–06).

4   CBS News/*New York Times* polls, 2003–2004.

5   ABC News/*Washington Post* poll, 27–30 Apr. 2003, 26–29 Oct. 2003, 18–21 Dec. 2003, 20–23 May 2004, 23–26 Sept. 2004. The Pew Research Center found similar results: approval of Bush's Iraq policy was 59 percent in January 2004 (after the capture of Saddam) and 40 percent in April 2004. Pew Research Center polls, 2003–2004.

6   ABC News/*Washington Post* polls, 2003–2004. During this period, the number of Americans who thought the Iraq War had contributed to long-term U.S. security never fell below 51 percent. In contrast, a *Time* poll asked on 3–5 August 2004: "Do you think that the United States' actions in Iraq have made the world safer or more dangerous?" In response, 52 percent said the war had made the world more dangerous. An *Investor's Business Daily/Christian Science Monitor* poll asked on 2–5 August 2004: "And generally speaking, would you say the U.S. military action in Iraq is helping to make the world a safer place or not?" The results were 48 percent "is helping," 49 percent "is not helping." That same month, 49 percent of respondents thought the Iraq War was creating more terrorists, while only 25 percent thought it was reducing their numbers. PIPA, "U.S. Public Beliefs and Attitudes about Iraq," 20 Aug. 2004.

7   ABC News/*Washington Post* poll, 20–23 May 2004. *Investor's Business Daily/Christian Science Monitor* poll, 2–5 Aug. 2004. PIPA, "U.S. Public Beliefs and Attitudes about Iraq."

8   Pew Research Center surveys, 2003–2004. PIPA, "U.S. Public Beliefs and Attitudes about Iraq." Harris poll, 10–15 Aug. 2004. CBS News poll, 11 May 2004.

9   A. B. Krueger, L. C. Johnson, R. Perl, and P. Probst, "Measuring Success in Combating Terrorism," Third Annual Princeton Colloquium on Public and International Affairs: Rethinking the War on Terror, 2005; M. Scheuer, *Imperial Hubris. Why the West Is Losing the War on Terror* (Dulles, Va.: Potomac Books, 2004)

10 J. Mueller, *The Remnants of War* (Ithaca: Cornell University Press, 2004), 134–136.

11 K. Gannon, "Afghanistan Unbound," *Foreign Affairs* 83 (2004): 35–46. A. Lieven, "Don't Forget Afghanistan," *Foreign Policy* 143 (2003): 54.

12 D. Byman, "Scoring the War on Terrorism," *National Interest* 72 (2003): 75–84; S. Biddle, *Afghanistan and the Future of Warfare: Implications for Army and Defense Policy* (Carlisle, Pa.: Strategic Studies Institute, 2002); M. E. O'Hanlon, "A Flawed Masterpiece," *Foreign Affairs* 81 (2002): 47–63.

13 "Fact Sheet: Plots, Casings, and Infiltrations Referenced in President Bush's Remarks on the War on Terror," Office of the Press Secretary, White

House, 6 Oct. 2005. U.S. State Department, *Patterns of Global Terrorism* (Washington, 1995–2003).

14 O'Hanlon, "Flawed Masterpiece," 47.

15 B. Woodward, *Plan of Attack* (New York: Simon and Schuster, 2004), 9–23; R. A. Clarke, *Against All Enemies: Inside America's War on Terror* (New York: Free Press, 2004), 231–232. M. P. Leffler, "Bush's Foreign Policy," *Foreign Policy* 144 (2004): 26. See Bush's speeches of 29 Jan. 2002, 1 June 2002, 12 Sept. 2002, and 6 Nov. 2003.

16 A. H. Cordesman, *The Iraq War: Strategy, Tactics, and Military Lessons* (Westport, Conn.: Praeger, 2003), 247. M. O'Hanlon and A. L. de Albuquerque, "Scoring the Iraq Aftermath," *National Interest* 74 (2003/04): 31–36.

17 M. O'Hanlon and A. L. de Albuquerque, "Gauging the Aftermath," *National Interest* 76 (2004): 24–26. Y. Primakov, "Auditing Arrogance," *National Interest* 76 (2004): 8–11; A. Debat, "Vivisecting the Jihad," *National Interest* 76 (2004): 18–23. M. O'Hanlon and A. L. de Albuquerque, "Iraq Index Archive: Tracking Variables of Reconstruction and Security in Post-Saddam Iraq," Brookings Institution, Saban Center for Middle East Policy report, 2003–2005. *Economist,* 29 Jan. 2005, 22. See, e.g., L. Diamond, "What Went Wrong in Iraq," *Foreign Affairs* 83 (2004): 34–56. J. Fallows, "Blind into Baghdad," *Atlantic Monthly* 293 (2004): 53–74.

18 J. R. Schlesinger, "Transferring Sovereignty," *National Interest* 76 (2004): 6. W. E. Odom, "Retreating in Good Order," *National Interest* 76 (2004): 33–36; O'Hanlon and de Albuquerque, "Gauging the Aftermath." D. Byman, "Constructing a Democratic Iraq: Challenges and Opportunities," *International Security* 28 (2003): 47–78; A. Taheri, "Thinking through Liberation," *National Interest* 76 (2004): 26–29. *www.thelancet.com.* O'Hanlon and de Albuquerque, "Iraq Index Archive."

19 V. Cannistraro, "Terror's Undiminished Threat," *Foreign Policy* (2003): 69.

20 E. Voeten and R. Brewer, "Public Opinion, the War in Iraq, and the President," American Political Science Association Conference Paper, Chicago, Sept. 2004. R. C. Eichenberg and R. J. Stoll, *The Political Fortunes of War: Iraq and the Domestic Standing of President George W. Bush* (London: Foreign Policy Centre, July 2004).

21 In one survey in April 2004, there were no significant differences between men and women in their assessment of whether the United States was winning the war on terror, but some 65 percent of women and only 56 percent of men stated that the United States was doing moderately badly or very badly in Iraq. Wisconsin Public Radio and St. Norbert College Survey Center, 14–21 Apr. 2004.

22 Rasmussen Reports poll, 15–17 Oct. 2004. Pew poll, 3–6 Nov. 2005.

23 O. R. Holsti, *Public Opinion and American Foreign Policy* (Ann Arbor: University of Michigan Press, 2004), 173. A Harris poll, 10–15 June 1999, found that support for the sending of NATO and U.S. troops into Kosovo was stronger among Democrats (72 percent) and weaker among Republicans (55 percent).

24 Gelpi, Feaver, and Reifler, "Success Matters."

25 S. P. Huntington, *American Politics: The Promise of Disharmony* (Cambridge, Mass.: Harvard University Press, 1981), 236–245.

26 Students filled out the forms anonymously and without knowing the objective of the experiment.

27 Broken down by party and group, international support, intelligence, and majority support were statistically significant (Mann-Whitney U test, all Z values > 3.15, all p < 0.001). The other three variables were not significant (all Z < 1.64, all p > 0.05). For Republicans, there were no statistically significant differences between groups (all Z < 1.99, all p > 0.05). We used exact significance tests because sample sizes in some cells were small.

28 A. J. Berinsky, "Assuming the Costs of War," paper delivered at the American Political Science Association annual meeting, Chicago, Sept. 2004. W. A. Boettcher and M. D. Cobb, "Echoes of Vietnam? Casualty Frames, Casualty Tolerance, and Public Perceptions of Success and Failure in the War in Iraq," paper delivered at the annual International Studies Association convention, Honolulu, Mar. 2005. Pew Research Center, "Iraq Support Steady in Face of Higher Casualties," 17 Sept. 2004.

29 R. Jervis, "The Confrontation between Iraq and the U.S: Implications for the Theory and Practice of Deterrence," *European Journal of International Relations* 9 (2003): 315–337. Wisconsin Public Radio and St. Norbert College Survey Center, 14–21 Apr. 2004. CNN/USA *Today*/Gallup poll, 26–28 Mar. 2004.

30 PIPA, "Misperceptions, the Media, and the Iraq War," 2 Oct. 2003; S. Kull, C. Ramsay, and E. Lewis, "Misperceptions, the Media, and the Iraq War," *Political Science Quarterly* 118 (2003–2004): 569–598.

31 Pew Research Center polls, 10–16 Apr. 2003, 20 June–2 July 2003. *Time*/CNN/Harris polls, 16 July, 18 Nov. 2003.

32 *Newsweek* poll, 8–9 Apr. 2004. ABC News/*Washington Post* polls, 2003–2004. Harris Polls, October 2003–June 2004. Pew Research Center polls, 2004.

33 *Time*/CNN polls, 18–19 Nov., 30–31 Dec. 2003.

34 CBS News polls, 14–15, 22–22 Dec. 2003. *Newsweek* poll, 8–9 Jan. 2004.

35 *www.usatoday.com*, accessed 15 Mar. 2006.

36 Pew Research Center for the People and the Press, "Public Support for War Resilient: Bush's Standing Improves," 17 June 2004.

37 Associated Press–Ipsos poll, 4–6, 18–20 Mar. 2003.

38 R. Alt, "Tet 2?" *National Review Online*, 8 Apr. 2004. Rory Carroll, "Iraq Insurgents Snatch Victory from Defeat," *Guardian* (UK), 24 June 2004. Fox News poll, Oct. 2003.

39 PIPA, "Misperceptions, The Media and the Iraq War," 12–20; Kull, Ramsay, and Lewis, "Misperceptions, the Media, and the Iraq War."

40 For this question, sample size was 94. Students filled out the forms anonymously and without knowing the objective of the experiment. The order of this question among other questions was randomized. The first group (*New York Times*) consisted of 31 Democrats, 9 Republicans, and 8 others; the second group (*Fox News*) of 26 Democrats, 17 Republicans, and 3 others.

41 A logistic multiple regression controlling for sex and partisanship revealed that the purported news source had a fairly strong influence on whether or not people saw the event as a victory (although this effect was of borderline statistical significance, $p = 0.053$). Partisanship also had an independent sig-

nificant effect, such that Republicans discounted Fox News less than other people (p = 0.001).

42 Fox News/Opinion Dynamics poll, 8–9 June 2004; ABC News/*Washington Post* poll, 17–20 June 2004.

43 Fox News/Opinion Dynamics poll, 21–22 Apr. 2004; Pew Research Center poll, 1–4 Apr. 2004.

44 CBS News/*New York Times* poll, 23–27 Apr. 2004; Fox News/Opinion Dynamics poll, 21–22 Apr. 2004.

45 CBS/*New York Times* poll, July 2003–July 2004. ABC News/*Washington Post* poll, April 2003–December 2004.

46 CBS/*New York Times* poll, 7–9 Mar. 2003; Fox News/Opinion Dynamics poll, 8–9 Sept. 2002.

47 CNN/*USA Today*/Gallup polls, 23–25 Aug. 2004, 3–5 Sept. 2004.

48 Dana Milbank and Mike Allen, "U.S. Shifts Rhetoric on Its Goals in Iraq," *Washington Post*, 1 Aug. 2003.

49 See Bush's speech of 7 Sept. 2003.

50 A. B. Kruger and D. D. Laitin, "'Misunderestimating' Terrorism: The State Department's Big Mistake," *Foreign Affairs* 83 (2004): 8–13; *USA Today*, 11 June 2004.

51 *seattletimes.nwsource.com/html/nationworld/2002243262_terror16.html.*

52 J. Mueller, "The Iraq Syndrome," *Foreign Affairs* 84 (2005): 49.

53 J. Surowiecki, *The Wisdom of Crowds: Why the Many Are Smarter Than the Few and How Collective Wisdom Shapes Business, Economies, Societies, and Nations* (New York: Doubleday, 2005).

Chapter 10. Conclusion

1 N. Machiavelli, *The Prince*, trans. P. E. Bondanella (Oxford: Oxford University Press, 2005), ch. 13.

2 R. Mandel, *The Meaning of Military Victory* (Boulder: Lynne Rienner, 2006), 206 (of manuscript).

3 S. Budiansky, *Air Power: The Men, Machines, and Ideas That Revolutionized War, from Kitty Hawk to Gulf War 2* (New York: Viking, 2004), 430.

4 R. C. DiPrizio, *Armed Humanitarians: U.S. Interventions from Northern Iraq to Kosovo* (Baltimore: Johns Hopkins University Press, 2002), 93; T. G. Weiss, *Military-Civilian Interactions: Humanitarian Crises and the Responsibility to Protect* (New York: Rowman and Littlefield, 2005), 124–125. For evidence of growing skepticism see CBS News/*New York Times* poll, 6–9 Dec. 1994; ABC, CBS, NBC News, CNN, Associated Press poll, 8 Nov. 1994; *Time*/CNN poll, 29–30 Mar. 1995; NBC News/*Wall Street Journal* poll, 19–22 Oct. 1996.

5 DiPrizio, *Armed Humanitarians*, ch. 6; "Summary of U.S. Government Policy on Bosnia," U.S. Department of State, 16 July 1998; Marcus Cox, "State Building and Post-Conflict Reconstruction: Lessons from Bosnia," Centre for Applied Studies in International Negotiation report, Jan. 2001. PIPA poll, 13 Feb.–20 Apr. 1998.

6 Curt Tarnoff, "Kosovo: Reconstruction and Development Assistance," Congressional Research Service, report for Congress, 7 June 2001; F. Fukuyama,

"Nation-Building 101," in T. Halstead, ed., *The Real State of the Union: From the Best Minds in America, Bold Solutions to the Problems Politicians Dare Not Face* (New York: Basic Books, 2004), 250–260; B. Posen, "The War for Kosovo: Serbia's Political-Military Strategy," *International Security* 24 (2000): 39–84; L. Freedman, "Victims and Victors: Reflections on the Kosovo War," *Review of International Studies* 26 (2000): 335–358.

7 J. Dobbins, J. G. McGinn, K. Crane, S. G. Jones, R. Lal, A. Rathmell, R. Swanger, and A. Timilsina, *America's Role in Nation-Building: From Germany to Iraq* (Santa Monica, Calif.: RAND Corporation, 2003), ch. 7. Pew Research Center poll, 15–19 Mar. 2000.

ACKNOWLEDGMENTS

We have incurred a great many debts to friends and colleagues in completing this book, and it has been hard to keep score on all of them.

The key pillars of the project were the Widener Library and Grendel's Den in Cambridge, Massachusetts, and we offer our thanks to the able management of both institutions. We are especially grateful to Robert Jervis and Robert Mandel for their time, effort, enthusiasm, and ideas in critiquing the manuscript, which was considerably improved as a result. Stephen Peter Rosen has provided essential and insightful support to both of us and deserves our greatest gratitude. As anyone who has spent any time with John Mueller will know, he is a wonderfully creative conjurer of ideas, and we were grateful for the chance to discuss our project with him. Dominic Johnson owes a special thanks to Jeffery Boswall for offering friendship, encouragement, and opportunities over the years, and without whom no books would have been written. Marc Jason Gilbert went above and beyond the call of duty in sharing expert advice on the Tet offensive, and Jesse Ferris and Patricia Johnson gave us excellent help in understanding the Yom Kippur War. When we submitted a fifty-page single-spaced paper on perceptions of victory for the International Studies Association Conference, Paul Kowert received it with remarkable good grace and provided excellent comments.

We would also like to thank the following people for their help and expertise in developing the various ideas that led to this book: Samuel Adams, Pierre Allan, Graham Allison, Jan Ångström, Steve

Biddle, William Boettcher, Terry Burnham, Michael Cobb, Christina Davis, Colin Dueck, Isabelle Duyvesteyn, Colin Elman, Drew Erdmann, Maria Fanis, Peter Feaver, Christopher Fettweis, Ben Friedman, Adrian de Froment, Dennis Hood, Michael Horowitz, Yuen Foong Khong, Kurt Taylor Gaubatz, Fred Greenstein, Xavier Guillaume, Daniel Kahneman, Hanspeter Kriesi, Ellen Langer, Rose McDermott, Mark Molesky, Timothy Naftali, Jackie Newmyer, Johan Yohanan Plesner, Katrina Rogachevsky, Sebastian Rosato, Eldar Shafir, Erin Simpson, Diane Snyder, Martin Stein, Rob Trager, Mark Wilson, and Richard Wrangham.

Special thanks are due to the John F. Kennedy Memorial Trust and the Frank Knox Memorial Trust for funding our first period of research at Harvard University, without which we never would have met to argue about perceptions of victory. We thank the faculty, fellows, and staff at the Mershon Center at Ohio State University (especially Richard Herrmann and John Mueller), the Olin Institute for Strategic Studies at Harvard University (especially Stephen Peter Rosen, Monica Toft, and Ann Townes), the UCLA Global Fellows Program (especially Ronald Rogowski and Francoise Lionnet), the Princeton University Society of Fellows (especially Leonard Barkan, Michael Wood, and the superhuman Mary Harper), the Woodrow Wilson School of Public and International Affairs (especially Anne-Marie Slaughter), and the Branco Weiss Society in Science program at ETH Zurich (especially Olaf Kübler, Helga Nowotny, Katrin Sträuli, and, for his particular support and enthusiasm, Branco Weiss).

We are exceptionally grateful to our editor at Harvard University Press, Michael Fisher, who provided excellent guidance throughout the project, and Camille Smith, who successfully defended her title as the world's best manuscript editor. The text is far stronger (and shorter) for their efforts. We also thank Philip Schwartzberg, of

Meridian Mapping, Minneapolis, for the excellent maps in the book.

Two people did not choose to analyze perceptions of victory but nevertheless had to learn to live with the project. Dominic Tierney would like to offer his love and thanks to Amy Oakes, who was constantly helpful, supportive, and inspiring. Dominic Johnson would like to express his love and thanks to Gabriella de la Rosa for her never-ending support, ideas, and patience.

Both authors would like to add that any remaining errors are not the fault of our many helpful colleagues–instead they are Dominic's responsibility.

INDEX